THE COMPLETE
DAY
SKIPPER

THE COMPLETE
DAY
SKIPPER

A practical guide to coastal cruising and the RYA Day Skipper syllabus

STEVE REEVE

David & Charles

ISBN 0 7153 0058 X

Typeset in Times Roman by
ABM Typographics Ltd, Hull
and printed in England by
Redwood Books, Trowbridge
for David & Charles
Brunel House Newton Abbot Devon

Contents

Acknowledgements

Artwork: Steve Reeve and Judy Hill
Photography: Steve Reeve, Imogen Bowden and Alan Bowden
The author would like to thank:
Sadler Yachts for the use of various photographs, diagrams and plans
The Controller of Her Majesty's Stationery Office for permission to use extracts from Admiralty Charts, extracts from NP735 and NP204 (Admiralty Tidal Prediction Form)
John Crocker of the Hydrographic Office for assistance with the instructional charts
Thomas Reed Publications Ltd for tidal information from Reeds Almanac
Macmillan Publishers Ltd for tidal information from The Macmillan and Silk Cut Nautical Almanac
Mrs J. Wilson, Information Office of Trinity House Lighthouse Service
Mrs Heather Deane, Deputy Public Relations Officer of The Royal National Lifeboat Institution
Mr T S Anderson, Staff Officer, HM Coastguard
Guy Linley-Adams, Pollution Officer, Marine Conservation Society, for his help in the production of the chapter on pollution
Autonnic Research for photographs of navigational equipment
Avon Inflatables for photographs of liferafts
Northumbria School of Navigation for the navigation exercises
Halfway Yacht Club, Thorpe Bay, where I learned to sail
Mum and Dad for help with word processing and proof reading

Preface

My aim in writing this book has been to provide a detailed text for the RYA Day Skipper course, and a clear, easy-to-follow guide to basic boat-handling skills. By studying it the student will learn all the traditional techniques required to complete a safe and enjoyable daytime passage in familiar waters.

Those parts of the book that relate directly to the theory course investigate each topic in far more detail than is required by the syllabus, and by doing so they provide a sound foundation for further study of the subject.

One of the attractions of our sport is that one never stops learning, and the Day Skipper course should be seen as the first step along the path of knowledge. By presenting the material in a logical manner my hope is that it will be readily understood, even by those who are new to sailing. To help students test the extent of their understanding I have set questions at the end of many of the chapters: the answers are at the back of the book. The charts used for these exercises are the instructional chart 5061 and the 1993 revised edition of instructional chart 5055. Both were prepared by the Hydrographic Office at the request of the RYA for use by RYA recognised schools. Once principles and techniques have been grasped firmly they should be applied on the water.

Throughout the text I have largely avoided the use of the personal pronoun, to the extent of using the term 'helm' to refer to the person steering. Suffice it to say that both sexes are equal in all aspects of sailing.

Steve Reeve

Introduction

The Royal Yachting Association (RYA) evolved from the Yacht Racing Association, which was founded in 1875 as a response to the complications produced by the number of different methods being used to measure yachts. The Yacht Racing Association drew up a code of sailing rules that led to the foundation of the International Yacht Racing Union in 1907.

The Royal Yachting Association did not come into existence under that name until 1952, by which date its sphere of influence had considerably widened. Then, as now, its prime responsibility was to protect the interests of all those who use the sea and inland waters, in whatever type of boat. Today that includes everything from windsurfers to offshore power boats. The RYA now manages Olympic sailing teams, and administers yacht racing. It runs a comprehensive training scheme for sail and power and liaises with the government on relevant matters. The RYA provides legal advice as well as finance and insurance schemes devised especially to suit the needs of the sailor.

The RYA National Cruising Scheme

In the UK there is as yet no statutory obligation for those who go to sea in boats of less than 80 tonnes to have any form of qualification, and in this respect boating is very different to motor sports and flying. However, with increasing concern at the number of accidents at sea and the ever increasing burden on the rescue services, it is likely that this situation will change, especially as the UK becomes more integrated with Europe. Some countries already require the skipper of a boat to have a certificate of competence, while UK insurance companies are beginning to offer discounted premiums to those who have RYA qualifications.

The most important reason for gaining a qualification is to get more enjoyment from your sport and to take pride in your increasing ability. That there are risks involved in

going to sea cannot be denied: you may run aground, or you may get lost! The intention of the cruising scheme is to minimise the risks and increase your enjoyment. Whether you are going to skipper a boat in the near future or simply want to be a more than useful crew you must have a thorough working knowledge of the theory before putting to sea. On passage through the English Channel in the middle of a gale is not the time to be reading a navigation manual.

The logical progression through the RYA scheme would be:

RYA standard	Course type
Competent Crew	Practical
Day Skipper	Shore-based theory
Day Skipper	Practical
Coastal Skipper/ Yachtmaster Offshore	Shore-based theory

(Successful completion of each of the above leads to the award of a course completion certificate.)

Coastal Skipper	Practical or oral examination
Yachtmaster Offshore	Practical examination
Yachtmaster Ocean	Shore-based theory (certificate)
Yachtmaster Ocean	Examination or submission of log

There is no need to start at the first level. If you feel that you have sufficient experience you can start at the Coastal Skipper level, for example.

While the significance of an examination is probably obvious, that of the course completion certificate is perhaps less so. Essentially, if you follow a theory or practical course and reach a satisfactory standard you will be awarded a certificate to prove it.

The RYA scheme should be seen as consisting of theory and practical courses that are both complementary and progressive. A student who has completed a theory course will find the practical course easier and more rewarding, because the instructor will not have to teach the basic principles that should have been studied before the student took to the water.

THE DAY SKIPPER SHORE-BASED COURSE

This is a course in basic seamanship, navigation and meteorology. It is for those who wish to reach a sufficient level of competence to be able to skipper a boat through a short coastal passage. It is suitable for those who have absolutely no boating knowledge and also for those with either dinghy or basic coastal cruising experience.

The Day Skipper syllabus is detailed in the *RYA Cruising Logbook, G15/93.* You should have a copy of this because it gives the syllabus of each course, informs you of the entry requirements for certain examinations and provides space for you to keep a detailed record of your sailing experience. You must keep this up-to-date, because it will be needed as proof of your experience if you want to complete certain examinations or courses.

The general content of the syllabus falls under the following headings:

Terminology	Meteorology
Ropework	Passage planning
Anchorwork	Pilotage
Safety	Compass
Tides	Drawing instruments
Navigational	Position fixing
publications	Course to steer

The practical Day Skipper course covers the same ground, but also includes boat-handling skills under sail and power. The aim is to bring the student to the standard necessary to skipper safely by day a family cruiser in familiar waters.

Theory and practical courses are run by a variety of RYA-recognised schools. The theory course may be followed at a night school over the normal academic year, as a short intensive course or by correspondence. Uniformity is maintained by means of all RYA-recognised teaching establishments using the same ten exercises as classwork or homework. All students, irrespective of their school, then complete the same two RYA assessment papers, which cover the whole of the syllabus. One paper has short questions chosen from all aspects of the syllabus, concentrating on ropework, magnetism, collision regulations, buoyage, distress signals and meteorology. The remaining paper has four questions. Three are on position plotting and finding the course to steer, and the fourth is on working out the height of the tide.

The student who follows a correspondence course will complete the assessment papers at home under examination conditions. This means that an invigilator, who may be a family member or a friend, observes them completing the papers and then writes a note to that effect. The papers are then marked by the correspondence school.

You do not have to be perfect to obtain the certificate: it will be awarded even if you make a significant error, as long as you show that you understand the principles that have been taught. Should you fail one of the final assessment papers you may retake it as soon as you like, using a similar exercise.

CHAPTER 1

The Development of Sailing

The origins of sailing date back to the Bronze Age, when waterborne transport was used on rivers such as the Nile, and on lakes such as Titicaca in the Andes. There the first boats were dug-out canoes fashioned from large trees by craftsmen using stone tools. In other parts of the world, such as Polynesia, the earliest boats were made from logs bound with reeds.

A square-rigged Viking longboat.

Some 4–5,000 years ago sails were first added to boats. These were square sails held by a short central mast. A large paddle-shaped oar was used to steer the boat. Early Mediterranean civilisations, such as those of the Phoenicians and Greeks, traded great distances in these vessels, while they and the Romans and Egyptians had warships powered by oar and sail. The advantage of the sail was that the slave rowers could be rested, so that fast overall speeds could be maintained. The disadvantage of the square sail was that you could only head downwind. The square sail, however, did carry the Vikings down the great Russian rivers and across to North America, and it should be remembered that the passages westward across the Atlantic were against the prevailing wind and so were all the more remarkable.

The Egyptians were among the first to use the lateen sail, which has evolved into the modern triangular shape. The trapezial lateen, with its short luff, was rigged to a yardarm set obliquely to the mast. This rig is still seen today in the Arab dhows of the Red Sea and The Gulf.

The Chinese introduced the lugsail, which was one sail stiffened into sections by bamboo slats. The main advantage of this sail was that it was easily reefed.

In Europe, the designers of medieval ships realised that the amount of cargo that could be carried was governed by the size of the boat, and that the power delivered by a sail was proportional to its size. They also realised that using a single mast meant they would have to hoist an impossibly large sail and would need a large crew to handle it. The solution they found was to construct boats with two or three masts carrying multiple sails of relatively small dimensions. In these boats, with their square rig, wide beam and high freeboard, they explored the oceans by sailing as often as possible downwind in the trade-wind belt. The boats they developed for trade in coastal waters reflected that function in their design, with their combined fore and aft rig, as can be seen in the development of barques, brigantines and ketches.

The first hint of sailing boats being used for pleasure can be found in the Dutch word *jaght*, which was used in the early seventeenth century to describe a light vessel used for commerce or pleasure. At that time, and for much of the following two hundred years, the Dutch were the dominant maritime power. The nature of their coastline, with its many inland seas and waterways, meant that it was frequently more comfortable to travel by water than by land. Charles II of England, having been given a jaght, had several more designed by the Pett brothers. These he used in a series of races with his brother and other members of the aristocracy.

In 1663 William Petty designed a double-hulled boat that may be seen as the forerunner of the catamaran. This boat was undoubtedly modelled on sketches of some

Polynesian outrigger canoes made by European explorers. Petty's design was fast, but unfortunately it sank during sea trials. That proved to be the end of catamarans for the next three hundred years.

The use of the sea for recreation did not develop fully during the eighteenth century because it was hindered by war – notably the Seven Years War, the War of American Independence and the Napoleonic wars. The threat from pirates was also significant, and any sailing that took place, apart from that for trade, was largely restricted to areas close to the shore. That some were more adventurous in their cruising is evidenced by the attack in 1777 on the yacht *Hawke* in the English Channel: chased by an American privateer she fled to Calais.

The royal yachts of the eighteenth century tended to be functional rather than recreational, and closely resembled miniature men-of-war, even to the point of having small cannon.

In 1749 the first recorded race between more than two boats took place – from Greenwich to the Nore lightship in the Thames estuary, and then back again. The Prince of Wales presented a trophy. Not long afterwards the Cumberland Sailing Society had a large fleet of yachts racing on the Thames between Blackfriars and Putney.

The end of the Napoleonic wars in 1815 introduced a period when the seas were relatively safe. Cowes became the centre for the rapid development of leisure sailing with the foundation of the Royal Yacht Club, renamed the Royal Yacht Squadron in 1833. The following years saw a rapid growth in sailing for leisure among the aristocracy and wealthy industrialists. This soon spread beyond Britain, with the Royal Swedish Yacht Club, in 1830, being the first club to be founded outside the British Empire.

The mid and late nineteenth century saw the heyday of the clippers. These very fast streamlined boats had a combined fore/aft and square rig. The success of the British Empire was directly related to the success of these trading vessels.

The first official race in North American waters, off New York in 1845, led to the Hundred Guinea Cup off Cowes in 1851. The latter is now accepted as being the first America's Cup match race.

During the mid nineteenth century the first solo crossings were made of the Atlantic and Pacific, and in 1898 Joshua Slocum completed the first single-handed passage around the world.

In 1869 Edward Middleton, in a 23ft yawl, became the first to sail around England single-handed, via the Forth-Clyde canal, and soon afterward the spread of cruising in the UK was underlined by the foundation of the UK Cruising Club (1880), and later by the UK Cruising Association (1908). The novel *The Riddle of the Sands*, by Erskine Childers, was centred on cruising, while the first book was entirely devoted to the subject, *Yacht Cruising*, by Claud Worth, was published in 1910.

The years of war, followed by the Depression, inevitably prevented an upsurge in sailing during the early years of the twentieth century, although the America's Cup defences attracted considerable attention. Sir Thomas Lipton's *Shamrock IV* came within one race of victory in 1920, and Tommy Sopwith lost narrowly in 1934 with the Nicholson-designed *Endeavour*. The first Fastnet race took place in 1925, the winner being the converted pilot boat *Jolie Brise*. The Royal Ocean Racing Club was formed by the owners of the boats in that first race.

Again war intervened, and for some twenty years the development of sailing was held back. Its resurgence in the 1950s, as Britain came out of the post-war period of austerity, culminated in the first OSTAR in 1960. Finally, the development of mass-production methods and of materials such as glass-reinforced plastic, together with the growth of leisure time, led to an explosion of interest in small-boat cruising in the early 1960s.

CHAPTER 2

The Boat

Buying a boat

Apart from the purchase of your home, buying a boat will be the biggest financial commitment of your life. A bad decision may not only put you off sailing, but may also cause you considerable financial problems.

You must think seriously about your reasons for buying a boat as opposed to chartering or having a part-share in one. Will you use it often enough to justify the purchase? Will you use it every weekend and for longer passages each year? If the answer is yes then you can justify the expenditure. The prospective boat owner who would use a boat on only a handful of occasions during the year would be better advised to consider the alternatives.

Work out the annual cost of a boat and put that alongside the planned frequency of use. Beyond the initial capital investment you have to consider the cost of mooring, insurance and maintenance. Add to these the interest that could have been earned if the capital tied up in the boat had been invested. You will probably have to borrow some of the money to buy the boat, so the monthly repayments should also be included in your calculations. A conservative estimate of the combined cost of mooring, insurance, repairs and loan repayment would be £4,000 a year. That is a substantial sum of money, even if you will use the boat frequently.

Do you have to own a boat? You could join or set up a small syndicate to share the purchase and running costs. That would significantly reduce the cost of your sailing, but may mean that you would not have the use of the boat every time you felt like a sail. Furthermore, it needs only one person in a syndicate to leave the boat unprepared for the next user and tension develops. Chartering is a sensible option to consider. A thirty-five footer may cost £1,000 for a week, but divided between five people that becomes very cheap sailing. You could have several weeks' charter in a year without getting anywhere near the cost of boat ownership.

Having decided, despite the cost, that you wish to own a boat, you then have to decide on the type. The choice will be governed by factors such as the nature of the passages you are likely to be making: if you are planning to day-sail close to the shore then you will not want a boat that would suit more extended passages. The size of the boat you choose will also be affected by the size of your crew or family. Larger boats will have separate cabins, which give much needed privacy on longer passages. On a passage of several days duration the lack of privacy in a small boat may cause unnecessary tension. You also have to decide on the keel configuration. A bilge keel would be ideal for making coastal passages in shoal waters, but a fin keel would be desirable if you are likely to be making extended offshore passages.

Once you are clear about the type of sailing you plan to do, and have considered the financial constraints, your choice of boat will be relatively limited. The next problem is to obtain objective information: the manufacturer's brochure will provide much information, but it will not be objective. Magazine test-reviews are excellent sources of information, but do remember that any such test, however objective, inevitably contains some of the writer's personal bias. *Yachting Monthly* runs a 'Second Opinion' service, through which you can write to a boat owner who has the type of boat you are interested in and ask for their opinion. Again, most owners will be fond of their boats and are unlikely to be very critical. They may even gloss over negative points.

You will also have to make the choice between new and second-hand, which is not always easy. New boats have the obvious advantages of looking bright and clean and being without an osmosis problem. The price

A small bilge keeler (*top*).

A deep fin keel.

may also look attractive, but what does it include? It may include equipment that you do not want, and may not include equipment that you do want. You may have a preference for one manufacturer of equipment and find that the boat is supplied with a different make. If this is the case then it is worth discussing with the boat manufacturer

exactly what equipment you would like installed. You will almost certainly have to buy a liferaft, dinghy, danbuoy, flares and fenders. You can hardly set off without them. The sail wardrobe is likely to be minimal, and certainly will not include a spinnaker. The cost of such 'extras' will run into thousands rather than hundreds of pounds.

A major disadvantage of a new boat is that it will not have been run in. It takes two to three seasons of hard sailing to adapt a boat to your requirements. This is particularly true of stowage space and hand holds.

A second-hand boat is very different. It may well have a full inventory, so you will not need to make any further purchases. All the same, you should look at this carefully, because that full inventory might include tired sails, a liferaft that needs a service, and faulty electrical equipment. If some of the equipment is old it may well be impossible to obtain replacement parts. A major plus of buying second-hand is that you will get a larger boat for the same amount of money. Also, the boat will probably have been run in and be ready for serious sailing. Perhaps a final advantage is that the second-hand boat will be ready to sail away, while you will have to wait for your new boat to be built.

Whether you decide to buy new or second-hand you must have at least one lengthy sea trial, preferably more. Try the boat on every point of sailing in all possible conditions, and try every manoeuvre under sail and engine.

Another possibility is to buy a hull and complete it at home. Several leading manufacturers supply boats in various stages of completion. Boat building is hard work and requires basic DIY skills, but it will save money. The amount saved will depend on what proportion of the boat you complete yourself and how efficient you are. You could reasonably expect to save 20% on the finished price, so it is definitely worth considering. It would be sensible to buy the hull and deck bonded together, with the keel, rudder, ballast, engine bearings, skin fittings and main bulkheads fitted. Some manufacturers supply off-the-peg kits to complete the boat, or you can save a little more money by buying your own internal fittings. Do remember that the manufacturer will order in bulk, and can therefore buy at much lower prices than you will find. Most manufacturers will be happy to provide you with guidance as you proceed. You need somewhere sheltered to complete the boat, with access to a power supply. Home completion takes time, but that allows you to spread the cost over a long period, because you do not need to buy anything until it is actually required.

Whatever you buy, you will inevitably need finance. The best advice is to shop around and look at the various possibilities. Personal loans are available from banks and finance houses, but the latter also offer marine mortgages, with the loan secured on the boat. They usually require a 20% deposit and repayment periods of five to ten years.

The boat must be insured to its full value, which is the purchase price plus the replacement cost of all the equipment. You must also have third party liability of at least £½ million. Most policies will cover the boat for a given period in commission, so if you want to extend this you must tell the insurance company. Your policy will also indicate the sea area to which you are restricted, usually Brest–Elbe. If you think a particular passage will take you beyond this then, again, make sure that you inform the insurance company. The same rule applies if you intend any single-handed sailing. As with a car policy, a small excess of £50–£100 will lead to a reduction in the premium. The maximum no-claims bonus of 20% is reached after four years.

Hull construction

For 5,000 years the natural material for boats of all sizes was wood. Whatever the construction method the end product was no more than an open wooden container with caulking used between the planks to prevent leaks. Today, although a vast proportion of boats are made from other materials, the same basic design concepts hold true.

WOODEN BOATS
There are three main methods of wood construction – clinker, carvel and chine.

Clinker The origin of this can be seen clearly in the Viking longboat. The first stage of construction is to build a frame of timber ribs. It is these that frequently survive from Viking boats. Overlapping planks of wood are then laid fore and aft over the timber frame. The Vikings would have secured these planks with wooden pegs, but today copper rivets are used. It is because the wood has to be thick enough to take the rivets that the boats are so heavy. These labour intensive production methods make clinker boats slow and expensive to build.

Carvel This is very similar to clinker, but perhaps an improvement because the planks are laid flush with each other. Each plank is slightly bevelled so that there is a V-shaped groove between the individual planks. Caulking is pressed into the grooves to make the boat watertight. Such boats are sturdy, durable and heavy.

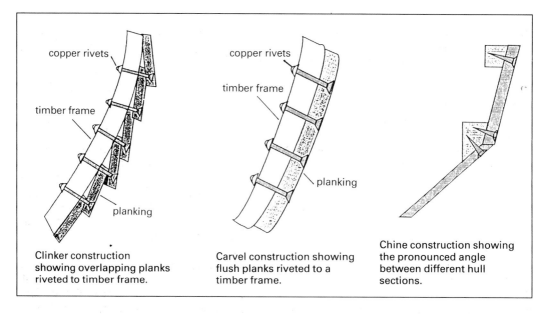

copper rivets

timber frame

planking

Clinker construction showing overlapping planks riveted to timber frame.

copper rivets

timber frame

planking

Carvel construction showing flush planks riveted to a timber frame.

Chine construction showing the pronounced angle between different hull sections.

Chine Plywood revolutionised the industry and allowed the first mass production of small boats. The strips of wood are glued together, with adjacent strips having opposing grains. The disadvantage of plywood is that it can be bent in only one direction. In the construction of the hull the wood is curved in a fore-aft direction. This means that it cannot be bent across its width to produce the natural curve of the side of a hull. To overcome this problem the wood is laid in sections of two to three planks with a pronounced angle between each section. The name given to this is chine. Plywood is a popular material for amateurs because it is cheap and easy to use. Where a smooth hull shape is required it is laid in thin strips to produce a more rounded shape. This is described as double or multi-chine.

OTHER MATERIALS
Wood is undoubtedly very attractive when new or looking new, but the maintenance costs in terms of money and time are high. It also suffers from the disadvantage of having relatively little resistance to swelling or shrinking, rot and marine borers. Cold-moulding, using waterproof glue and veneers of wood saturated with epoxy resin, has over-

Clinker construction.

Single chine construction in plywood.

come some of these problems but the production costs are high. Not surprisingly, many manufacturers are using other materials.

GRP A look around a present-day marina will emphasise the lack of variation in modern cruiser design and construction. It is often said that the greatest fault with modern cruisers is their tendency to look alike. In detail this similarity may well turn out to be superficial, because although GRP stands for glass-reinforced plastic the plastics (resins) vary considerably and the reinforcement may not be glass.

The theory behind strengthening the resin is the same as that of adding strength to concrete piles by inserting steel rods. There are a great variety of fine fibres used to reinforce the resin. E-glass, with its extruded glass filaments, is widely used on mass-production boats because of its strength, stiffness and relatively low cost. An alternative is kevlar. This expensive material provides high tensile strength and low weight, so it is ideal for racing yachts. The material of the future was at one time considered to be carbon fibre. Although strong it is brittle and unidirectional, so it can only be safely used where there is a specific directional strain.

Whichever resin or reinforcement is used, the production process will begin with the construction of a prototype in wood, from which the female fibreglass mould is made. This is smoothed to a perfect surface with wax and polish and coated with a releasing agent. The resin is then brushed over the mould to form the outer surface of the hull. Fibreglass layers are laid over the resin, with further resin being brushed in. Several layers of resin and fibreglass are built up like this until the required thickness is reached. Once the resin has set hard and cured, the hull is lifted out of the mould. The same mould is used to produce a series of hulls: this is mass-production in boat building.

A hull produced in this way has a pleasantly rounded form with smooth curves. It is easy to maintain and is leakproof. The only potential problem with fibreglass is osmosis, but this is relatively rare. Osmosis is apparent as a blistered surface – a result of water penetrating the outer part of that surface and then combining chemically with compounds in the resin or fibreglass. The problem has

long since been recognised by manufacturers, who have responded by altering manufacturing processes to eliminate it. Such manufacturers now guarantee their hulls against osmosis. However, when buying a second-hand GRP boat you should get a qualified marine surveyor to check it. If your present GRP boat is more than five years old you should regularly check for blistering. If you are unlucky enough to find that you have a problem it can be cured quite easily by specialists, though at a cost. The greater the spread of the osmosis in the hull the greater the cost. Prevention is obviously better than cure, and you can now overcoat your hull with a water-resistant barrier.

Ferrocement This was quite widely used in commercial and naval vessels in the first half of the twentieth century. The skeleton of the boat consists of layers of steel rods laid at right angles to each other. This is covered with wire mesh to form the hull shape. The hull is then plastered, inside and out, with fine cement.

The advantages of ferrocement are that it is leakproof, is impervious to corrosion and is rot and fireproof. It is also durable and will withstand massive impact, for though it may be deformed it rarely splits. It makes heavy but good sea boats that are suitable for long distance passages but do tend to look less attractive than those that are made of other materials.

Metal Many amateur builders, starting from raw materials, use steel if they possess welding equipment and basic skills. Strength is the great advantage of this material, together with the fact that it may be repaired relatively easily. The major disadvantage is its weight and its susceptibility to corrosion.

In the 1970s and 80s various light alloys and marine-grade aluminium were used in racing yachts. Although expensive and requiring specialist construction facilities they did produce boats that were light, strong and rigid. The major problems with aluminium are corrosion and electrolysis.

The layout of a modern cruiser

BELOW DECKS
The interior of a boat is as important as its deck layout, engine and rig: sailing should be

a comfortable and enjoyable experience. The below-deck accommodation of a typical 26ft cruiser is surprisingly roomy. Many small boats with well planned interiors are effectively more spacious than some larger boats. Most manufacturers of 25–26ft boats claim that they are five or six berth. That is not the same as saying that you would enjoy a passage with five or six people in a boat of that size! Two people, or a couple and two young people would be ideal, although for day trips four or five would be a perfectly reasonable number. For a passage of any length a crew of more than three people would find the lack of privacy and stowage space a problem. You are unlikely to be making long passages at this stage, so a twenty-six footer is more than adequate. (It should be remembered that Sadler 25s have been raced successfully in the OSTAR and AZAB events.)

Of the six berths on such a boat the quarter berth is by far the most comfortable during a passage. The forecabin is an especially un-comfortable berth on passage but does make an ideal cabin for young children when the boat is moored. A further problem with this cabin is that most owners stow their sails in the massive lockers located under the berth. The Houdini hatch to and from the foredeck is usually sited at the aft end of the forecabin, and whilst providing that cabin with plenty of light it does mean that it tends to be used as something of a passageway from deck to cabin.

The middle of the double berth in the main cabin will almost certainly be the folding saloon table, which may also double as the navigation table. In a boat of this size this is the only practical solution. In the Sadler 26 the chart table slots over the quarter berth so that the navigator may sit on the companion-way steps to use it. Usually the main saloon table is folded out of the way during a passage unless it is to be used by the navigator. If you are going to use the main-cabin berths to sleep in during a passage you will need to fix lee cloths to them to prevent you falling out as the boat heels. You will find that the lack of privacy makes it very difficult to sleep in these berths.

Ideally, the navigational instruments should be placed close to both the companionway and the chart table. When short-handed this will allow those on watch

The interior layout of a Sadler 26.

to check the chart or instruments quickly without being off watch for more than a few seconds. The chart table must be large enough to take at least a chart folded in half. You need shelving for books in the same area, and a console repeating cockpit instruments. The VHF set should also be close at hand.

The galley should include a gimballed cooker and oven, although smaller boats do tend to lack the space for the latter. You will need an icebox and a sink with pressurised water. There should be ample work surfaces, protected by fiddles, and good stowage space. All lockers must have robust catches that will not break and will not pull out of their fittings or come loose in a seaway.

The heads are usually found between the main cabin and the forecabin. These efficient pump-operated toilets do occasionally block, so they must be treated carefully. The hanging locker is usually positioned opposite the heads.

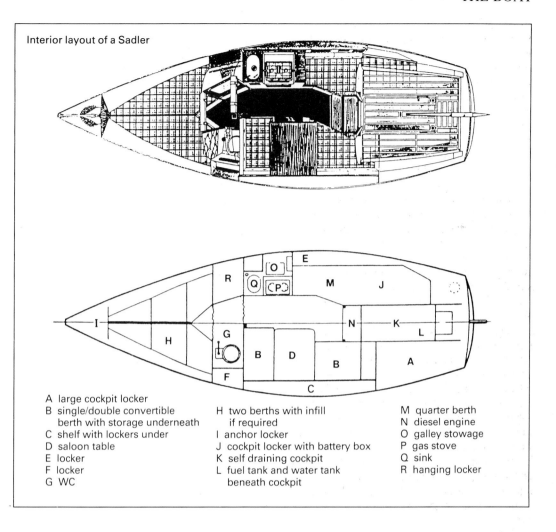

Interior layout of a Sadler

A large cockpit locker
B single/double convertible
  berth with storage underneath
C shelf with lockers under
D saloon table
E locker
F locker
G WC

H two berths with infill
  if required
I anchor locker
J cockpit locker with battery box
K self draining cockpit
L fuel tank and water tank
  beneath cockpit

M quarter berth
N diesel engine
O galley stowage
P gas stove
Q sink
R hanging locker

Headroom will generally be at its greatest in the aft part of the cabin, but even there it will only just reach six feet (1.8m). This may seem low, but it is really only a problem to the very tall. Even those slightly taller than average will find the height more than adequate. As you go further forward the headroom rapidly decreases.

DECK LAYOUT

The deck layout is obviously of great importance. That of the small family cruiser is fairly standard.

The foredeck is an exposed area in which to work so it must have a strong pulpit. This affords protection to the crew when working headsail changes or the anchor. There will also be cleats and fairleads here, located either side of the anchor well.

The raised part of the deck is called the coachroof. This has windows along its sides and at least one ventilator on top. The latter helps air to circulate in the main cabin. Hand holds run along the length of both sides. Access to the forecabin is through the hatch positioned at the forward end of the coach roof. The main cabin is accessed through the companionway at the aft end of the coachroof. This access is closed by a sliding hatch and washboards. Hand holds should be situated on either side of the companionway, both inside and outside. These will help the crew to get into the cockpit in heavy weather. There should also be at least one lifeline clip-on point near the hand holds.

The cockpit of a small cruiser is invariably at the aft end. In a medium sized or large cruiser it may be in the middle, in which case

19

there is an aft cabin. The cockpit consists of a self-draining well surrounded by seats. It is because this is the safest part of the boat, that the winches and cleats are positioned on top of the coaming, thus allowing as many of the controls as possible to be managed without leaving the safety of the cockpit. Navigational instruments such as the compass and the log will usually be positioned in the aft bulkhead of the cabin, so that they face into the cockpit. There should be two or three small lockers in the cockpit in which to stow food and drink for those on watch, together with a torch and tools. Access to the main locker is often from this point, and the bilge pump handle should also be situated here.

On the pushpit you should have a dan-buoy, two horseshoe lifebuoys and a heaving line of at least 30m. One of the lifebuoys should be attached to the danbuoy, which is a lightweight telescopic tube with a poly-styrene float. A heavy weight at the base keeps it upright in the water. The top of the buoy is equipped with a light and a flag, to help mark the position of a crew member should they fall overboard.

Boat electrics

The electrical system on your boat is used to start the engine and run the navigational instruments, navigation lights and cabin lights. Almost certainly the boat will have a 12V DC system powered by one or two batteries. These are charged either by a dynamo or alternator on the main engine or by a separate generator. Many cruisers now use separate charging units such as solar panels or wind vanes.

BATTERIES
Assuming you have an inboard engine you should have two batteries: one for starting the engine and one for all your other electrical needs. The logic behind this is that it then becomes much more difficult to run out of power. The dangers resulting from loss of power are the lack of navigation lights and the inability to start the engine (unless you can hand-start it). The lack of an engine will cause problems when berthing the boat or if the sails are insufficient to get you out of a dangerous situation. The engine will not start if the batteries are flat. With a two battery system, as one becomes low on charge it is

possible to start the engine with the other and recharge it. For this to be successful you must not have the two batteries wired together. In that situation the battery with the greater charge would discharge into the other until they were both at a similar level. You would then have *two* batteries that were low on charge.

With batteries wired separately you will need a battery selection switch, allowing you to decide whether to use both batteries or just one. To start the engine you switch to the engine battery, then, when the engine is running, you switch on the other battery so that both are being charged. When you stop the engine you turn off that battery, but keep the other on if you are using any of the instruments. (As you should keep a constant listening watch on channel 16 this means that you will always have the instrument battery switched on.)

For the batteries to remain in good condition they must be kept fully charged. They must be securely mounted so that they cannot possibly move, irrespective of the amount of heel or pitching of the boat, and should sit in a tray to take any spill that does occur. The locker in which they are stowed must be well ventilated so that there is no possibility of a build up of explosive gas. Always switch off both batteries before leaving the boat.

Lead acid batteries lose their charge rapidly, so must be charged regularly. They also deteriorate rapidly if neglected. Alkaline batteries cost more but have a longer life and tend to be more tolerant of neglect.

Starting the engine is a major drain on the battery, though only for a short period if the engine is in good condition. Ignition may require 1,000–1,500A, which will at most take 2–3 seconds with a warm engine. But if the engine is very cold the starter motor may have to turn it over for some 30 seconds before it fires.

ELECTRICAL SYSTEMS
Salt water does not suit electrical systems, so the circuitry has to be planned very carefully. All the materials used must be waterproof and resistant to corrosion. Wiring must be accessible and kept as far as possible from any area where water collects. The wires should be clipped at frequent intervals to prevent them working loose.

All electrical systems should focus on the switch panel. This consists of rows of switches and fuses. The external face holds the switches, which are labelled according to the instrument or light that they operate. Behind each switch, on the reverse face, there is the fuse block, where the wires terminate. The positive cable from the battery runs to the battery switch, where it is interrupted, and then on to the positive connection on the switch panel. The negative cable runs straight from the battery to the negative connection on the panel. From the fuse blocks the lighter cables run to the instruments and lights. The cables from the battery must be relatively short and certainly should not have a combined length in excess of 6m (19.7ft). They should also be of a diameter sufficient to prevent them heating up and wasting energy.

The switch panel should be positioned in a dry location close to the battery so that the cable length is minimised. It should be wired in such a way that when it is taken away from the bulkhead you have ready access to the wiring coming in to it.

When an instrument or light fails to work you should first check the wiring at both ends, clean the connections and check the fuse. If it is an instrument which has a sensor, check that the sensor is connected. Should it still fail to work you will have to consult the faultfinding section of the manufacturer's manual.

Electronic instruments

COMPASS

The compass is the heart of the boat's navigation system. It works on the basis that a magnetic needle suspended so that it swings freely will come to rest pointing to the magnetic pole.

There are various types of compass on the market but all function in much the same manner. An enclosed bowl contains a graduated card which swings freely over a liquid, which helps to dampen the motion. The helm lines up the lubber line on the glass with the required heading on the card. Small magnets attached to the card help to ensure that the north indicator on the card points to the magnetic pole, although correction for deviation is still necessary.

The compass must be sited so that it may be easily read from the normal helming position. The lubber line on the compass must be parallel to, and preferably lie on, the boat's centreline. It must be at least 4ft (1.2m) from the engine and you must avoid placing any electrical or metallic objects close to it. For night navigation the compass needs a subdued light so that it may be looked at without causing an adverse effect on night vision.

On a small cruiser it is virtually impossible to find an ideal location for the compass. Positioned in one bulkhead it is clearly not on the centreline, and because of the slight curvature of the bulkhead it is not parallel to the

Two types of steering compass.

Range of electronic equipment produced by Autonnic Research.

centreline either. When the helm is on the opposite side to the compass it will be difficult to read accurately. Placed on or close to the companionway it *will* be on the centreline but will be frequently kicked by those moving from cabin to cockpit. On a small boat the bulkhead location is probably the best compromise.

LOG

A speed-and-distance log plays a vital role in calculating position and course to steer because it records both the distance you have travelled through the water and your speed through the water.

The trailing mechanical log is reliable and robust with little need for maintenance. The registering unit is mounted on the pushpit when the log is in operation. A small spinner is attached to a line which in turn is connected to the registering unit. The spinner is towed behind the boat and rotates as a result of the fins on its body. The registering unit simply counts the number of rotations and gives the boat's speed in tenths of a mile. To avoid twists and knots in the end of the line you should take hold of a bight of the line and let that out before the spinner. When retrieving the spinner hold a bight of line and release the end from the taffrail unit. That end should then be fed into the water while the spinner is hauled in; the remainder of the line is hauled in from the spinner. Modern spinners are a dull colour so that they are no longer a lure to fish. You should nevertheless have a spare line and spinner.

Similar to the above is the trailing electrical log. A short electrical line attached to the spinner transmits a pulse to the registering unit as the spinner rotates. Like the trailing mechanical log it is relatively inexpensive, reliable and accurate.

The electrical impeller log has a tiny rotator that is positioned through the hull. The rotator is connected by electrical wire to the registering unit. As the rotator turns it transmits an impulse to the unit. The number of impulses is converted to distance through the water, from which speed through the water is calculated. Although more expensive, this type of log is long lasting and avoids the need to tow a spinner.

Should your log fail, you may make a fairly accurate calculation of speed through the water by using what is known as a Dutchman's log. Measure out a suitable length of your deck and find a tight ball of paper or attach a bottle to a rope. Throw the paper or bottle into the water ahead of the boat and time it along the measured section of the deck. If the object takes 2 seconds to travel a measured (deck) length of 10ft your speed is:

$$\frac{10 \times 60}{2 \times 100} = 3\text{kn}$$

ECHO SOUNDER

Echo sounders vary widely in both complexity and cost. The day skipper who is only making short coastal passages certainly needs no more than the basic unit. The transducer, which with modern accuracy does not need to go through the hull, should be near the centreline, forward of all seacocks. Flow from the seacocks would otherwise lead to an error in depth measurement. The transducer sends a pulse of ultrasonic sound to the seabed and measures the time it takes to reflect back. Displays are either digital or rotating LED. The latter show two flashes: as the signal is sent to the seabed, and as the signal returns from the seabed which therefore gives the depth.

A basic unit will measure the depth from the transducer to the seabed, whereas you require the depth from the surface to the seabed. Such an echo sounder will therefore always under read. To be accurate in your tidal calculations you need to know the distance from your transducer to the waterline. More sophisticated units may be calibrated to take this into account. Such units also have shallow water and anchor alarms. The nature of the flash on some LED units will give an indication as to the material on the seabed. You should be aware that it is possible for an echo sounder to produce false readings from layers of seaweed or shoals of fish.

The display unit must be positioned some distance from the VHF set because that transmits in the same frequency and irritating clicks may be picked up on the radio. The cable from the transducer should be well separated from other circuits because it radiates electrical noise which these systems may pick up.

Lead line As a back up to the echo sounder some boat owners carry a lead line with which to measure depth. These used to be marked at intervals by varied pieces of cloth, but are now simply marked in metres. A piece of tallow is set into the base of the lead weight so that some of the seabed material adheres to it. This helps to determine your position by correlating that material with the charted description of the seabed. Lead lines are particularly useful when navigating close to the limit in shoal waters. They are also used to confirm depths when anchoring.

MASTHEAD INSTRUMENTS

These are the anemometer and wind vane. The former consists of three cups that rotate on a spindle. Each rotation causes an impulse to be transmitted to the registering unit which converts it into speed. The wind vane points into the wind, the voltage of an electrical current within it varying according to the direction of the wind. This information is transmitted to the registering unit which calculates the voltage as an angle.

DECCA

This position finding system is a piece of relatively expensive equipment that the day skipper definitely does not need. Decca could make you lazy in your navigation at a time when you should be learning all the basic techniques. The advantage of it is that it gives a continuously updated position in latitude and longitude. It also provides you with a course to steer between waypoints and tells you how far off course you are and in which direction you should head in order to get back on course. Additionally, it will give you course and speed made good, and the ETA at the next waypoint.

The often quoted accuracy of Decca is 50m within 50 miles of the transmitter. The degree of accuracy is quite variable and there are dead spots along the coast where the Decca will not give you a position. You would therefore be very foolish to rely on this instrument alone. Treat it as a back-up to traditional chart plotting methods.

The engine

The small cruiser will have as its auxiliary either an outboard or an inboard, which will be either diesel or petrol driven. On a boat of any size an outboard really is impractical unless you fit cockpit controls. The alternative is leaning over the stern to adjust the engine while you should be looking ahead. The advantage of an outboard is that it has a good power-to-weight ratio and occupies less space, while the fact that it can be taken off the boat makes it easier to service. However, putting an outboard back onto its bracket when at sea or even on a mooring is very difficult and requires considerable strength and agility. Once out at sea taking the engine off is virtually impossible and all you can do is raise the bracket so that on an even keel the propeller is just out of the water. You then have a considerable weight on one side of the centreline, which will have a negative effect on the boat's performance: when you heel on the engine side the shaft will cause considerable drag. All in all, an inboard, despite the initial cost, will make your sailing that much more comfortable, enjoyable and safe.

INBOARDS

The choice between petrol and diesel is less clear cut, although the latter finds greatest favour with those yacht manufacturers who supply boats fitted with engines.

Petrol engines are cheaper and lighter and more easily maintained. They do, however, require a continuous electrical system, unlike the diesels which need electricity only when starting. The often quoted greater fire risk of petrol is perhaps exaggerated, but it does nevertheless exist. Diesel is safer because it has low volatility and is non-flammable at low temperatures.

Diesel engines are cheaper to run, their thermal efficiency being perhaps 50% greater than that of petrol engines. This is because their more effective combustion results in a greater proportion of heat energy from the fuel being turned into useful work. This efficiency of power production is important, as at best only about 30% of horsepower is translated into thrust through the propeller.

The compression system which causes diesel to ignite requires large castings, which explains why such engines are relatively heavy and expensive. They are also noisier, smellier and create more vibration. Their fuel system is more susceptible to dirt and they have exacting lubrication requirements.

Regardless of the type of fuel it uses, the engine should be positioned as low as possible on the centreline, about one-third of the length of the boat from the stern. The engine compartment should be accessible through removable panels so that maintenance may be carried out. It also needs to be dry and well ventilated. The propeller shaft connects with the propeller through the sterngland, which is a point that must be regularly checked for leaks. The compartment must be insulated to reduce noise and the vibration that will be felt throughout the boat. It should be fitted with an automatic fire extinguisher, and a bilge pump that can be operated from the cockpit. Diesel fuel tanks should be stainless or lead-coated steel, to combat diesel's corrosive nature.

The cockpit should contain a good bank of engine monitors so that you are made immediately aware of any problem. These monitors should include a tachometer, oil pressure gauge or warning light, water temperature gauge or warning light, and voltmeter or charging light.

The typical cooling system is one in which an engine-driven pump draws water up from the sea. This then passes through an oil cooler and around the cylinder block and the exhaust manifold before being discharged over the side. The temperature is controlled by a thermostat. The major drawback of this system is the inevitable build-up of salt in the internal engine passages. This can be avoided by using an enclosed fresh-water cooling system in which fresh water is pumped around the engine after being cooled by salt water. It is very important that you keep the inlet strainers clean and, in an enclosed system, make sure that the header tank is topped up. The whole cooling system must be frequently checked for leaks, because any shortage of cooling water will lead to overheating and engine damage. Before departure you must also check the oil level in the sump and gearbox.

The engine must have clean air and clean fuel. Dirt in the fuel is perhaps the more serious problem, so fit extra filters in the fuel supply lines and regularly inspect them. The tank should be drained at the end of the season and thoroughly inspected. This implies that it must have a good inspection hole.

Your engine must be serviced at least once a year. If you intend to lay it up for several months especially in winter, then you need to take certain precautions, as outlined in the manufacturer's manual. In practice, to prevent deterioration during the winter the engine just needs to be run for fifteen minutes every two to three weeks. If you have an enclosed cooling system fill it with antifreeze.

There are many reasons why an engine may fail to start. The battery might be too low, and attempting to start with such a battery can damage your starter motor. Loose connections might be the problem, or the starter motor might be jammed. Assuming you have sufficient fuel, the problem might be a blocked fuel line, a choked fuel pump, dirty filters or a flooded carburettor. Most diesel engines may be crank started if necessary. If the engine cuts out while running, the most likely cause is an electrical problem. Overheating usually results from a lack of oil or a fault in the cooling system. This is most likely to be caused by a blocked water intake or the fact that you have simply forgotten to open the seacock.

If air has entered the fuel system you will have to bleed the whole system before you will be able to start the engine. An airlock is most likely to be a result of running out of fuel, or of a leak from the suction side of the fuel line.

OUTBOARDS

Most boat owners will wish to have an outboard for the dinghy, as there will be times when it is too far to row ashore from an anchorage. At the very least the engine will provide a back up should you break or lose one of the oars. Most crew treat the oars as the auxiliary. An 8–10ft dinghy will be perfectly manageable with a 2hp engine. There is no point in getting a bigger engine if it just adds weight to the yacht when stowed. The dinghy's transom will be designed to take a maximum horsepower, which you must not exceed. These small outboards use an expensive petrol–oil mix, and are all too easily dropped into the water or stolen. For these reasons most insurance companies will insist that they are valued separately on your policy.

The outboard should be clamped to the transom in such a way that the cavitation plate just above the propeller is level with or just below the bottom of the boat. You must make sure that the engine is vertical when running and that the water inlet is well beneath the surface. Before you reach the shore, stop the engine and tilt it forward, so that the propeller is not damaged on the seabed.

CHAPTER 3

Clothing

Whatever the temperature on land, it will invariably feel colder when you put to sea. This is because even on a dry day the atmosphere at sea is very damp. The moisture which inevitably gets into your clothing is evaporated through the process of drawing latent heat of vaporisation from your body. Water conducts heat twenty-five times faster than air, so the fact that you have replaced the air close to your body with clothing that has water trapped in it makes the situation that much worse. The wind speeds up this process by constantly removing the saturated air from close to your body, so allowing evaporation and cooling to continue. This is the 'wind chill' factor. The body's core temperature should be maintained at about 37°C. Hypothermia begins to set in when it falls below 35°C, so only a very small drop in body temperature is needed for problems to start. You must realise that hypothermia can very quickly become fatal.

Even the limited degree of discomfort brought on by feeling cold and wet will lower the efficiency of the crew to a dangerous level. Cold and damp reduce physical strength, making it much easier to lose your grip while working on deck. They also affect the senses, so that the mind no longer thinks clearly, which may lead to potentially dangerous navigational errors.

The first-time crew who has yet to decide on what to buy should take the following into consideration. Your clothes need to be organised to keep out damp and cold. Thermal underwear, including full-length pants, is sensible in cold conditions. Remembering that air trapped within and between layers of clothing is a poor conductor of heat you should have two or three thin layers over your underwear. This will reduce the loss of body heat. A woolly hat is very important because otherwise much heat will be lost through your head. Wear warm trousers, not jeans. Jeans take a long time to dry out, and

cling uncomfortably to the skin so that there is no room for a layer of insulating air. Long warm socks with comfortable sea boots or deck shoes will protect the lower legs and feet and give added grip when working on deck. In heavy weather, boots, not shoes, must be worn.

You must have waterproofs, and wear them whenever necessary. Even in moderate conditions you are likely to get wet. The quality of waterproofs varies tremendously, but it tends to be the case that the better foul-weather gear is the more expensive. It is well worth paying £300–£500 for the comfort and protection of clothing that will keep you both warm and dry. Before you make your purchase it is important that you try wearing the waterproofs over your heavy-weather sailing clothes, to ensure that you are quite happy with the fit and degree of comfort.

A lightweight middle-layer jacket.

Musto ocean trousers.

Ocean trousers plus chest harness and safety line.

Musto ocean jacket and integral harness.

The range of clothing available is bewildering. Getting fully kitted out for the worst possible conditions can easily cost you in excess of £500. In the first instance it is not wise to spend so much, but you do need to think carefully about what you are going to buy. Try to borrow specialist clothing so that you can try it out at sea and decide what suits you. Consider the type of sailing that you are going to be doing in the next two or three years. If you do not expect to venture far beyond your home port or the immediate bay, then there is little point in buying a dedicated ocean suit. However, if you are planning longer coastal passages then you should consider such a suit. The conditions that require an ocean suit are just as likely to be found close to the shore as in mid ocean. Above all, remember that this clothing will keep you comfortable in even the most extreme conditions. Eventually it would be sensible to have a range of clothing that allows you to change as the conditions dictate.

The three-layer system

Most clothing systems now consist of just three layers. This is because research has proved that while efficient clothing will trap air and so insulate the body, it is equally true that too much clothing, or clothing that is very dense, will disturb the warm layers of air that build up around the body.

To be clothed effectively against all possible weather and sea conditions you need:

1. *Thermal underwear*
2. *A middle layer*
3. *An outer waterproof layer*

These three layers ensure that you are separated from external water and from perspiration but do not disturb the layers of air around the body. If you wear a good waterproof without the correct undergarments you are likely to feel uncomfortable and will still become cold and wet, regardless of its quality. This is because although you are well protected from external water the garment will retain body-generated heat, which leads to eventual cooling and a sensation of being wet.

THERMAL UNDERWEAR
In one hour your body may produce up to a third of a pint (165cc) of water through perspiration. The warm moist air trapped between the outer garment and your body will be cooled as it comes into contact with the garment. This causes the vapour to condense, and you will then have water drops lying on the underside of the outer garment as well as on your skin and inner garments. The drops will eventually become a film of water that is highly efficient at transporting away your body heat. Thermal underwear is made of non-absorbent fleece that conducts the water away from your skin so that your body remains surrounded by a film of warm air rather than cold water. You therefore feel warm and comfortable. It is available as one-piece suits, as separate shirts and trousers and as long and short socks.

MIDDLE LAYER
The middle layer should be warm and showerproof, so jackets and trousers may be used as normal sailing clothes until conditions require foul-weather gear to be put on top. They should be made of a lightweight fleece so that they feel comfortable between your other layers and through a wide temperature range. That way you will not have to keep changing clothes as the temperature fluctuates.

OUTER LAYER
The role of the outer layer is to protect you during heavy weather, keeping out water and wind and fitting snugly over the inner layers.

All the major manufacturers incorporate similar design features into their clothing. Outer garments tend to have a built-in chest harness so that you do not require a separate one. Above the neck you will find that you are well protected by a high collar that has a Velcro strap to prevent water entering from the front. A stow-away hood with a spray visor completes the protection by allowing you to cover your whole head – except for your eyes of course, you do need to be able to see! The wrists and ankles are elasticated to prevent water entry and are backed up by Velcro straps. The zips are protected by storm flaps, again to prevent the ingress of water. Areas like the knees and seat, that are likely to wear quickly, are reinforced. Finally there are deep pockets and reflective strips. The latter will play a vital role should you go over the side.

Precautions in fine weather

The effect of fine weather also needs to be considered. Sun, clear skies and a gentle breeze will rapidly lead to sunburn for the unwary. You must therefore make liberal use of preventive creams and must protect sensitive parts of the skin, such as the back of the neck, with light clothing. On a bright day the glare from sun and sea may cause headaches, so always have a pair of sun-glasses available.

Personal buoyancy

You must never set sail without some form of individual buoyancy being available for each crew member. Such buoyancy comes in two forms, the buoyancy aid and the lifejacket. Both tend to be a little uncomfortable, and restrict movement to a certain extent.

A buoyancy aid, manufactured to a British Marine Industries Federation standard, will do no more than help you stay afloat. It is of no use if you cannot swim or are unconscious. On the other hand, a lifejacket manufactured to British Standard (BS) 3595 will keep you afloat on your back with mouth and nose clear of the water at an angle of 30–60° even if you are unconscious.

If your sailing is confined to sheltered waters during daylight, then a buoyancy aid may be acceptable, but you should really wear a lifejacket even then. At night and/or offshore there is no doubt that you must wear a lifejacket.

As yet, although the manufacture of personal buoyancy is governed by safety regulations, the wearing of it is still the choice of the individual. Clearly if you are single-handed you must wear buoyancy, as should all crew on deck in heavy weather or poor visibility. Non-swimmers must wear it at all times, and everyone should wear it when in a dinghy, whatever the conditions.

Lifejackets are either self-inflating on immersion or must be manually inflated by pulling a cord. The modern type are slimline when deflated, which makes them less cumbersome and more likely to be worn. Most manufacturers design them to be attached to their own brand of outer jacket, so this is yet another point to be considered when buying. Some have a non-metallic whistle and a light, as well as reflective strips. They should also have a crutch strap or a strap from neck to waistband to prevent them from being dragged over the head. On some an integral harness is fitted, which is obviously a good idea, although if your outer jacket has one this may be superfluous. Lifejackets are always bright yellow or orange because these are the most visible colours in water. When buying one you must make sure that it is a good fit. This is probably as important as the quality of its manufacture.

Safety harness

A safety harness, connected to a line, has the single role of preventing you from going over the side. If you have to make a choice between wearing a lifejacket or a harness then it must be the latter: it is more important to be stopped from going over the side than to be kept afloat after you have gone. (The only exception to this rule is when visibility is poor, as we shall see.) With modern designs it is quite possible and comfortable to wear both at the same time, so you should not have to make this choice. As already stated, modern outer garments often have an integral harness, as do some lifejackets. You should have a separate harness for warm weather or for working aloft.

In terms of when to wear a harness the same rules apply as for lifejackets. However, in poor visibility you should wear a lifejacket without a harness. This is because if you are run down the boat will probably sink rapidly and you do not want to be dragged down with it. It is the skipper who has the final responsibility for deciding what is to be worn. Young children must wear both at all times.

The British safety standard for a harness is BS 4224. The common chest harness is made of broad webbing which goes over the shoulders and crosses the chest and back. At the front it has a quick-release catch, with which to free yourself in case of difficulty, and a safety line. The latter, 2–3m long, is made of nylon rope or webbing and has a safety catch at the far end. The catch is used to hook on to secure points on the boat. The line should preferably have a second catch halfway along its length. This is used as a secondary hook-on point, allowing you to move freely around without ever unhooking. Always hook on to strong points that are bolted through the deck, such as chain plates and stanchion bases. The line must be relatively short so that if you do fall you are pulled up short of the water. For this reason you should always hook on to the windward side when practical, because you are more likely to fall in the direction of the boat's heel, which will be to leeward. The danger in going over the side while hooked on is that you may be dragged through the water. Even at the relatively slow speed of a sailing boat this can lead to injury or drowning.

It is because of the importance of a good fit that it is essential that lifejackets and harnesses are, as far as possible, assigned to individuals. They must be stowed so that they are readily accessible, preferably in individual lockers. It is equally important that they are regularly serviced and checked.

Checklist of essential clothing

1. *Thermal underwear, or at least two or three light shirts or pullovers.*
2. *Woollen trousers.*
3. *Thermal jackets.*
4. *Waterproof jacket and trousers.*
5. *Thick socks and sea boots.*
6. *Non-slip deck shoes for when sea boots are not required.*
7. *Warm head gear.*
8. *Warm waterproof gloves.*
9. *A complete change of clothing.*
10. *Sun-glasses.*
11. *Lifejacket.*
12. *Safety harness.*

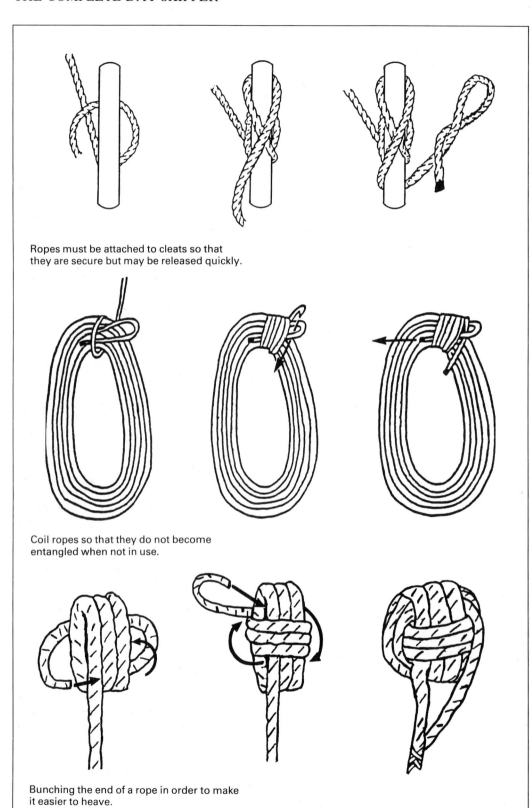

Ropes must be attached to cleats so that
they are secure but may be released quickly.

Coil ropes so that they do not become
entangled when not in use.

Bunching the end of a rope in order to make
it easier to heave.

Rope

The running rigging of a boat is invariably rope, although a halyard may have an inner core of wire. Rope has a wide range of uses on a boat. It is used as a warp for the anchor, lines to attach to mooring points, halyards to hoist sails and sheets to control them.

Types of rope

Until relatively recently all rope was produced from natural fibres such as cotton, hemp, manila and sisal. Threads of these fibres are spun into yarns which are then twisted into strands. The strands are then 'laid-up' or twisted into rope. The rope is held together by virtue of the fact that yarns are laid in one direction and the strands in the other. Some synthetic ropes are also manufactured in this way.

Laid-up rope may only be coiled in one direction, determined by whether it is left- or right-handed in manufacture. If right-handed it is coiled clockwise; anti-clockwise if left-handed.

Laid-up rope.

Braided rope.

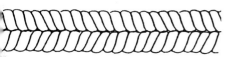

Plaited rope.

The alternatives to laid up rope are plaited and braided ropes. Their interwoven structure means that they will not kink and may be coiled either to the left or the right. A disadvantage of this structure is that it cannot be repaired by splicing without the use of special tools. Plaited and braided ropes are generally more flexible than the laid up variety, which when wet tend to be particularly stiff to handle. Clearly, these ropes are best for sheets, which must not be allowed to kink. While sheets and halyards are usually braided, mooring warps tend to be laid up.

Ropes made from natural fibres have largely disappeared from the modern boat. The development of synthetic rope has made the handling of sheets and other ropes much easier. BS 4928 covers the manufacture of synthetic ropes. The major synthetics are nylon, polypropylene, Terylene and Kevlar. The manufacture of these differs from that of natural fibre in that the yarn is made in continuous lengths which are then either laid-up into strands or braided and finally weaved into rope. The major advantages of the synthetics are their greater strength, lightness and rot resistance. The disadvantages are that they tend to be slippery and more difficult to control, especially when wet.

Nylon has considerable tensile strength and a high degree of elasticity (up to 20%), giving it good shock absorbency and making it strong and hard wearing. Multi-plait nylon is therefore ideal as an anchor warp and three strand nylon is ideal as a mooring line. Alongside a tidal pontoon the continuous swell will produce cyclical loading which may cause nylon rope to fail due to stress. This can be avoided by using a snubber (a shock absorber). The braided variety of nylon is the best as it will lay better when it is uncoiled and should not develop into a 'cat's-cradle' if stored for a long period.

Polypropylene will do the same job but tends to wear quickly and thus needs to be renewed frequently. It is, however, cheaper. You need to bear in mind that because of its lower breaking strain it needs to be of relatively greater diameter, and is best used where there is little applied pressure. It is frequently used as a short warp and has the valuable property of buoyancy, which makes it ideal for use as a dinghy painter or danbuoy line.

Terylene is nearly as strong as nylon but is not designed to be as elastic. It is therefore ideal for halyards if pre-stretched (ie Dacron). For the same reason braided Terylene should be used for control lines that take heavy loads. Terylene resists wear, and so is excellent as a long warp for a kedge or as head and stern ropes to cope with tidal rise and fall. When used as a mooring warp it should have a snubber. For sheets, sixteen-plait Terylene is best, because it is easy on hands and its frictional surface means it grips the winch better than do other types.

Kevlar is a relatively new material which is non-elastic and very strong but is also expensive and not very resistant to chafe.

A cruising boat needs to have at least six warps, excluding the bower and kedge anchor warps:

    1 bow rope the length of boat x 2
    1 stern rope the length of boat x 2
    2 springs the length of boat x 1.5
    2 breasts the length of boat x 1.5
(Allowance needs to be made for the tidal range of your normal cruising area.)

For a 33ft boat the head and stern ropes should be 14mm in diameter while the springs should be 10–12mm and the anchor warp 16mm.

Care of rope

Ropes do not last for ever. The durability of a rope is obviously determined by the quality of its manufacture, but the amount of use and the care involved in that use will also play a major part in determining its life span. All ropes must be kept clean, and that means regular washing to remove salt and grit. The latter, if allowed to get inside the rope, will cause chafe and therefore internal weakening which will not be visible. Ropes must therefore not be left lying where dirt will be ground into their internal structure by the treading action of feet. Washed ropes must be hung to dry naturally, because excessive heat will cause damage. Any kinks must not be pulled out but 'chased' to the end. When dried, a rope must be coiled and hung, not stowed flat.

Different ropes should be used for specific jobs and must never have dual roles. Mooring ropes, for example, inevitably become dirty and pick up grease which would be transferred to sails if they were also used as sheets. Chafe is the biggest danger to ropes of all kinds, so those used as mooring lines or anchor warps should be enclosed by short sections of plastic tubing, or wrapped in rags, where chafe is likely. Ropes used as guys, halyards or sheets should be regularly changed 'end for end' so that chafe is redistributed and their life consequently prolonged.

Winches and rope handling

Although perhaps not the most obviously dangerous aspect of sailing, ropes can cause injuries. Rope-burns can occur, and fingers can get trapped around cleats and winches, if care is not exercised in their use.

Winches are there to take the strain when you are hauling halyards or sheets. They allow you to achieve the maximum purchasing power on a rope. One turn of a sheet must first be taken around the winch in a clockwise direction, as that is the direction of rotation of most winches. Do not put any more turns on the winch at that stage otherwise the sheet may jam. Begin by hauling in hand-tight, then, as the load on the sheet increases, put two or three more turns around the winch in order to increase the friction. You will then need to use the winch handle. Insert the handle into the central socket so that it engages the ratchet mechanism. It is easier to winch in the remaining sheet with two crew, but one may do it alone. When two are doing it, one winches while the other maintains tension by 'tailing' the running end and gathering in more sheet as the winching continues. When you are winching alone, avoid the tendency to guide the sheet onto the winch with one hand while the other operates the winch handle. The hand not using the winch should, if holding the sheet at all, be clenched so that the fingers are not exposed. Never have any part of your hand between the sheet and drum. When the sail is correctly trimmed it is cleated and the handle is removed from the winch. The advantage of the self-tailing winch with its built-in cleat is immediately obvious, especially for the short-handed crew.

Tension must be eased off a winch, never suddenly released. First uncleat the sheet and gradually ease turns off the drum, with the palm of your hand placed against them. When you feel all the tension has gone from the sheet you may then cast off. If you need to release a sheet more rapidly you should flick the turns off the top of the winch, having first uncleated.

Although winches make rope handling relatively easy, problems do still occur, particularly the 'riding-turn', where one turn on the drum is jammed beneath another. This usually occurs because there are too many turns on the drum, but it may also be because the lead onto the winch is set at the wrong angle. The riding-turn acts as a lock, preventing a sheet from being winched in or eased out. Should a headsail sheet become jammed like this then it may well create serious problems. In order to release the jam the pressure needs to be taken off the sheet. This is usually best achieved by using a rolling hitch to attach a line to the sheet at a point close to the winch. If the other end of the line is then attached to a second winch and tensioned it should be relatively easy to release the pressure on the jammed sheet.

Attaching a rope to a cleat is simple, but do remember that putting several turns around the cleat does not give added security but does prevent quick release. Take just one or two turns behind the cleat and around the base. Then make two or three figure-of-eight cross turns, finishing with a round turn jammed hard behind the top of the cleat to stop the rope. This will prevent the coil working loose and coming off the cleat. Take the rope in one hand, close to the cleat, and coil it clockwise around that hand. Just before you reach the end put your hand through the coil and pull a bight of the standing part of the rope back through the coil and twist it two or three times. Then place the bight over the top horn of the cleat so that the coil hangs neatly. With the self-jamming cleat a single turn around the cleat will be adequate.

At all times, ropes must be ready for use and not entangled. Untidy heaps of rope on the deck or in the cockpit can cause accidents, and may even result in someone going over the side. They can also lead to gear failure, and if allowed to enter the water may

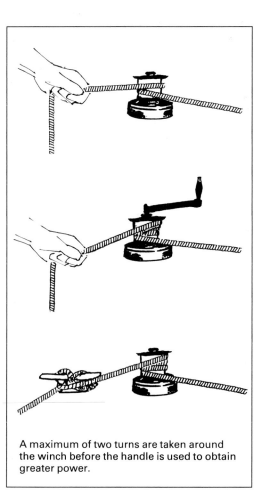

A maximum of two turns are taken around the winch before the handle is used to obtain greater power.

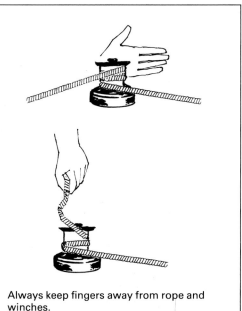

Always keep fingers away from rope and winches.

FIGURE OF EIGHT

This is a stopper knot, tied at the end of a line, especially a sheet, to prevent it running through a block. It will not jam and is easily untied.

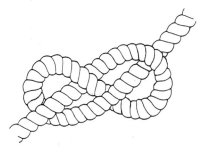

Figure of eight.

CLOVE HITCH

This may be used for temporarily securing rope to a mooring ring or spar. It is also useful for securing fenders to the guardrail for short periods. Used with two loops it may be placed over a bollard and made more secure with a half hitch. You must bear in mind that it will only hold well when under constant strain perpendicular to the object to which it is secured. As a clove hitch can slip, unwind or jam it is often better to use an alternative knot.

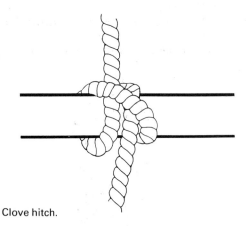

Clove hitch.

ROLLING HITCH

This knot is similar to the clove hitch but has an extra turn. It is used either for fastening a rope to a spar or chain, or for fastening a rope to a thicker rope in order to take the strain temporarily, for example when releasing a riding turn. With the former use the pressure must be applied in a linear direction.

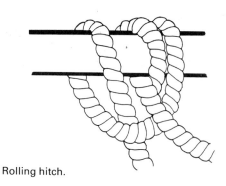

Rolling hitch.

REEF KNOT

The reef knot is used for fastening reefing ties or bandages. This knot is insecure and so has no other safe use.

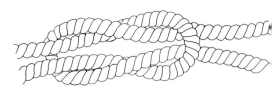

Reef knot.

BOWLINE

A good, easy-to-tie, general purpose knot, a bowline is particularly useful for making a temporary eye in a mooring warp so as to put the line over a bollard, or for attaching a sheet to a sail. In the latter case if it is not tied tightly a flogging sail might well cause it to come undone.

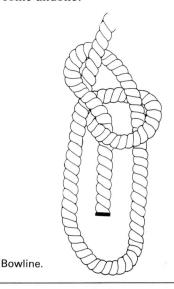

Bowline.

SHEET BEND

This is the knot to use when you want to fasten two ropes together. It is especially useful where the two ropes are of differing thickness or material.

Sheet bend.

DOUBLE SHEET BEND

A more secure version of the single sheet bend, this provides an easy method of making fast to an eye so as to fasten sheets to a sail. It may also be used to fasten a rope to the eye of an eye splice.

With both sheet bends the bight should be formed in the thicker of the two ropes. It would also be sensible to seize the ends by lashing them to the standing part with twine.

ROUND TURN AND TWO HALF HITCHES

This is the most widely used knot for mooring because it minimises chafe. It is excellent for securing a rope to a ring or post, for attaching fenders to a boat, or a dinghy painter to a mooring. It is very easy to tie and adjust. It is also very secure and may be let go under tension. Although it will never untie it may jam if overloaded.

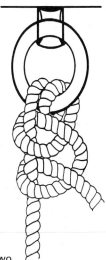

Round turn and two half hitches.

FISHERMAN'S BEND

This is the only knot to use for securing the anchor warp to the anchor ring. It is very secure and minimises chafe on the warp.

Double sheet bend.

Fisherman's bend.

35

foul the propeller. To avoid these possibilities, rope should be coiled and stowed
when not in use.

There are various methods of coiling a
rope in preparation for heaving or stowing.
The majority of ropes are laid or twisted in a
right-hand or clockwise direction and must
therefore be coiled in that direction. While a
halyard coil is usually placed over a cleat a
sheet coil is normally placed on the deck so
that the sheet runs from the top. A coil that is
not required immediately should have a half
hitch made around its body with its own end.
Coils left for a period of time in a locker are
likely to become entangled with other gear,
so a seizing of twine should be placed around
them at two or three points. You must have
one coil, unseized, ready for emergency use
at all times.

There will be occasions when you need to
'heave', or throw, a line. These might be to
give or accept a tow, or to pass a line to a
helper on the quay or pontoon. To get distance and accuracy you need to follow a few
simple rules. The rope to be heaved should
be coiled, and the coil evenly divided between your hands. Stand straight, with your
feet well spaced to give a good footing. If
right-handed, your left shoulder should be
turned towards your target. Build up
momentum with a pendulum action and then
release by letting the first coil go and allowing
the second to run through your hand. To improve accuracy and distance, bunch the leading end of the rope with an easily released
knot.

Whipping

Whipping is a method of preserving or, more
correctly, repairing frayed rope ends. All
rope ends will eventually fray unless they are
somehow sealed. Synthetic ropes may be
heat-sealed to preserve (or repair) frayed
ends, but fraying will inevitably recur. Although it is possible to use a back splice
(where the rope is weaved back into itself)
this usually so enlarges the end of the rope
that it will not pass through the eye of a fairlead or block. It is therefore best to use traditional waxed or Terylene whipping twine to
make the repair. For this you will need a
good clean clasp knife with a sharp but slim
blade, a roping palm, needles and Vaseline.

Splicing

There are several different types of splice.
They are used to join ropes by weaving the
ends together, to repair rope ends and to put
a permanent eye in a rope end. Such tasks are
relatively easy with laid up rope but with
plaited and braided ropes you will require
special tools.

Knots

A typical dictionary definition of a knot
would be 'a fastening made by tying together
pieces of rope'. An alternative definition
would be 'a lump in a rope as formed by a
tangle'. Tangles must be avoided! They may
look strong but can actually be very weak, or
be so intertwined that the rope cannot be released quickly, thus causing problems.

The correct methods of tying the various
knots must be learnt, and practised until they
become second nature. You must also know
their respective uses.

Knots are used to join ropes together and
to enlarge rope ends to prevent them running
through blocks. They are also used to tie
ropes to rings, cleats, bollards and sails. The
term 'bend' describes a knot which joins two
ropes, while a 'hitch' is a series of loops which
jam when pulled tight, but will release when
the pressure is relieved. Knots, bends and
hitches should be used sparingly as they reduce the breaking strain of an individual rope
by up to 50%.

Questions

Answers are on page 223.
1. Which type of rope would you use for the following?
   a) A danbuoy line.
   b) A main halyard.
   c) An anchor warp.
   d) A mooring warp.
   e) A genoa sheet.
2. Which type of cordage is shown in the diagram?

3. What would you use the following for?
   a) A round turn and two half hitches.
   b) A clove hitch.
   c) A bowline.
4. Which knots would you use for the following?
   a) Tying a bandage.
   b) Stopping the end of a sheet.
   c) Joining two ropes of differing thickness.
   d) Attaching a rope to a chain or spar.
5. Which type of knot is shown in each of the following diagrams?

a)

b)

c)

d)

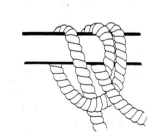

Running with the spinnaker boom well aft and a headsail
set to reduce the power of the spinnaker.

CHAPTER 5

Boat Handling

You must develop a complete understanding of how your boat responds in varying conditions under sail and power. Although the characteristics of the rig and engine play an obvious role in this response, the overall shape of the boat as produced by the design of the hull and superstructure plays an equally important role.

Beneath the waterline you may have a long keel, a deep or shallow fin or a bilge keel. Above the water you may have a Bermuda-rigged schooner or a two-masted ketch. You may have the high coachroof of a motor sailer or the low coachroof of a racing cruiser. The hull may be heavy and beamy or it may have a streamlined, light displacement shape. The stern may be cut almost vertical, or you may have a counter that slopes aft. All of these affect the response of the boat.

The first thing to do is study the response characteristics of your boat while it is moored. Any movement in response to wind or stream will not be the result of sail or power, but of the overall design of the boat. The natural tendency is for windage on the above-water part of the boat to cause the bow to point downwind and the stern upwind. However, this windage effect is opposed by the resistance of the immersed part of the hull, and the keel, rudder and sterngear. A further complication is introduced by the asymmetry of the above- and below-water surface areas. One end of the boat will offer greater area to the wind than the other, and one end of the boat has a greater underwater surface area than the other.

By studying your boat you should be able to determine the approximate location of the point at which the greatest amount of windage is concentrated: that is the centre of effort of the wind. The point at which the maximum resistance to water is located is called the centre of lateral resistance.

A cursory consideration of the profile of the typical cruiser will show that the centre of effort must be ahead of the centre of lateral resistance. You would therefore expect the boat to pivot around a point between the two, so that the bow blows off the wind. On turning downwind the boat will present a constantly changing profile to both water and wind. Eventually, when the boat is 90°, or more, to the wind, the centre of effort will lie directly downwind of the centre of lateral resistance. The forces are then said to be in equilibrium and the boat will drift with a constant angle to the wind until there is a change in one of the forces: either a decrease or an increase in the wind or a change in the stream. The rate of drift of the boat will be about 10% of the wind speed.

To find out how your boat behaves in different wind and sea conditions you should take it out in light to moderate winds with a gentle sea and experiment. The ideal starting point is with the boat close-hauled. Let the helm go free to see what might happen if your tiller or rudder was damaged. Many production boats will continue heading into the wind with greater steadiness than if there was a hand on the helm. Such boats will tend to bear away in a gust and then slowly luff up again. If your boat is not balanced then it will not easily make progress to windward. It may be that because of the underwater profile, the state of the sea, or the sails being carried, the boat develops significant lee helm and bears away to the point where it may even gybe. Alternatively, if it develops weather helm it may luff up and then tack itself through the wind so that it lies head-to-wind with the headsail backed. Should your boat bear away or luff up like this and show no tendency to self-correct then you need to change the set and/or trim of your sails. If that does not succeed then try increasing or decreasing the sail according to the conditions. With experience you should be able to make some progress upwind without the helm.

It is not as easy to control the heading of a

boat when you are sailing off the wind. On letting go the helm the boat will either tack and lie head-to-wind with the headsail backed or will simply luff up and lie with the sails flapping. Should you have a large headsail set then it is possible that the boat will head off downwind. Again, you will have to adjust your sails to achieve a balance.

The effect of the stream is to move a floating object over the seabed in a given direction at a given rate. At any one time and location an object, whether it be a supertanker or piece of driftwood, will move over the seabed in exactly the same direction and at the same rate as would any other.

The significance of the stream lies not just in the way it drifts you across the seabed, but also in its effect on your speed. For your boat to be under control the rudder needs to bite hard into the water. To achieve this you must have forward power through the water. If the stream is going in the same direction as you are then your speed over the seabed will be equal to the boat's speed plus the speed of the stream. In confined waters this may be too fast for comfort. In order to stop you will have to put the engine into reverse, but this may not be as easy as it sounds because the very act of going hard astern to counteract the stream will cause the boat to deviate wildly off its track. This is a result of prop walk. Clearly it is easier to manoeuvre when you are going into the stream. Your overall speed over the seabed will then be equal to the boat's speed minus the stream's speed. In this situation, slight adjustments of power and helm will allow you to move gradually in the required direction.

A two-bladed propeller.

Effects of the engine

Your boat will almost certainly be an auxiliary sail cruiser. That is to say that the engine is an auxiliary, an extra. Even though the boat is primarily powered by sail it needs an engine for manoeuvring in harbour and for maintaining passage speed. You may argue that the engine is very much part of your safety equipment because it provides back-up propulsion should your rig fail. It will also help to get you into harbour before deteriorating weather arrives or you have to fight a foul tide. The engine might fail, however, and so you must be competent enough to complete any manoeuvre under sail that you might normally carry out under power.

An auxiliary engine is inevitably a compromise. It provides the power for the above manoeuvres but it does have definite disadvantages: the engine and fuel tank add significant weight to the boat and by doing so are detrimental to its sailing performance; the propeller creates drag which also affects performance (although you can buy propellers that substantially reduce this problem by folding into a streamlined shape). When sailing the vibrations from the spinning propeller can be very irritating, especially if you are trying to sleep in the quarter berth.

The effect of the movement of the propeller through the water is quite complicated in that it produces lateral as well as forward or reverse movement. This lateral movement is particularly significant because it is most pronounced at low speeds, and therefore has implications for manoeuvring in marinas and harbours.

The propeller acts in several ways. It grips the water in the same way as a swimmer and literally pushes the boat through, while at the same time ejecting a stream of water astern (when in forward gear). The size of the propeller and the lack of grip provided by the water mean that it initially finds it difficult to grip, and so most of its energy is used in ejecting the slipstream. Once the boat gains some momentum the propeller begins to grip the water more easily and the slipstream is reduced. The boat is steered by angling the rudder across the slipstream so that half the slipstream is deflected.

A further action of the propeller is that it attempts to turn the boat sideways because of the twist built into the shape of its blades.

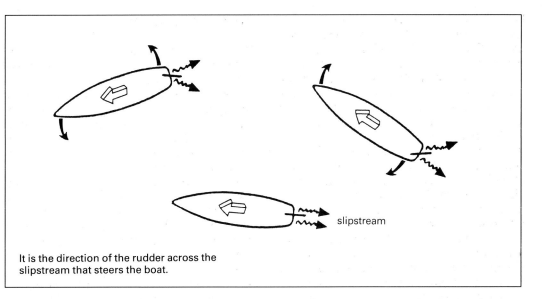

It is the direction of the rudder across the
slipstream that steers the boat.

This tendency, known as prop walk, is increased by the rapid increase of water density with depth. There is therefore a marked and significant difference in density across the lower and upper blades as the propeller rotates. A useful analogy is with a rower who is much stronger on one side than the other, and so finds it very difficult to keep the boat pointing in a straight line. The effects of the prop walk increase with increasing propeller diameter and decreasing speed of rotation.

Clearly it is important to know the direction in which your propeller rotates, as that controls prop walk. A right-handed or clockwise turning propeller not only produces forward drive but also pulls the stern to starboard so that the bow drifts to port. The same propeller in reverse rotates in the opposite direction and so drives the boat astern, causing the bow to turn to starboard and the stern to port. Should you have a propeller that rotates the other way then just reverse the above directions. You can determine whether you have a left- or right-handed propeller (in forward mode) by looking at the direction of rotation of the shaft or by looking at the propeller itself, which should be stamped either left- or right-handed.

When going astern you must remember that the point about which the boat pivots will move aft, so the bow will swing through a wider arc. Unless you have a firm hold on the helm you will find that the water will push the rudder hard over.

The rudder is not particularly effective

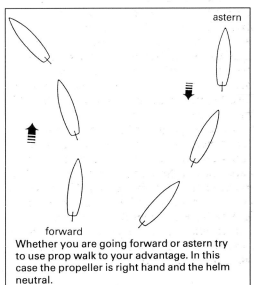

Whether you are going forward or astern try to use prop walk to your advantage. In this case the propeller is right hand and the helm neutral.

when going astern because it only forces half the slipstream in the required direction. The greater the momentum of the boat the longer it will take to answer the helm. The first effect of moving the rudder is to cause the boat to drift out of the turn. The amount of this drift is determined by the underwater profile of the boat, the speed of the boat and its weight. A heavy bilge keel will drift further out of the turn than will a deep keeled boat.

Rather than worrying about these prop walk effects you should learn to use them to your advantage in tight manoeuvring situations. One point to remember is that a boat

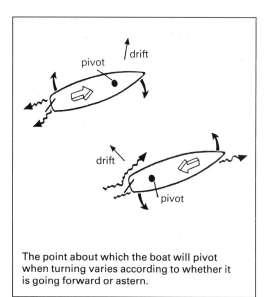

The point about which the boat will pivot when turning varies according to whether it is going forward or astern.

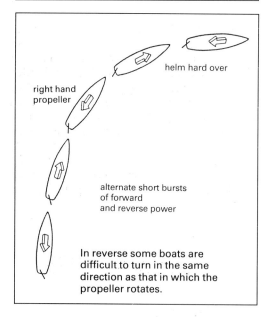

In reverse some boats are difficult to turn in the same direction as that in which the propeller rotates.

will turn a tighter circle in the opposite direction to that in which its propeller rotates. A right-handed propeller will therefore produce a tighter turn to port than to starboard. All things being equal, you will therefore choose to turn to port when manoeuvring. The opposite holds true for a left-handed propeller. In reverse gear this effect is even more significant, and some boats prove very difficult to turn in the same direction as their propeller rotates. Should circumstances force you to reverse in that direction then you will need to keep the helm hard over and al-

ternate short forward bursts of power with short bursts in reverse. The typical auxiliary cruiser will usually turn in about one and a half lengths with full helm and engine ahead.

Anchoring

The aim of anchoring is to remain stationary offshore in a safe situation, perhaps in order to seek shelter from deteriorating weather, to go ashore, or simply to rest. The art is to so place the anchor that you settle at exactly the required spot and swing clear in safe water with the anchor firmly bedded in. To anchor successfully you must have the correct equipment and a sound, well executed plan.

EQUIPMENT
You will need:

- *two anchors;*
- *a combined chain and warp of at least five times the HW depth;*
- *a trip line (not always used);*
- *an all-round white anchor light;*
- *a large black ball (to hoist in the rigging during day to indicate that the boat is anchored).*

The main, or 'bower', anchor has to be heavy enough for the size of the boat. For boats of up to 40ft in length, a safe guide is 1lb (0.45kg) of anchor for every 1ft of boat. You should err on the heavy side. An anchor that is too small will eventually lead to problems. It will certainly drag in poor holding ground or in heavy weather.

The kedge anchor, which may be a size smaller than the bower, must be of a different type in order to increase your options. The kedge has a variety of uses apart from being a back-up to the bower in difficult conditions. It may, for example, be used to hold a boat in position against a foul tide, or to help refloat a grounded boat.

ANCHOR TYPE
The four most commonly used anchors are the fisherman, Danforth, plough (or CQR) and Bruce.

Fisherman Although this is the traditional anchor it is seldom used today. A good general-purpose anchor, it holds well in mud, clay and shingle. It has the advantage of being able to be stowed flat if the stock is unshipped, although if it is not well secured it may cause damage to the deck. The main disadvantage of this anchor is that it needs to be much larger, and 50% heavier, than a Danforth or CQR of equivalent holding power. This is because it will hold a strain of only 7–10 times its own weight. It has few moving parts to jam, but the flukes may foul the chain or the boat and it is generally unwieldy to use.

Fisherman's anchor.

Bruce The Bruce is a relatively new anchor with a very high hold–weight ratio of approximately 25–30 times its own weight. It is especially good on a short line as it digs in well. It holds well on rock, sand and mud, but not kelp. The one-piece design, with no moving parts to foul, makes it a very good anchor which is easy to break out. Its disadvantage is that like the plough it is difficult to stow.

Bruce anchor.

Danforth This is a flat anchor with twin flukes and the stock built into the head. It has an excellent hold–weight ratio, being particularly good in soft sand and soft clay. It does not hold so well in hard sand or seaweed, and may slide some distance before biting if the seabed is shingle or rock. If a tripping line is not used the Danforth may be difficult to

break out of mud. Its other disadvantages include the possibility that a pebble may jam its hinge in the open position, or that its movable parts may injure your hands. However, its design makes it unlikely to foul its own cable and allows it to be stowed flat, unlike the plough.

Danforth anchor.

Plough (or CQR) The plough, so named because of its shape, was the first stockless anchor for small boats. It has similar holding characteristics to the Danforth, but is harder to stow, and its moving parts may cause it to capsize or injure a hand. Based on the concept of swivel geometry, it will sheer round without breaking out, which is advantageous in strong tidal streams or a fluctuating wind. It holds well on all ground except rock, kelp and hard sand, and may prove difficult to break out of mud unless a tripping line is used.

Plough or CQR anchor.

Anchor line
An anchor's holding ability is also influenced by the catenary, or curve, of its line. This is determined by the line's weight and length. The best hold occurs when the first part of the line is horizontal, rather than steeply inclined from the anchor. This is because if the initial pull is largely horizontal then that tends to

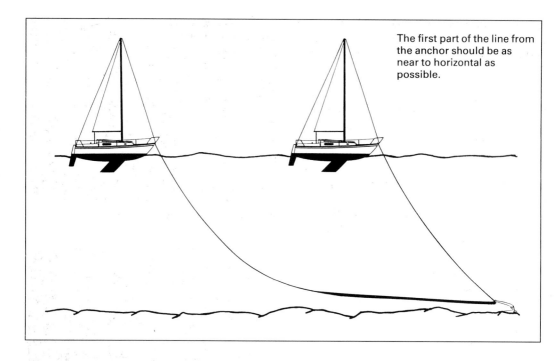

The first part of the line from the anchor should be as near to horizontal as possible.

dig the anchor into the seabed. The implication is that you should have an all-chain line. However, because of the cost and stowage problems of chain most boat owners have to compromise and have a line that is mostly warp. At the very least the first 5–10m leading from the anchor must be chain in order to ensure an initial horizontal pull.

The length of the line is of as much importance as its weight. This length, the scope, is expressed as a multiple of the depth of water at high water. With an all-chain line a scope of 4 : 1 will be adequate because the line will hang down in a catenary and so produce a horizontal pull. Indeed, in quiet weather the boat may well lie to the chain with no pull being exerted on the anchor. One advantage of chain is that it reduces the swinging circle of the boat. With a short length of chain attached to nylon warp the ratio should be no less than 6 : 1. The minimum length of your anchor lines should be 60m for the bower and 30m for the kedge. In heavy weather, or with poor holding ground, the scope must be significantly increased.

The warp used should be either three strand nylon or anchorplait and should be one size larger than a mooring warp. The chain should be 8mm in diameter for a 25ft boat, so that with a 15kg anchor your ground tackle will be able to cope with a force of up

to 2,000kg. The anchor line must be marked every 2m so that you know how much you have paid out. The easiest way to mark chain is to paint the links. With rope it is best to sew in scraps of coloured material.

The bitter end of the anchor line must be secured to an eyebolt in the chain locker by a line that is long enough to be hauled out on deck if necessary. The weak links in the anchor line will be the point at which the warp is joined to the chain and the point at which the chain is joined to the anchor. The pin of the shackle joining the chain to the anchor must be moused with a small piece of wire so that it will not undo as it moves around on the seabed.

Stowage of the anchor and chain, which may have a combined weight of over 80kg is a problem. Most medium sized boats have the anchor/chain locker well up in the bow, which is exactly where you do not want such a weight if you wish to get the maximum speed from your boat. Any possible solution will depend upon the interior layout of your boat.

CHOOSING AN ANCHORAGE
There are various points to consider when choosing an anchorage:

Depth Is the water deep enough? Use Admiralty tidal curves to calculate the depth for the period you will be anchored. There may be adequate depth at high water but not enough to float you at low water, and you would then have to wait for the tide to rise again before you could depart. At low water you should have enough water to float, plus half your draught for clearance, and enough to ensure that you are not likely to swing out of this required depth. At high water you may find that where there is a gently sloping seabed you have a long row ashore; at low water this becomes an impossible walk over deep mud.

Use the available tidal information to make sure that you are not anchoring in a strong tidal stream.

Poor holding ground – rock and weed.

Shelter Is the anchorage sheltered from the present wind and swell, and from any forecast weather changes? An open roadstead between headlands is a suitable place if the headlands reduce the seas and if the bay is a weather shore. Any location at which the fetch is limited, thus reducing maximum wave size, will be favourable. Steep sided estuaries can produce violent downdraughts and are less secure than those backed by wooded rolling hills, which make excellent windbreaks. Never anchor on an exposed lee shore in a strong wind, and make sure that conditions are not going to change and put you in that position.

A clay bed with no obstacles makes a good anchorage.

Seabed Is the seabed suitable? The holding power of different materials varies. Soft mud, for instance, has only one-third the holding power of sand or clay. Kelp, pebbles and rock generally give a very poor hold. Pebbles and weed may easily jam the moving parts of an anchor so that it loses its effectiveness. Foul ground, such as wrecks, must obviously be avoided. The quality of the holding ground may be determined by consulting the chart and local pilot. If the ground is poor or simply does not suit your anchor then you will have to go elsewhere.

Even if not prohibited this is not a good anchorage.

Swinging room Have you sufficient swinging room? Your boat will swing constantly with the changing wind and tide, and you must be careful not to swing into other boats or into a navigation channel. At the same time in the same location other boats will swing at different rates and in different directions. Clearly this may well lead to collision and damage.

A boat that has substantial windage and a small underwater area is more affected by wind than by tide. A boat with a long deep hull tends to lie more to the tidal stream than to the wind. Some designs will sail around the anchor while others will tend to sheer to one side, where they stay. All this you must bear in mind when you arrive at an anchorage.

There may well seem to be sufficient space between the boats for you to anchor, but you will not know the location of the individual anchors or how the boats are lying to those anchors. You may find that you anchor in an apparently safe location only to be fouled when the tide or wind changes.

Other factors that need to be borne in mind are whether the anchorage is prohibited, and the proximity of traffic lanes. A common reason for prohibition is the presence of shellfish or oyster beds or a pipeline.

PREPARING THE EQUIPMENT
1. *Fasten the anchor on deck close to the anchor roller.*
2. *Lay on deck the amount of line to be veered.*
3. *Flake the chain on deck to make sure that there are no kinks or jams that would prevent the smooth running of the line.*
4. *Cleat the line at half scope and full scope.*
5. *Put the fenders out if you plan to anchor close to other boats.*
6. *Have the engine running in neutral in case of emergency.*

EXECUTION OF ANCHORING
As you approach your chosen harbour or bay take constant bearings on landmarks so that you arrive at the precise point at which you wish to anchor. If there are other boats in the anchorage look at how they lie to their anchors. Decide on the most likely direction that you will drag, usually downwind, and approach from that direction. Have a few practice runs to get the feel of the anchorage.

If you are approaching from downwind, with the wind and tide in the same direction or at a right angle to each other, come in close-hauled. The crew must unlash the anchor and check that the 'bitter' end is secure to the boat and that the anchor is secure to the line. The correct amount of line must be flaked out on deck so that there are no kinks. As you close the anchorage come head to wind and let the sails fly. The boat's headway will carry it to the point over that on the seabed at which the anchor is to lie. As the boat stops and then gathers sternway the crew should lift the anchor clear of the anchor roller and, on seeing a pre-arranged signal from the helm, lower it gradually from the bow so that the chain does not end up lying on it. Veer the line up to the first cleated position. Grasp the cable forward of the roller and you should feel the anchor drag and then bite. At that moment gradually begin to veer the remainder of the scope. Should there be little sternway because of a light wind or gentle stream then use the engine in reverse for a few seconds to ensure that the anchor line does not lie in a heap on top of the anchor on the seabed.

When the remainder of the scope has been veered out put the engine gently astern, no more than half a knot, to check that the anchor holds. If it becomes obvious that it is not going to hold then either let out more line or raise the anchor and start again. Finally, check that you are not going to swing into any problems.

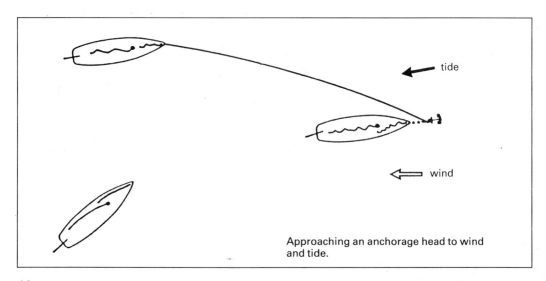

tide

wind

Approaching an anchorage head to wind and tide.

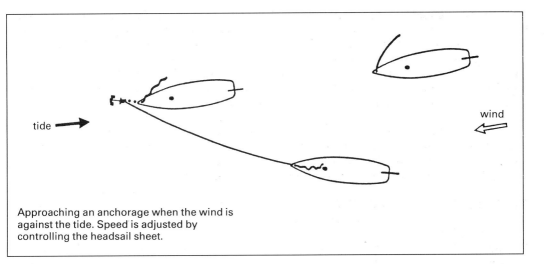

Approaching an anchorage when the wind is
against the tide. Speed is adjusted by
controlling the headsail sheet.

If the wind is against the tide then approach with the wind, stemming the tide, with the mainsail lowered. At the chosen spot let the headsail fly, or lower it, and then proceed as above. The boat will drift with the tide against the wind.

If the tide is against the wind but the latter is stronger then approach from upwind under headsail with the main lowered. At the chosen spot let the headsail fly, or lower it, and release the anchor. Although you continue as before, the boat will, in this situation, swing head to wind and drift back against the tide.

When anchoring with the engine always turn the boat to stem the tide at the chosen spot. Go slowly astern and lower the anchor, taking care to avoid entangling the cable in the propeller.

Once you have anchored hoist a black ball in the bow, or an all-round white light at night, and check again that the bitter end of the cable is secured. Check the depth with the echo sounder and set the depth alarm if one is available. Complete your deck log and tidy the boat. Fix the position of your anchor by taking bearings on shore objects. Around that position on the chart draw a circle equal to the radius of the cable you have veered. Check the position regularly: if you find that you are out of the circle then you are dragging.

DRAGGING ANCHOR
Apart from drifting away from the position circle there are other clues to indicate that you might be dragging. If the cable is tending

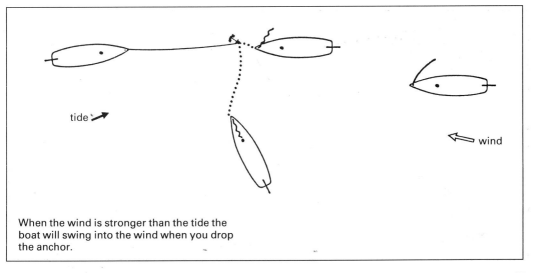

When the wind is stronger than the tide the
boat will swing into the wind when you drop
the anchor.

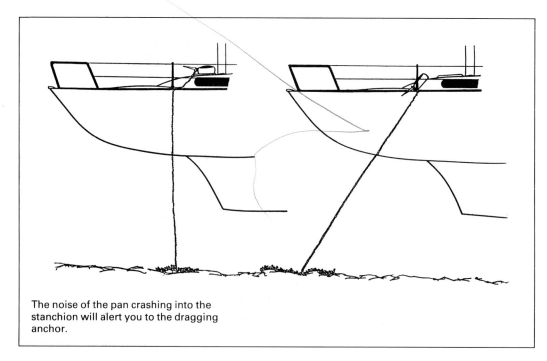

The noise of the pan crashing into the stanchion will alert you to the dragging anchor.

to snatch (that is, if it is alternately slack and taut) this is one sure sign. Others are grasping the cable and feeling vibrations, and hearing a distinctive rasping sound inside the cabin.

Various alarms may be used to warn of dragging while it is still at an early stage. For example, all good echo sounders have an anchor watch whereby an audio-visual alarm is triggered if the boat moves into deeper or shallower water. There are also numerous simple non-electronic alarms. One involves sinking a weight attached to a taut line to the seabed. The bitter end is passed through the eye at the base of a stanchion, laid across the deck and secured to a potentially noisy object such as a length of chain or a frying pan. The chain (say) is attached on deck in such a way that it will not move easily. (You must have some slack in the chain because no boat stays stationary for long and you otherwise run the risk of being regularly woken by false alarms.) If the boat drags, the weight on the seabed will initially stay in place, but pressure will be applied to the line so that the section lying on deck becomes taut and pulls the object hard into the stanchion, creating a loud noise.

Alternatively you could wedge the forehatch open and pass the line around the wedge so that when it becomes taut as a result of drag the wedge will be pulled out, slamming the hatch shut.

When the wind strength forecast is not clear it is possible to make a wind alarm to indicate increased strength and hence the likelihood of dragging. Tie a weak rope to the anchor line ahead of the bow and bring 2–3m of that line onto the deck and secure it by the weak rope to a deck cleat. Then attach a short length of chain to the line on deck. As the wind increases so the pressure on the

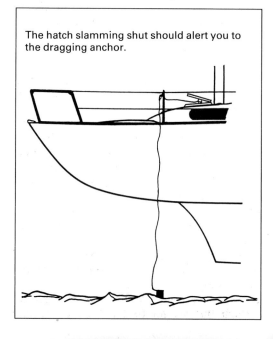

The hatch slamming shut should alert you to the dragging anchor.

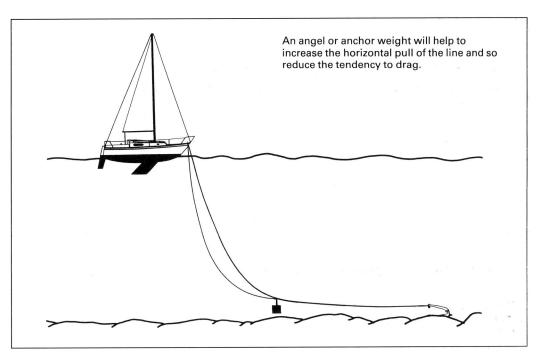

An angel or anchor weight will help to increase the horizontal pull of the line and so reduce the tendency to drag.

anchor line will increase until the weak rope breaks. The line will then drop back into the water and the chain will rattle across the deck.

In order to prevent drag it is necessary to understand why it occurs. There are two major reasons for it – excessive yaw and/or the shaft of the anchor being lifted above the horizontal. If excessive yaw develops it produces a sideways snatching action which will wrench the anchor out of the seabed. The best remedy is to lay a second anchor (see below). For an anchor to hold well the shaft needs to be flat and the flukes need to dig into the seabed. When the line is lifting the shaft above the horizontal the holding power is dramatically reduced. A lift of only 15° will reduce the holding power by 50%. With an exposed coastline and a long fetch the procession of long rolling waves which come with an onshore wind will produce considerable oscillating shock loads on the anchor line, which goes taut and snubs hard as each wave crest passes. The answer is either to veer more line or to use an angel (an anchor weight).

All that is required is a 10kg weight shackled to a line. It is possible to purchase ready-made weights but it is cheaper to find an empty paint tin and fill it with concrete. Attach this weight to the anchor line and allow it to slide down it for about 20m; secure the bitter end to the foredeck. This will increase the catenary of the line and therefore decrease its tendency to snatch. The angel will also reduce the lifting effect of the line on the shaft by directing the pull at a lower angle. The result will be greatly increased holding power. You may also use an angel to reduce the scope, and thus decrease your swinging circle while maintaining the same holding power.

LAYING TWO ANCHORS
You may decide to lie to two anchors when first anchoring or be forced by changing circumstances to lay a second. Two anchors will limit the swing of the boat, which is essential if the area of safe water is restricted, and will give you extra security in heavy weather. There are many methods of laying them, but both must be strong enough in their own right to hold the boat if the other should drag.

If you decide from the outset that conditions dictate the use of two anchors, lay the first as described above but veer twice as much cable as you would normally require. Drift back until, at the end of this scope, the anchor bites. Then drop the second anchor under the bow. Heave on the first while veering the second. When the second anchor bites the boat should be halfway between the

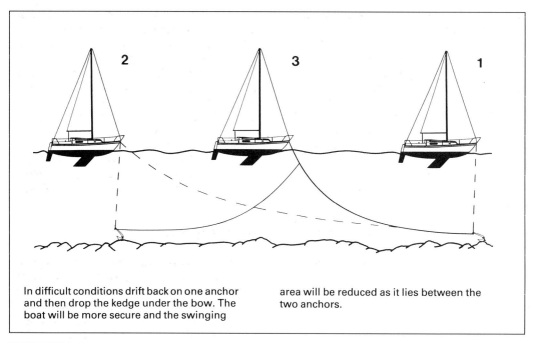

In difficult conditions drift back on one anchor and then drop the kedge under the bow. The boat will be more secure and the swinging area will be reduced as it lies between the two anchors.

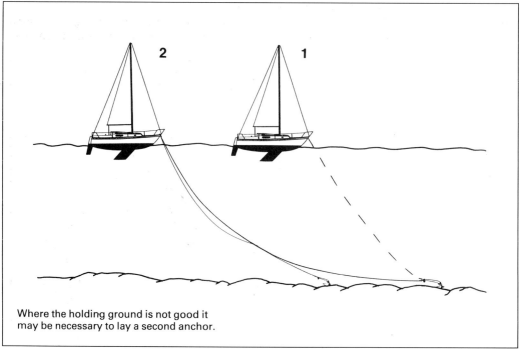

Where the holding ground is not good it may be necessary to lay a second anchor.

two. Shackle the second line to the first, if using chain, or, if using warp, join the two lines with a rolling hitch. In both cases the point of attachment should lie well below the keel. The bitter end of the second line will come aboard with the first line. The boat will then swing through a smaller than usual circle, on both lines, without fouling. If you should wish to reduce swing still further, perhaps because of restricted room, then attach the first line to the bow and the second to the stern. It is always best to have slightly more pull on the bower otherwise the kedge is likely to drag.

Two anchors may be laid in tandem should you consider that conditions are such that holding may not be good. Proceed as usual up to the point at which the bower line has been veered to half scope. Then bend the kedge line to the bower line and lower the kedge. Drift back to full scope on the bower. The kedge will not act until the bower drags. The two lines should not foul while the direction of pull remains constant but might if swing in excess of 90° develops. A variation on this is to lay the kedge first, well ahead of the bower. The kedge will then drag until the bower bites; if the bower drags then the kedge should check it.

If a veering wind is forecast you can use two anchors to minimise possible problems. Anchor as before but with the bower to port followed immediately by the kedge lowered under the starboard bow at about 45° to starboard. The angle should be no greater, otherwise the strain on the individual anchors will be too great. This angle between them should prevent them from fouling each other. As the wind veers pay out the second cable until the boat lies to both anchors.

If, having set one anchor, you find that the boat subsequently drags, it is easy to lay a second. One method of doing this is to back the headsail and steer the boat as far as possible to one side before lowering the anchor and drifting back. When using two anchors like this the ideal angle between the two cables is 35°. The holding power will then be twice that of a single anchor. If the angle increases beyond 35° then the relative holding power decreases from two fold to equal only that of a single anchor at 120°.

Weighing anchor

Preparation is as important for weighing as it is for arrival at an anchorage. In particular you must decide on which tack you wish to depart. This will be largely determined by the amount of room available for manoeuvre and the relationship between the wind and the tide.

If the wind and tide are together, hoist both sails and take up slack on the anchor,

A second anchor may be laid under the bow as the wind changes direction.

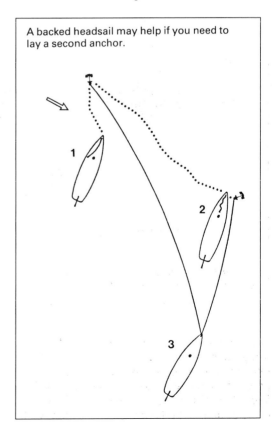

A backed headsail may help if you need to lay a second anchor.

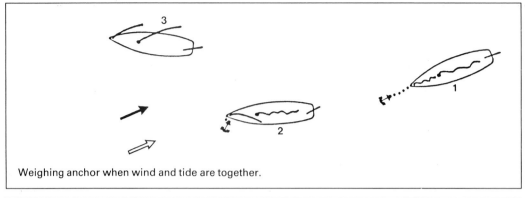

Weighing anchor when wind and tide are together.

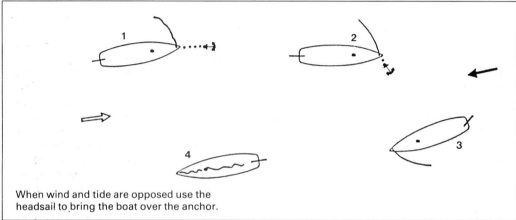

When wind and tide are opposed use the
headsail to bring the boat over the anchor.

feeding the line into the anchor locker until
you are directly over the anchor. At that
point the crew should tell the helm that the
anchor is 'up and down'. As the anchor
leaves the seabed give the boat a slight sheer
with the rudder and back the headsail so that
the mainsail fills. Sail gently while the anchor
is being lifted, and continue to do so until it is
secured on deck.

When the wind is against the tide hoist only
the headsail and use that to bring the boat
over the anchor. As the anchor breaks free
sail downwind until it is secured on deck and
then round the boat head to wind in order to
hoist the mainsail.

When the wind is across the tide hoist both
sails, but only allow them to fill to a small extent until the anchor is secured.

At times when it is vital to get the boat sailing immediately, such as in a crowded anchorage, then the headsail must be hoisted
from the outset in order to pay the bow off in
the required direction. The headsail will obviously get in the way of the crew raising the
anchor and there is therefore a danger of the

anchor damaging it, or at least making it
dirty. If there is adequate searoom, avoid this
by setting only the mainsail. Once the anchor
is secured you can fall off the wind in order to
pick up speed and then turn head to wind so
that you can hoist the headsail.

When you are weighing anchor whilst
using the engine it is best to motor to a position directly above the anchor. With the engine running slowly, raise and secure the anchor before turning the boat head to wind
and hoisting the sails.

FOULED ANCHOR
There is a temptation to say that this should
never happen, and that if it does it is a result
of carelessness. However, as it does happen
to even the most careful and experienced
sailors there must be more to it than that.

If the anchor gets caught on loose boulders
on the seabed then release may be very
difficult. One technique is to make a 0.3m
diameter collar and attach it to a line. Send
the collar down the anchor line and slacken
that line. If you are lucky the collar will slip

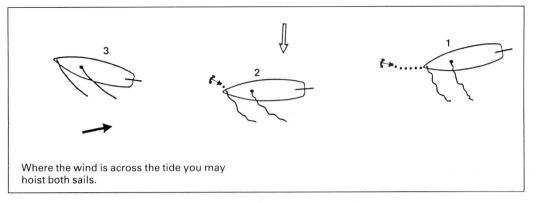

Where the wind is across the tide you may hoist both sails.

over the anchor shanks and you may be able to jerk the anchor free using the collar line. This method can also be applied by pulling the collar from a dinghy.

Another technique is to haul in the anchor line until it is vertical, attach a strong warp to a second chain, loop that chain around the anchor line and work it down the line in the hope that it will slip over the shank. The inboard end of the anchor line should be buoyed and set free and the warp attached to the second chain secured to a strong stern cleat. Then motor the boat in the opposite direction to that in which the anchor was laid. That should release the anchor.

There are numerous other reasons for an anchor becoming fouled. If you anchor where the rock is highly jointed or well bedded then the anchor might catch in a joint or bedding plane. Before attempting to rectify the situation draw a sketch map showing the lie of the rocks and fouled anchor to work out in which direction you should apply pressure to the anchor, then motor in that direction.

Heavy clay has such a clinging effect that an anchor, although not technically fouled may appear to be. The best method of release is to motor in various directions in an attempt to loosen the anchor. Kelp will have the same effect but may be distinguished by the fact that the anchor will yield slightly to an upward pull. Use the same technique as for clay.

It is often possible to sail the anchor out of the seabed. Hoist reefed sails and head off close-hauled. The boat will drag the anchor line after it but you must tack before the line stops the boat. On the new tack you will go back over what is by then slack anchor line. Haul in this slack until it begins to go taut. At that moment secure the line to a strong cleat and the momentum that the boat has built up should be sufficient to snatch the anchor from the seabed.

By studying the chart and pilot of the area in which you propose to anchor you should be able to avoid being troubled by identifiable hazards such as boulders, heavy clay, seaweed and wrecks. In the latter case, if you do become fouled your only hope will be the chain and collar described above.

Popular anchorages should be avoided, not just because they are crowded, but because the seabed is likely to be cluttered

An anchor fouled on boulders may be released by sliding a collar down the anchor line and over the shanks.

with debris such as anchors, wires, chains and concrete piles. If your anchor does become fouled by wire and/or chain you have a problem which movement may in fact make worse. The best solution is to try to pass a line under the obstructing chain and raise it as high as possible. Once it is raised secure it and then attempt to lower and clear the anchor.

The chain and collar technique may also work in this situation, particularly if you pull the collar from a dinghy. You could also attempt to drag the obstructing cable free or lift it to the surface from the dinghy. If all else fails you will have to cut the anchor line. Before you do this haul in as much as you can and attach a marker (a buoy or a fender) to the line below the point at which you intend to cut. This will make it easier to recover the anchor either at low water or with the services of a diver.

Trip lines, favoured by many skippers, can create as well as solve problems. Before anchoring take a 10mm diameter line and attach one end to a buoy and the other end to the crown of the anchor. The line should be just long enough for the buoy to break the surface, ie it should be of a length equal to the calculated maximum depth of water. The buoy will then float at a point more or less directly above the anchor. (A line that floats should not be used as it will snag a passing propeller, rudder or keel, while a line that is too long may cause fouling by snagging an obstruction.) Once the anchor has fouled allow some slack on the anchor line and lift the tripping line which should trip the flukes out.

Picking up a mooring

The factors you should consider when deciding on a place to moor are similar to those you should consider when anchoring. The only other things to bear in mind are whether the mooring is private (if it is and the owner returns you will have to move) and whether it is suitable for the weight of your boat. Mooring buoys usually have a weight limit marked on them. If the limit is less than the weight of your boat then it would be foolish to use that mooring.

As with anchoring, planning is the key to success. Picking up a mooring is a manoeuvre that you should practise many times in open water, clear of obstacles, before actually trying for real in a crowded harbour, as missing a mooring and becoming out of control in confined waters is more than likely to lead

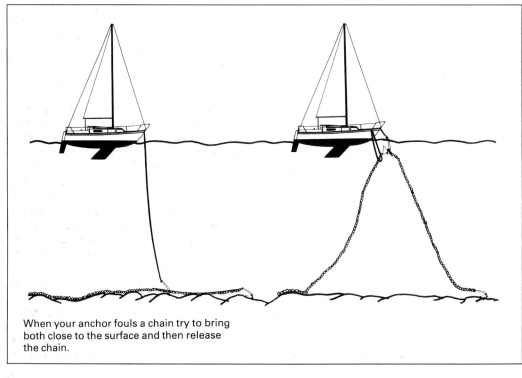

When your anchor fouls a chain try to bring both close to the surface and then release the chain.

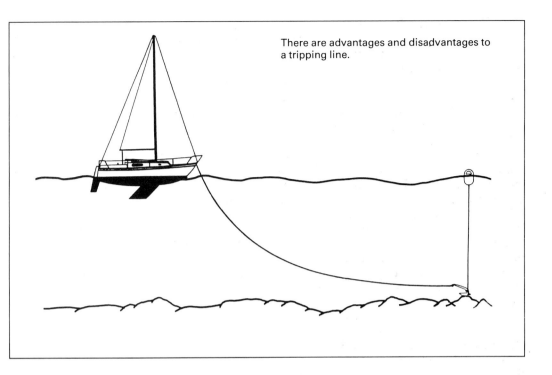

There are advantages and disadvantages to a tripping line.

A small buoy attached to a heavy mooring chain.

to serious damage.

You must consider the effects of tide and wind, as well as any nearby obstacles. Having planned your approach head towards the buoy with the engine in neutral, your fenders out on both sides, and your heaving lines and kedge ready. These are sensible back-up precautions that you will be thankful for should you get into trouble and need either to stop or motor out of danger quickly.

The crew, who has a vital role to play, must be in the bow with a boathook and line, ready

to grab the buoy. The line must run outside all rigging, stanchions, fittings and sheets otherwise it will snag. The bitter end must be made fast to a cleat. Back in the cockpit the helm is likely to lose sight of the buoy so it is important for the crew to indicate constantly its direction.

The buoy may be the type with a large ring on top to which you make fast or it may be a small one attached to a heavy mooring chain. In the latter case you should bring the buoy onto the deck and attach the large eye in its mooring chain to a deck cleat or samson post.

When you are mooring directly onto a large buoy the crew needs to grab the ring with a hook, put a line through it, and secure the line temporarily to a deck cleat. Once you are satisfied with your position they may then secure to the ring with a suitable knot and protect the line against chafe wherever necessary. It is important that they take care not to damage or dirty the headsail while doing all this.

The crew must never try to hang onto a buoy that is beyond their reach. If you have the boat stopped so that the bow is just to one side of the buoy you can use prop walk to

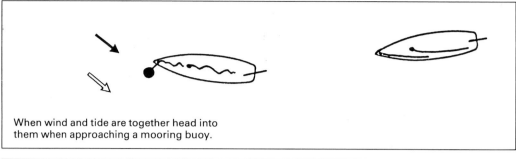

When wind and tide are together head into them when approaching a mooring buoy.

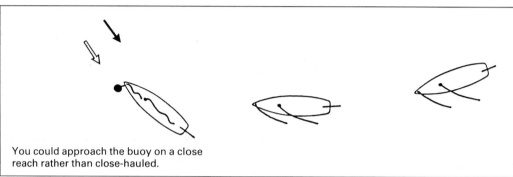

You could approach the buoy on a close reach rather than close-hauled.

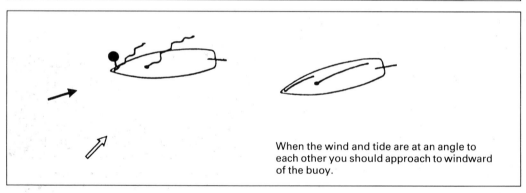

When the wind and tide are at an angle to each other you should approach to windward of the buoy.

keep the bow in that position.

When wind and tide are together approach close-hauled, downwind and downtide of the buoy. Aim slightly to leeward of it so that you luff up to it as you arrive. If you miss, bear away and try again. In a light breeze you may be able to luff up and carry your way for several boat lengths until you can pick up the buoy, but when the wind is stronger or there is a sea running the boat may be stopped dead as you try to luff up to it. Then the boat might well pay off and build up speed out of control.

In the same situation you could approach on a close reach. The advantage of this lies in your ability to control your speed with the sheets. Aim to undershoot short of the mark and then harden up, so as to close the buoy head to wind.

If the wind makes an angle with the tide so that you are going head to wind across the tide, then you must aim to windward of the buoy. If you do not, and the tide takes you downwind of the buoy, you will not be able to get back to it on that tack. There is no problem in going a little too far to windward, as you can always fall off the wind a little before hardening up.

When tide and wind are in opposition you must always stem the stronger of the two. If that is the tide then your initial approach will be from downwind. As you pass the buoy lower the mainsail and approach from upwind under headsail only. Play the sheets so that the boat sails just over the tide until reaching the buoy.

When the wind makes a right angle with

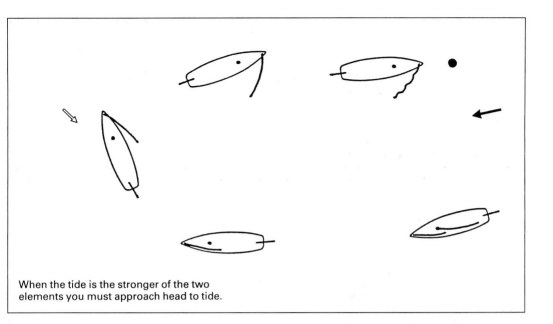

When the tide is the stronger of the two elements you must approach head to tide.

the tide you should make your approach by stemming the tide. As you close on the buoy control your speed with the mainsheet, and just before you reach it let the mainsail fly so that your way takes you up to it.

Leaving a mooring

The warp which has been made fast to the ring of the buoy must be replaced with a slip line when you are ready to leave the mooring. Where a small mooring buoy has been brought on board this should also be attached to the boat by a slip line.

Once again planning is the key to success. Which tack you depart on depends on the prevailing wind and tide conditions and the proximity of obstacles. You must choose a tack that takes you away from problems such

Crowded moorings such as this in the Coquet estuary in Northumberland demand great care when picking up or leaving a mooring.

as nearby boats and sandbanks. The first 200m are the most critical as that is where things are most likely to go wrong. The best

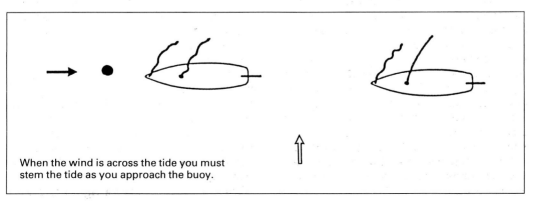

When the wind is across the tide you must stem the tide as you approach the buoy.

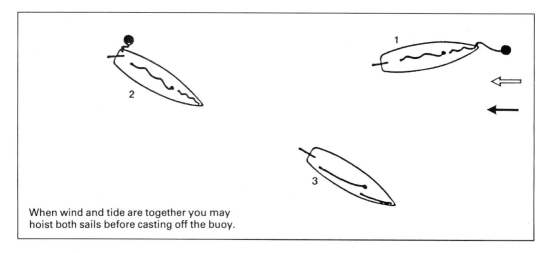

When wind and tide are together you may hoist both sails before casting off the buoy.

policy is to make slow progress towards the wind, as that will allow you to luff up if in difficulties, and to move at a slow speed, so that any collision will cause the minimum of damage. Bearing all these things in mind there are various ways of leaving a mooring.

If the wind and tide are in the same direction hoist both sails but let the sheets fly. Cast off by bringing the buoy back along one side to the stern. This will have the effect of turning the bow in the required direction. As the boat pays off let the buoy go and harden up.

Alternatively, hoist the sails and put the rudder hard over so that the boat sheers. At the point of maximum sheer back the headsail and cast off. The backed headsail will produce sternway, so reverse the rudder if necessary, thereby turning the boat from the wind. As the mainsail fills tack the headsail.

Wind against tide produces a potentially difficult situation, as the boat will tend to lie to the tide with the wind from the stern. To

A bilge keeler dried out in the Aln estuary, Northumberland.

correct this take the buoy to the stern so that the boat lies stern-to-tide and therefore head-to-wind. You can then hoist both sails and cast off in the required direction by backing the headsail.

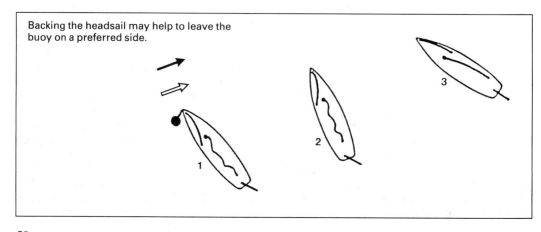

Backing the headsail may help to leave the buoy on a preferred side.

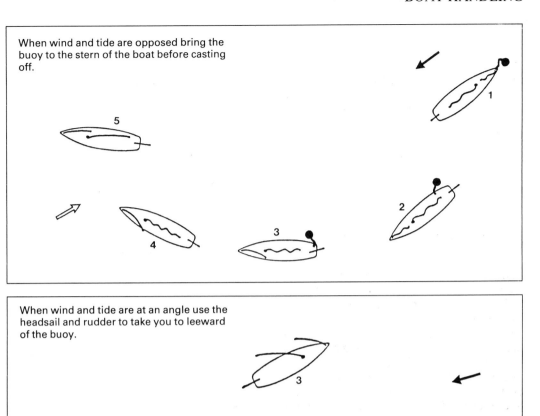

When wind and tide are opposed bring the buoy to the stern of the boat before casting off.

When wind and tide are at an angle use the headsail and rudder to take you to leeward of the buoy.

When the wind is across the tide hoist both sails but let the sheets fly. Push the helm hard over to sheer the boat, and sheet the headsail as for a close reach. As the sail fills cast off and the boat will sail off to leeward of the buoy. You can then sheet in the mainsail.

Mooring alongside

This skill is relevant not only to those pausing during a passage but also to the many boat owners whose permanent mooring is a pontoon berth. There will probably be long periods when owners are away from such boats, so they must have confidence in the integrity of the warps holding them to the berth. Inadequate, poorly secured warps will lead to a boat moving within its berth and being damaged or damaging its neighbours. Warps must therefore be of the correct

diameter and length and be attached to large cleats secured by bolts through the deck. They must be checked regularly for chafe and protected against this where possible. Fenders must be of the correct size for the boat and berth and be positioned in such a way that the boat's side cannot come into contact with the berth.

Again, plan! Expecting the impossible from an inexperienced crew will only lead to disaster. Do not be over ambitious or put unnecessary pressure on yourself, the crew or the boat. Have at least one practice run, then if you are still unsure go elsewhere. Make certain that if things begin to go wrong you know which way you are going to retreat.

All warps, plus a spare heaving line, should be coiled ready to take ashore. The bow line should be attached to the bow cleat and the stern line to the stern cleat. Ensure

The entrance to the Amble marina, Northumberland. This view is from the marina towards the Coquet estuary.

that they then run freely through the fairleads and pass outside all rigging, lifelines and sheets. The kedge should be ready in case of a problem and, for the same reason, if you are sailing in, the engine should be tested and left running in neutral. Sufficient fenders should be attached, a round turn and two half hitches being used on each.

The crew then stand outside the lifelines holding the coiled warps. On the signal from the helm they step ashore. They must not jump because a fall, as well as causing injury, would leave the boat unsecured. Temporarily secure the bow and stern lines and adjust the boat to its correct position between them. When this is achieved secure the bow and stern permanently and then attach other lines as required. Take excess warp back onto the boat and coil it neatly.

Where there is a choice of berths choose one to leeward of the pontoon. In a strong

The approach channel within Amble marina.

wind a boat on the windward side will be buffetted into the pontoon while a boat on the leeward side will be held just off it.

APPROACHING A MARINA

The approach to a marina berth is usually more difficult than that into an open quay. The berths and the separating pontoons lie at a right angle to the approach channel. Often the channel is not wide enough to make a 180° turn, so if you make a mistake in your approach it is difficult to retrace your steps and start again.

In approaching a pontoon berth it is vital to control your speed so that you stop before you hit the end of the berth. The greater your momentum the greater the distance you require in order to stop. You must therefore take the power off earlier rather than later. Do not rely on saving yourself by putting the engine hard astern: if you try that the effects of prop walk are likely to cause the boat to swing wildly from side to side.

Remember also that when manoeuvring in a confined space a tight turn is best achieved by short, sharp bursts of power. This drives a strong slipstream across the rudder and reduces forward motion to a minimum.

The availability of berths in a marina frequently leaves you with little choice as to your approach. If at all possible use the wind to drift you into the berth with the stream on one side of the bow. In the ideal situation occasional forward thrust will cause the boat to move sideways as required because the stream will counteract right-hand prop walk.

You should arrive at the berth from the far side of the approach channel with sufficient speed to retain adequate steerage. When the boat is just into the berth put the engine into neutral, and then into reverse when three-quarters in. The action of the engine going astern will stop the boat and either swing the stern gently into the berth, if you are mooring on the port side, or swing the stern out if you are mooring on the starboard side (assuming right-hand prop walk).

A strong wind makes marina manoeuvres more difficult. The wind tends to blow the bow downwind and you will need to counter this with steering and controlled prop walk. Putting the engine astern in a strong wind will cause the stern to turn towards the wind, a tendency which is very difficult to counteract.

With a following wind the boat will drift in under mast alone and little engine power will be required until you want to stop. You will then need more reverse thrust than you would if berthing into the wind. A following tidal stream makes for a very difficult situation. The engine thrust required to maintain steerage, plus the strength of the stream in the same direction, may mean that you make 3–4kn into the berth. That would be very difficult to control and, especially if there is also a following wind, you should think of going elsewhere until conditions change.

Where the pontoon has a broad end, or the plan of the marina allows, you may berth beam on temporarily by securing the bow and stern. You could then warp the boat into the berth. Where the pontoon end is narrow, as is

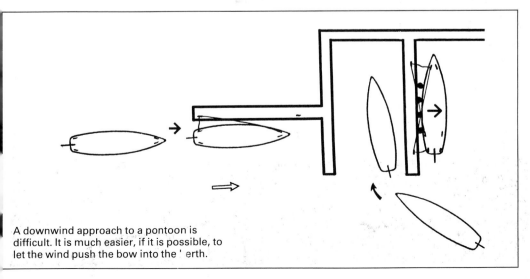

A downwind approach to a pontoon is difficult. It is much easier, if it is possible, to let the wind push the bow into the 'erth.

Narrow finger berths.

usually the case, the danger in this is that the boat may pivot on the end.

With a windward pontoon, approach bow-first from downwind in neutral and let the wind push the bow into the berth. Where the approach has to be downwind then enter the berth in reverse gear and get your stern line and aft spring ashore as quickly as possible and use them to slow the boat.

APPROACHING AN OPEN QUAY
Although it is never likely to be sensible to approach a marina berth under sail it is quite possible to approach a long open quay under sail in moderate conditions. The actual approach should be determined by the relationship between wind, tide and mooring. The stream should normally take precedence over the wind in your considerations, but this does depend on their relative strengths. The approach will normally be into the stream unless that is very weak and the wind very strong.

When wind and tide are together approach close-hauled until 10–15m off the berth. Turn head to wind, let the sheets fly and steer the boat alongside under its own way.

When wind and tide are in opposition sail upwind past the berth and drop the mainsail.

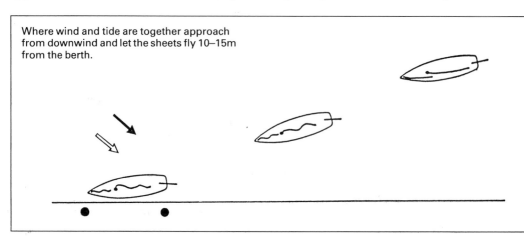

Where wind and tide are together approach from downwind and let the sheets fly 10–15m from the berth.

ail and motor cruisers berthed in Amble marina.

Run down to the berth under headsail only, using the sheets to control your speed. When you have sufficient way to reach the berth ease the sheets right out. Should you still have too much speed then gradually lower the headsail. Once alongside drop the head-sail. It is usually best to attach the stern line and aft spring quickly as brakes.

If the wind is onshore sail with the tide beyond the berth and then turn head to wind and lower the mainsail. Approach the berth under headsail on what will in effect be a broad reach, using the sheets to control your speed. When you have sufficient way to carry you to the berth let the headsail fly and turn the boat parallel to the berth, with the bow pointing slightly upwind. This will balance the tendency of the bow to be pushed in more than the stern. With the sails flying the wind will then push you into the berth.

In the opposite situation, with an offshore wind, you must again sail beyond the berth.

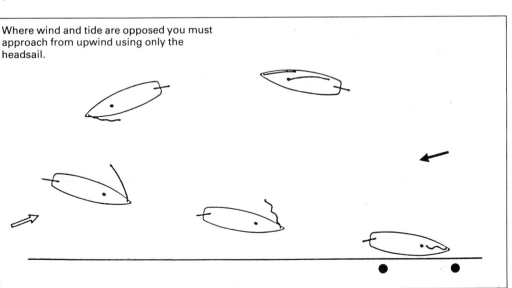

Where wind and tide are opposed you must approach from upwind using only the headsail.

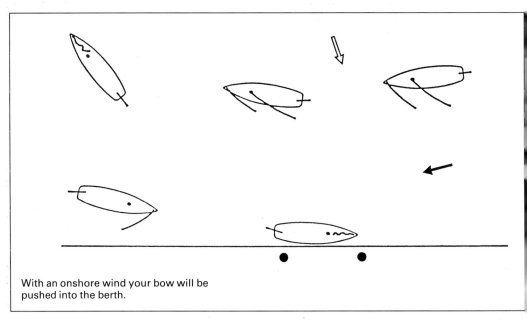

With an onshore wind your bow will be pushed into the berth.

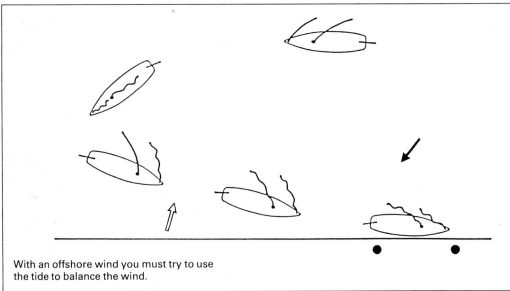

With an offshore wind you must try to use the tide to balance the wind.

Then turn downwind, letting the headsail fly, and approach under the main only, using the sheets to control your speed. Use the tide to push your bow towards the berth (lee-bow effect) and let the mainsail fly once you have sufficient way for the tide to push you in. In this situation it is best to come in under mainsail if the wind is forward of the beam. If it is aft of the beam use the headsail.

Under power your approach should be into the wind if the stream is weak. When the two are opposed you should usually approach into the stream. An approach from downwind of the berth is much easier than one from upstream.

When there is no wind and the stream is slack you should approach at an angle of about 30° to the quay, from a direction that will allow prop walk to pull you in. With just enough speed to maintain steerage you must aim the bow at the point at which you want it to come to rest. As the bow arrives at that point use prop walk to bring the boat parallel to the quay.

If circumstances dictate that you must

A Moody 35 in the English Channel.

The ship's cat

A ferry approaching Cowes, Isle of Wight.

Thames Barge.

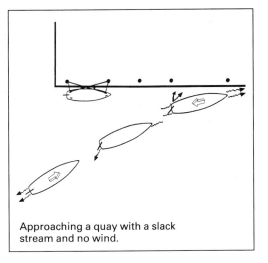

Approaching a quay with a slack stream and no wind.

A steep approach because prop walk is likely to drag the stern out.

arrive from a direction that will lead prop walk to drag the stern out then the angle of approach must be much steeper. In this situation aim the bow for the near end of the intended berth and stop about a length from the quay. A short burst of forward power with the rudder hard over will then bring the stern in. Avoid a prolonged burst of power because that would create too much forward momentum.

When a strong stream is the significant factor you should approach into the stream and at an angle of about 20° to the quay. Aim the bow at a point just ahead of the berth and use continuous small throttle and rudder adjust-

ments to slip sideways into it. If you use the stream carefully you will find that it will stop you, so there may be no need for reverse thrust. In a very strong stream you may find it necessary to maintain forward power until the warps are secured. If you do not have enough power the stream will cause the boat to sheer.

Should you be forced to approach downstream then you will find it very difficult to maintain a correct angle to the berth and will not be able to use the stream to slow your progress. In this situation your approach must begin as far upstream as possible with a very shallow angle. Using occasional reverse

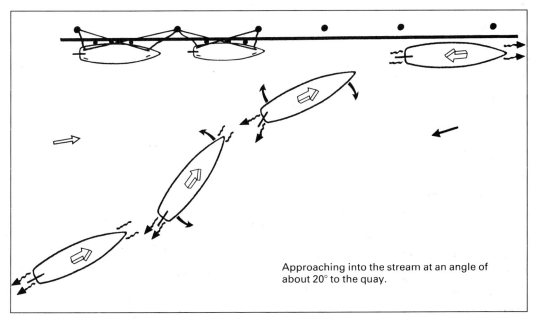

Approaching into the stream at an angle of about 20° to the quay.

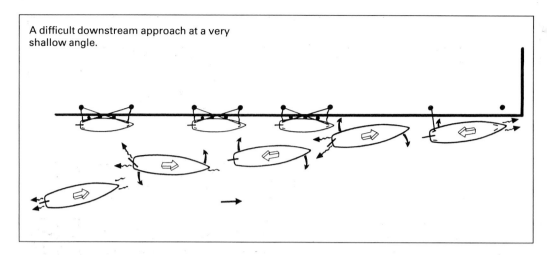

A difficult downstream approach at a very shallow angle.

thrust arrive more or less parallel to the berth and secure a quarter warp as quickly as possible.

When the stream is not significant you should approach into the wind. The final positioning will require forward thrust with the helm hard over. This will force the bow out while the wind pushes the stern in. As the bow comes out the wind will drive it back in. Continue like this until parallel and alongside the berth.

When the wind is from astern it will tend to drive the boat forward and to draw the stern away from the quay. If this approach is against the stream then that can be used to slow the boat, with reverse thrust at the last moment. Where there is no stream you will have to use frequent bursts of reverse thrust to keep speed to a minimum. If this tends to push the boat out you will have to put the helm hard over so that the slipstream keeps it in towards the quay.

Should you be under power and the wind onshore then stop the boat parallel to and clear of the quay. The wind will then push you into the berth. An offshore wind is a little more difficult to deal with under power. You have to counteract its tendency to push the bow out. As you come in at a sharp angle the crew must take both bow and stern lines over the bow and use these to manoeuvre the boat into the berth.

SECURING THE BOAT

Whichever method you adopt for your approach you will have to secure the boat once alongside. To do this you need to appreciate the role of each of the warps used.

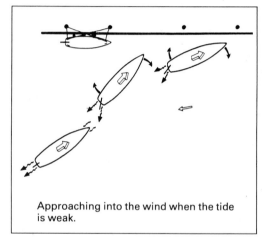

Approaching into the wind when the tide is weak.

The long bow and stern ropes secure the boat to the berth. They should be equal to at least twice the boat's length or three times the tidal range, whichever is greater. The longer these two warps are the less adjustment they will need, although they will need adjusting at half tide. They must be strong because they carry the main load of the boat. The two springs are to stop the boat ranging fore and aft. They should be a minimum of one and a half times the boat's length or the tidal range, whichever is greater. The two breast ropes hold the boat into the berth, which is particularly important when you are getting on and off. They too should be at least one and a half times the boat's length.

The organisation of these warps varies according to whether you are moored to a pontoon or a tidal wall. Mooring to a pontoon tends to be easier because the pontoon

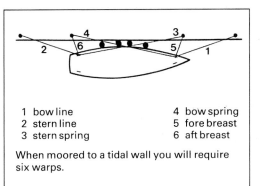

1 bow line	4 bow spring
2 stern line	5 fore breast
3 stern spring	6 aft breast

When moored to a tidal wall you will require six warps.

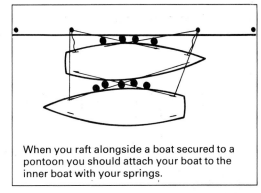

When you raft alongside a boat secured to a pontoon you should attach your boat to the inner boat with your springs.

will ride up and down with the tide. There is therefore no need for bow and stern ropes. The springs may be quite short and should be cleated half-way along the side decks and led to points on the pontoon that are opposite the bow and the stern. They need to be taut to lessen the tendency of the boat to surge with the tidal stream. The breasts, on the other hand, need to be slack otherwise the wash of passing boats will cause the boat to snatch at them as it rolls and rebounds on its fenders. When you are alongside a boat which in turn is alongside a pontoon you should have your breasts going to the pontoon. That way the bulk of the load will be on these and not the inner boat. Tie yourself to the other boat with taut springs.

When moored to a tidal wall you do not need breasts but you must have long springs and bow and stern ropes. The springs need to be as long as possible in order to take up the vertical movement. They should run from bow to stern and cross each other in the middle. The head and stern ropes should be at least three times the tidal range.

The various warps must be adjusted individually. If, for example, at half tide you haul in the bow and stern warps so that they are hand-taut (as they should be) they will be fully taut and just starting to lengthen at low water. There must be some slack in all the warps to allow for the tidal range, the amount of slack being controlled by the size of that range.

All warps need to be protected from chafe where this is likely to occur. This may be done by putting rags between the warps and troublesome spots such as rings and bollards. Alternatively, short lengths of split plastic hosing may be used.

When harbours are particularly crowded,

Short lengths of plastic hose used to reduce chafe.

such as in high season, you may well have to secure to another boat and not directly to the harbour wall. This is called rafting. The disadvantage of berthing like this is lack of privacy. Some crew, on the other hand, might like the company that such a situation provides. Having decided that you have no alternative try to find a boat larger than your own, because you will not lie very easily against a smaller boat. Approach the boat close to and, if anyone is on board, ask if it is all right to come alongside. They have tied up where rafting is common so they should be expecting it and can help you to secure alongside.

Avoid rafting in places where only the inshore boat is secured to the quay. You would be very uncomfortable there because you would range considerably fore and aft. The procedure for coming alongside is exactly that as for coming alongside a pontoon. You do not have to be facing the same direction as

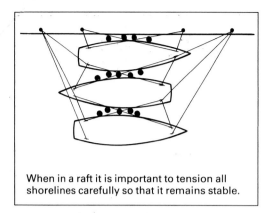

When in a raft it is important to tension all shorelines carefully so that it remains stable.

the inner boat. In fact it may be a distinct advantage to be facing the other way so that your masts are staggered and the spreaders do not become entangled.

Temporarily attach your bow and stern lines to the bow and stern cleats of the inner boat. It should have the usual bow, stern and spring lines to the quay wall, and its helm lashed amidships. When you are secure take the bow and stern lines ashore, and attach your boat to the inner boat by breasts and springs. The tension of all the shorelines must be such that the raft does not become unstable.

Having secured the boat it needs to be tidied. The mainsheet and kicking strap must be uncleated, and the tension taken out of the topping lift so that pressure is taken off the boom. Uncleat the main halyard and lower the mainsail. Coil and cleat the halyard and detach the head of the mainsail from it. (The end of the halyard will need securing before it disappears to the top of the mast.) Take the sail off the boom and fold it correctly before placing it in its bag and stowing it below. The headsail must be similarly stowed. All spare warps should be coiled and stowed, the boat cleaned and the seacocks put in their harbour position. Finally the correct flag etiquette should be observed, logs updated and stores checked.

Leaving an alongside mooring

Once again there are numerous possibilities, but the art of 'springing off' is very useful, especially where there is a lack of room fore and aft. For springing off under sail the wind needs to be from such a direction that the headsail may be used at the beginning of the

manoeuvre. It is also helpful to be head to tide, because unless there is a very strong wind from the opposite direction the upstream end of the boat should be taken out first. Heading into a moderate to strong stream will give you more control. If the wind is much weaker than the tidal stream you will have limited control and should therefore use the engine. The line with the most tension on it is the one that you cast off last. You will need to have plenty of fenders aft because the boat will be turning on that point.

Windage is a major factor that you need to consider as you prepare to depart. Until the boat has sufficient momentum for the rudder to bite, the natural tendency will be for the wind to push the bow downwind and the stern upwind. This may result in the boat being beam-on to the wind as you attempt a turn. If you were to be caught by a gust at that moment you would have very little control. The crew standing in the bow adds to the windage effect.

With an offshore wind ahead of the beam there are two possibilities, neither of which should be attempted without sufficient space. Cast off all lines except one spring, which should be at least the length of the boat and should be led from the stern to the bow or vice versa depending on the required direction of departure. This line should be attached to the shore as a slip line so that it may be easily released from the boat. You then back the headsail and push the rudder hard over to starboard to turn the bow in the required direction. When that direction is reached cast off the spring and apply some port helm to straighten the boat.

Alternatively, hoist the mainsail and release all shore lines. The wind will then drift the boat out of the berth, although you will have to use the rudder to counteract the tendency of the stern to drift back in. Once clear of the berth trim the mainsail and then hoist and trim the headsail.

When the wind is abaft the beam you should hoist the headsail first. As before, cast off all shore lines but this time trim the headsail as you drift out with the wind. Once clear of danger you should turn head to wind and hoist the mainsail.

When you are going upstream do not put the bow too far out into the stream or you will be turned downstream. If going downstream the spring should be far longer and the engine

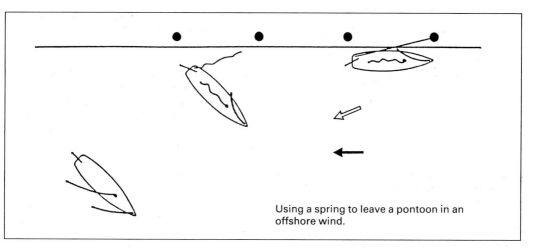

Using a spring to leave a pontoon in an offshore wind.

should be run astern slowly to keep the spring taut.

Should wind and tide conditions not allow, or if there simply is not room to manoeuvre under sail, you will have to leave under power. With your starboard side along the quay, if you just cast off and put the engine into forward the stern will drive into the quay. Using reverse thrust will simply drive the bow into the quay. You must try to turn one end of the boat off the wall using a spring so that the other end does not go into the wall. Before starting this manoeuvre try to get the boat as far off the quay as possible while keeping it parallel. Sufficient fenders need to be placed at the appropriate end of the boat.

If you are lying stern to the tide you should lead the spring from bow to stern and concentrate the fenders towards the bow. You will need to apply a little starboard helm so that the tide does take the stern out. Having the engine going slowly astern will help to keep the bow off the mooring. If you want to head upstream you will have to keep the spring attached a little longer while maintaining slow astern with the engine until the boat is almost completely around.

If you are lying head to tide you will not be able to use a bow spring in this way, although with negligible stream it will be possible to leave stern first under engine. Use a stern-to-bow spring with the rudder hard over to starboard and the engine slow ahead (if the propeller rotates clockwise in forward gear) to move the bow out gently. When the bow is clear you can slip the spring and then motor away in reverse.

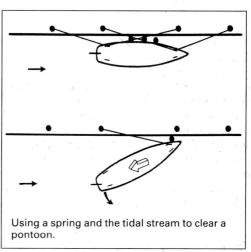

Using a spring and the tidal stream to clear a pontoon.

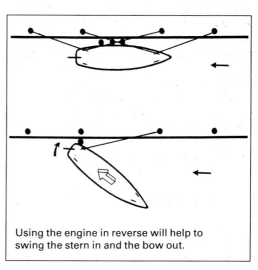

Using the engine in reverse will help to swing the stern in and the bow out.

To leave bow-first under power use the bow spring as a slip line and put the engine into reverse. With anti-clockwise rotation in reverse this will turn the stern towards the wall. Once the bow is well clear release the spring and motor forward. This is less effective than springing the stern off.

When the wind is abeam it will hold the boat onto the mooring, but with a limited stream it will still be possible to spring out. If the wind is forward of the beam you will need a stern spring and stern fenders. Go slowly astern with the rudder amidship so that the bow moves slowly out. Once clear cast off and go forward with the engine.

Should you wish to go downwind in this situation proceed in the same way but keep the boat turning until the bow is past the head-to-wind position. Motor slow ahead to keep the stern off the mooring while the wind blows the bow round until it is facing the required direction.

When the wind is abaft the beam you will need a forward spring and bow fenders. With some port helm and the engine slow ahead the stern will swing out. To turn the boat in this situation go slow ahead until the boat is past stern to wind and then go astern to keep the bow off the wall. The wind will then blow the stern round.

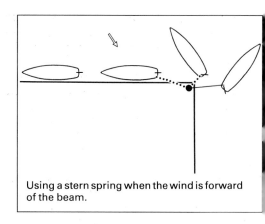

Using a stern spring when the wind is forward of the beam.

On those occasions when the berth allows you to move off directly ahead or astern you will have to decide which is the most appropriate for the conditions. The major problem in moving off ahead is to determine the direction in which the stern will turn. Moving off astern is possibly more difficult because the prop walk will be exaggerated and the rudder will not bite until some momentum has been achieved. In this situation move off in an arc until you have built up sufficient speed for the rudder to begin to work.

To move out of a narrow finger berth you have to plan your manoeuvre very carefully. Your bow will probably be facing into the

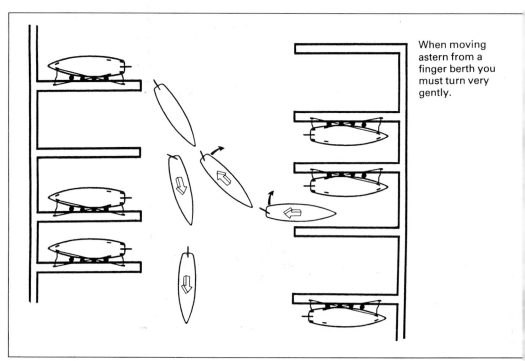

When moving astern from a finger berth you must turn very gently.

berth so you will have to reverse out. With the engine in reverse the boat will pivot around a point beneath the cockpit, and the slightest movement of the rudder will therefore cause the bow to swing so that the boat goes either into the pontoon or into the neighbouring boat. There is a technique to avoid this. Immediately before departure the crew holds the bow slip line while the helm holds the stern slip line. The engine is slowly put into reverse. The thrust must be very gentle so that there is no prop walk. Once you are happy with the line the boat is taking you let go both slip lines. When the boat is about half way out of the berth the rudder may be turned in the required direction. The stern will move in the direction that the rudder blade is pointing. (If you wish to turn the stern to port then this will be achieved quite

easily with reverse thrust and a right-handed propeller because the prop walk will turn the stern in that direction.) Continue to ease out on this gentle curve until you are about 3m from the opposite berths. Put the engine into neutral and then gently ahead with the helm hard over so that the rudder blade is pointing to starboard. Some 70% of the power developed will then be used to turn the boat so that it is facing in the right direction before forward momentum develops.

If you are in the middle of a raft of boats, leaving will be more difficult but not impossible. You must leave with the strongest element so that the raft will drift back together. Untie your bow and stern lines and bring them back on board. Next untie the spring and breast lines of the boat outside you. Depending on the direction in which you

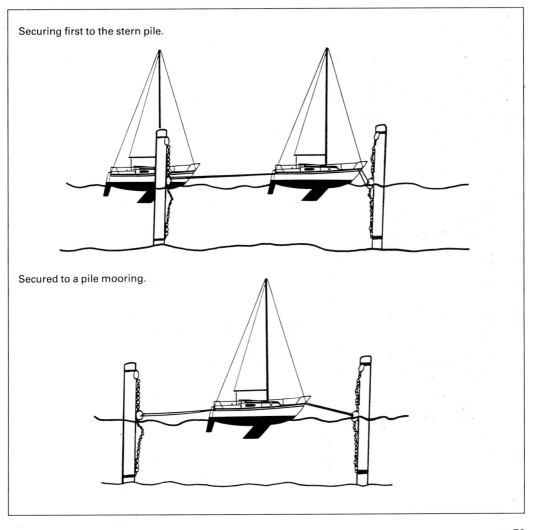

Securing first to the stern pile.

Secured to a pile mooring.

intend to head you untie its bow or stern line, lead it around your boat and back to the shore. This creates the space through which you can leave. Finally, release your breast lines and you will drift out with the strongest element. You may find that you have to leave one crew member on the raft to tidy it up as you exit, in which case you will have to return and pick them up from outside the raft.

Pile moorings

These consist of two piles, driven into the seabed, to which you tie up fore and aft. The point of attachment is normally a ring which slides up and down the pile on a chain. This movement of the ring is important because it means that you do not have to adjust your lines as the boat rises and falls with the tide. The only significant problem with pile moorings is the danger of colliding with them: as they tend to be encrusted with barnacles this can cause damage to the boat.

Pile moorings can be difficult to approach in a wind or tide of any strength. As you approach have long stern and bow lines ready and a third prepared for any emergency. The crew should be forward with a telescopic boathook. Ideally you should have two crew. One to hold the boat in position just clear of the pile, the other to secure the line to the ring. If the tide is weak and the wind negligible, stop the boat with the shrouds next to the first pile. With the stern line outside all rigging secure it to the ring on the pile with a round turn to limit chafe and a long bowline so that it is easy to reach if below water. Motor up to the second pile while paying out the stern line, making sure that it does not foul the propeller. Stop the bow at the pile and secure the bow line to the ring. Finally, adjust both lines so that the boat lies quietly between them.

If the tide is strong then head into it. In fact mooring to piles is easier when there is a moderate tide because the flow of water across the rudder maintains manoeuvrability. Keep the pile forward of the boat's natural pivoting point though or the boat will swing around it.

In a cross wind your action will depend on whether the wind is forward or aft of the beam. With the former, drop the headsail and approach under mainsail, using that to control your speed. Aim to stop with your shrouds close to the forward pile, and secure. Lower the mainsail and drop back to the aft pile and secure the stern line. You may then adjust the boat between the two.

When the wind is on or aft the beam, lower the mainsail and use the headsail sheet to control your speed. Stop to leeward of the aft pile and secure the stern line. Sheet in slightly and sail to the forward pile, with the bow slightly to windward, while carefully paying out the stern line. Finally, secure to the forward pile when alongside and adjust the boat between the two.

When wind and tide are together you must head into them. Under power, secure first to the forward pile and then pay out the bow line as you drop back. Finally you secure the stern line and adjust the boat between the two.

When there is already a boat secured to the pile come alongside and make fast bow and stern lines to that boat. Secure your springs and breasts to it and then use the dinghy to take the bow and stern lines to the piles.

When leaving a pile berth you should head bow to tide because that will give you greater control over speed and heading. Rig the bow and stern lines as slips and keep the stern line slack. If the wind is forward of the beam then hoist the mainsail only and sheet that in as you steer off, preferably to leeward of the forward pile. As the boat gathers way, slip the stern and then the bow line. When clear of the mooring you can hoist the headsail.

With the wind on or aft the beam act as before but this time hoist only the headsail. Slip the lines as you sheet in, and turn onto the desired heading. As soon as you are clear turn head to wind and hoist the mainsail.

Drying out

Some harbours dry out at low water, and at a place such as this your aim should be to ensure that the boat will dry out against the wall, balanced on its keel, while the enormous leverage of the mast counteracts any tendency to list outwards.

Although bilge keels have a considerable advantage over fin keels when sailing in shoal waters, fin keels are actually better than bilge when it comes to drying out. The latter tend to lean outwards, with consequent problems, while the fin will lean inwards if set up properly.

It is important that you view the prospec-
ive berth beforehand, if at all possible. In
particular you need to know the nature of the
seabed: both the direction of its slope and the
nature of its material, which could be gravel,
clay, sand or mud. Ideally the ground parallel
to the wall should be even for the whole
length of the keel so that the whole keel will
take the ground more or less simultaneously.
If one part of the keel were to ground first
then the rest might pivot on that point, with
either the bow or stern going into the wall. If
the ground slopes out from the wall then
there is a danger that the keel will slip out so
that the hull and rigging fall into the wall. The
same problem will occur if the keel slips into
the hole left by a previous and larger boat.

It is also important that you check the
range of tide, because it will affect the time of
drying and for how long the boat will be dried
out. If, for instance, you dry at two-thirds
ebb on a big range the warps will need frequent adjustment. When staying for a long
period it is best to find a shallow area where
you will float for only a short time. The warps
will then need less tending.

The plan is to hold the boat firmly against
the berth, parallel to the wall, with a slight inward list of about 5°. This 'false' list can be
induced by laying the anchor chain along the
deck. The boat should be held to the wall by a
line, running from the mast to the shore,

which must be able to move up and down as
the boat settles on the bottom. A snatch
block on the main halyard, with a shore line
attached to it, will allow this movement. The
boat will then be able to ride up and down
with the tide while a steady pull is maintained
by the shore line. The greater the tidal range
the longer the bow and stern warps and
springs must be. To create maximum inward
pressure the bow and stern warps must be

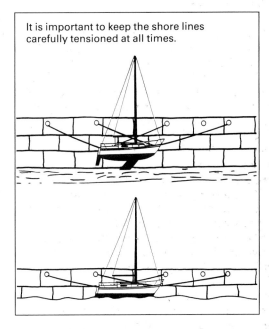

It is important to keep the shore lines carefully tensioned at all times.

Drying out with a deliberate 5° inward list.

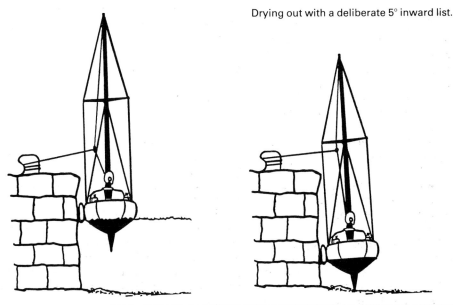

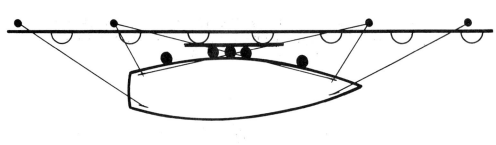

A plank will protect the boat and the fenders.

attached to the outboard quarters. They must also be secured as far aft and forward as possible so they do not lie at too steep an angle at low water. The springs must be crossed and supported clear of the fenders. To keep tension on the head and stern warps at all times slide a weight half-way along each. At about half ebb make all the lines hand-taut so that as the tide falls the hull will be drawn in against the wall on taut lines. In case of emergency it is helpful to have a spare bollard or mooring ring to which lines may be attached quickly.

To protect the boat and fenders a plank should be placed between the fenders and the wall. This plank must be attached by lines to either the boat or the wall – if to the latter the lines will need continuous adjustment. The fenders should be so positioned that the boat leans into the wall with them at deck level or just below on the topsides. If they are too high they may well be pushed up and out of position, whereas if they are too low the rail may touch the wall. A boat with a deep fin keel may have to be shored up at the bow and great care must be taken when moving around inside it.

Questions

Answers are on page 223.

1. What should be the minimum length of scope with:
   a) Chain?
   b) Chain and warp?
2. Which warps should you use in the following situations?
   a) Alongside a tidal wall.
   b) Alongside a boat that is secured to a pontoon.
3. Study the chart extract. For each of the nine possible anchorages (A–I) explain why you would or would not use the anchorage. The wind is a

moderate breeze from the south-west. The tidal streams are not relevant in this example but the depth of water is significant: it is given in metres and decimetres to show soundings and drying heights.

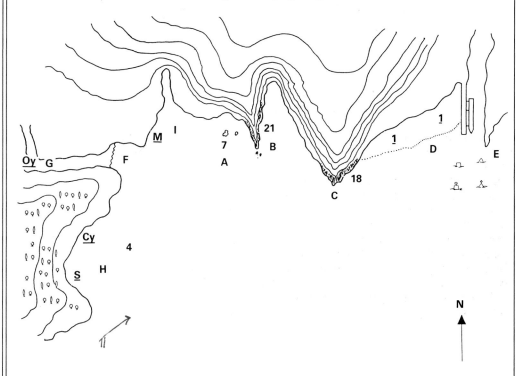

4. Study the imaginary bay.
   a) Assuming the tide to have a greater effect than the wind, explain how you would approach:
   i)   The anchorage;
   ii) The mooring buoy;
   iii) The open quay.
   b) Explain how you would depart from each with the same wind and tide relationship.

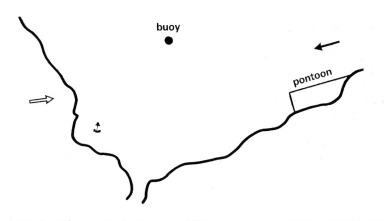

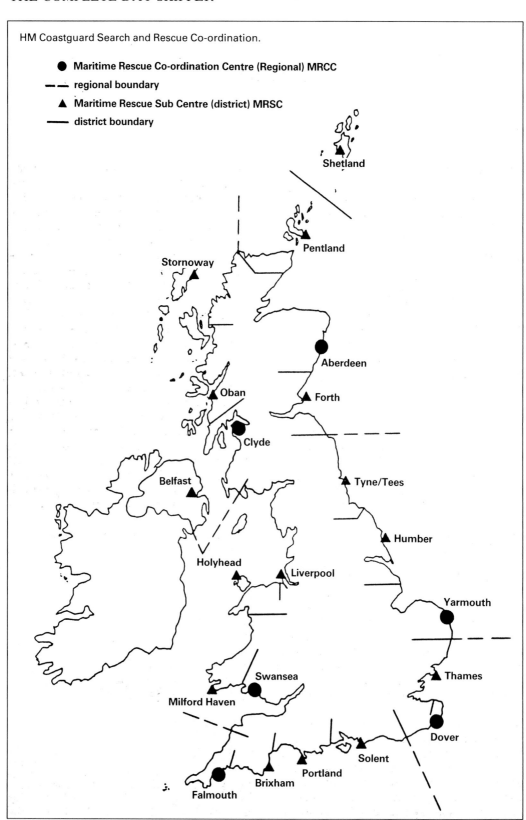

HM Coastguard Search and Rescue Co-ordination.

● Maritime Rescue Co-ordination Centre (Regional) MRCC
— — regional boundary
▲ Maritime Rescue Sub Centre (district) MRSC
——— district boundary

Shetland

Pentland

Stornoway

Aberdeen

Oban

Forth

Clyde

Belfast

Tyne/Tees

Holyhead

Humber

Liverpool

Yarmouth

Swansea

Thames

Milford Haven

Solent

Dover

Brixham

Portland

Falmouth

CHAPTER 6

Safety

Coastguard

The coastguard, now a civilian uniformed section of the Department of Transport, was established in 1822 in an attempt to combat smuggling, while the Merchant Shipping Act of 1854 put the Board of Trade in charge of life-saving and gave it the power to take over private life-saving companies. The coastguard service was placed under the control of the Admiralty as a result of the Coastguard Act of 1856, and consequently acted as a naval reserve during the middle of the nineteenth century. Nevertheless, in the fifty years 1859–1909 the service was involved in the rescue of some 20,000 people. It was not until the Coastguard Act of 1925 that the service was officially made responsible for life-saving and coastal watchkeeping. The same act brought it completely under the control of the Board of Trade. The service was further strengthened by the Coast Protection Act 1949, which required officers to report activity likely to damage the foreshore.

The coastguard is responsible for all civil maritime search-and-rescue operations around the UK coastline and 1,000 miles out into the North Atlantic. To achieve this it co-ordinates the work of the RNLI lifeboats, the Royal Navy and Royal Air Force rescue teams and assistance from commercial vessels and aircraft. It also maintains cliff-rescue teams and inflatables for inshore emergencies, as well as helicopters in the Shetlands, Hebrides and Solent. Its other operational duties are to provide the Channel Navigation Information Service and assist with pollution control.

The coastline is divided into six Search-and-Rescue Regions, each with a Maritime Rescue Co-ordination Centre and a number of Sub-Centres which control smaller district areas. All these rescue centres maintain a constant listening watch on the distress frequencies, while each sector of a district has four-wheel drive vehicles with which to patrol the coastline. The service employs 500 regular officers and 6,500 auxiliaries. The latter are part-time volunteers who participate in coastguard rescue teams and help to maintain a continuous visual and radio watch.

The coast-watch aspect of the service means that a coastguard is likely to be the first to discover a pollution incident. When such an incident is discovered the service not only reports it to the Marine Pollution Control Unit but has the power to call out immediately spray tugs and aircraft if this is deemed necessary. The coastguard is also the first to deal with any unidentified object found on the foreshore or in the water.

Introduced in 1972, the Channel Navigation Information Service is operated from the Langdon Battery centre near Dover. A twenty-four hour radio safety service for shipping in the Dover Straits, it broadcasts information on VHF channel 11 every sixty minutes, or every thirty minutes in poor visibility. (The information varies from details

RAF Air Sea Rescue helicopter based at Boulmer, Northumberland.

Yacht and Boat Safety Scheme.

DEPARTMENT OF TRANSPORT
HM COASTGUARD
YACHT AND BOAT SAFETY SCHEME

Details of owner
Name
Address

Tel. No.
Signature
Date

Details of Shore Contact
Name
Address

Tel. No.

Name of Club
or Association

Form CG66

Name of Craft
How and where is the name displayed
Type of craft
Sailing or fishing number
Colours of Craft
Hull above water
   below water
Superstructure
Sail
Spinnaker
length   feet   metres
Details of any special identification features
Usual base
Usual mooring
Usual activity (eg fishing, racing etc)
Usual sea areas

Type of rig
Speed and endurance under power
Details of radio
HF MF Trans/Rec:
VHF Channels and call sign:
Other Equipment:
Type of distress signals carried
Dinghy type
Colour
Life raft type
Serial no.
Are life jackets carried?

Name of craft

Address of the Coastguard Maritime Rescue Centre who hold details of this craft

Telephone No.

IF YOU ARE WORRIED ABOUT THE SAFETY OF THIS CRAFT, PLEASE CONTACT THE COASTGUARD BY DIALLING 999, OR BY TELEPHONING THE ABOVE COASTGUARD CENTRE.

about misplaced or defective navigation marks to the location of surveying and cable laying operations.) It also keeps a complete radar watch on traffic using the traffic separation scheme so that any vessel abusing the international collision regulations can be identified and reported to its home country. The result is a greatly improved safety record in the Straits, with no major accidents since 1979. Problems do still occur there however, as with the sinking of a fishing boat in 1991. Then it was only the study of the radar track that proved that the fishing boat had been run down by a much larger vessel.

The coastguard provides safety guidance for boat owners, windsurfers and fishermen. This is set out in the booklet *Safety at Sea*, which should be read thoroughly by everyone using the sea. It details the general and specific safety equipment that you should carry and tells you where to obtain a weather forecast, both on land and offshore; it gives advice on using the VHF to contact the coastguard, on using EPIRBs (emergency position-indicating radio beacons) and on other methods of indicating distress; and it

Boulmer helicopter above the Northumberland coast.

explains how to make passage reports and, of equal importance, when not to.

Associated with this advice is the Yacht and Boat Safety Scheme. To participate in this you complete a card obtained from the nearest coastguard centre. On it you note a description of your boat and its equipment, your call sign and usual sailing area. The completed card is given to the centre, where it is kept on file. The tear-off section of the card, giving the boat's name and the name and telephone number of the Marine Rescue Centre holding the card, is given to a reliable person while you are on passage. If they are worried about your safety they can then contact the centre, which has all the information with which to launch a search, should one be necessary. You must remember to update the information on the card whenever there is a significant change in the details.

The importance of the coastguard service is indicated by the number of incidents it deals with each year. Among the average annual figures are:

Total incidents	7,000
Offshore incidents	3,100
Cliff and inshore incidents	500
Persons rescued	11,500

The figures for 1990 were:

Total incidents	7,076
Assistance rendered	4,602
False alarms	2,277
Hoax calls	197
Persons assisted	13,474
Lives lost	295

Falmouth region was by far the busiest, with 30% of the total incidents, while Aberdeen and Dover were the quietest regions. Solent was by far the busiest district, with about 10% of the total incidents.

Among the smaller vessels assisted in 1990 were:

Sailing craft	872
Power (pleasure)	860
Sailboards	331
Inflatables	163
Small craft	65

Hartlepool lifeboat visiting Amble marina.

Among the reasons for the 872 sailing craft incidents were:

Machinery failure	190
Capsize	165
Stranding	163
Sail/gear/mast failure	106
Adverse conditions	95

Royal National Lifeboat Institution

The RNLI started as a voluntary organisation in the early nineteenth century. The various local lifeboat societies that existed at that time needed national co-ordination, but the government showed no concern and no willingness to take the initiative. It was Sir William Hillary who took action founding the National Institution for the Preservation of Life from Shipwrecks. From his home on the Isle of Man he had not only seen many shipwrecks but had helped to rescue those in trouble. His institution was the forerunner of the RNLI, which came into being in 1854.

In 1824 the institution had 25 lifeboats provided by Lloyds and a further 14 provided by local benefactors. The total had risen to 91 by 1851, and to 300 by 1891. The increase in lifeboats accompanied the rise in seaborne trade during the nineteenth century. The government took control of the RNLI in 1854 but interfered so much in its day-to-day organisation that it reverted to its charitable status in 1869. The first steam powered lifeboat came into service in 1890, and the first diesel powered boat in 1932.

Until 1945 there were 300–500 rescues a year. The figure now stands at 4,000 a year. This increase reflects the growth of boating as

An Arun class lifeboat.

A Tyne class lifeboat.

A liferaft for six people.

a leisure activity. In total, since its foundation, the institution has saved some 120,000 lives. The increase in recreation related rescues has led to the use of inflatables for inshore work since 1963. These now account for about half of all launches and lives saved.

There are now 266 lifeboats distributed between 208 stations around the shores of the British Isles. Of these boats 140 are 16–21ft (4·9–6·4m) in length and the remaining 126 are 33–54ft (10–16·47m). The type and size of lifeboat on duty depends on the nature of the coastline. Some are suitable for shoal waters while others are more suited to deep water. Some lie afloat, some on a slipway and others have to be pushed across the beach by a tractor. The coastline is divided into areas with each area having the number and type of boats demanded by the nature of the coast.

The RNLI's aim, which influences the design of its boats and the organisation of rescues, is to be able to reach a casualty up to 50 miles from the shore within four hours and to be able to search and/or standby for a further four hours.

The request to launch a lifeboat usually comes from the coastguard and is addressed to the honorary secretary of the local lifeboat institution, who authorises the launch. Most stations with a large boat will have a full-time mechanic but the rest of the crew and staff will be volunteers.

Over £40 million is needed to run the service each year. This is raised by donations, membership fees and fundraising events. The importance of the service is underlined by the figures: in 1990 there were 4,937 launches and 1,601 lives were saved.

Heavy weather

When the wind is in excess of force 6 it is inadvisable to set out from harbour because away from shelter it may be very much closer to gale force. Once the wind reaches force 5 then the sensible cruising family will review their options, if they have not already done so on the strength of the weather forecast. Although force 7 is often described as a 'yachtman's gale', in reality force 6 is probably the limit for comfortable sailing in a boat less than 30ft (9m) in length. A larger boat will be relatively comfortable in a force 8.

It is the sea state as much as wind strength that should guide your thinking. Wave size increases in proportion to the wind strength once you get into the open sea. The precise size and shape of waves depends not just on the wind but on tidal streams, ocean currents and the contours of the seabed. The Beaufort scale and its related sea state notes make it very clear that wave size increases dramatically once the wind begins to increase beyond force 4.

Sailing cruisers are designed to withstand conditions that are far worse, both in terms of wind strength and wave size, than you are likely to encounter. The problems, particularly for the inexperienced, stem from the uncomfortable motion of the boat, the cold brought on by the effect of being soaked by flying spray and the general feeling of concern the situation produces.

This feeling of concern will reduce with experience. It is far better to gain this experience as a crew member with a competent, reassuring skipper. Take every opportunity to read articles about boats in heavy weather to familiarise yourself with the situation. The most important point is that if you are inexperienced you should not be in charge of a boat in these conditions. However, when you are more experienced and find yourself in heavy weather, your feeling of well-being will be that much greater if you have a thoroughly equipped boat and good foul-weather clothing.

There can never be any excuse for setting out in extreme conditions and putting the lives of your crew and search-and-rescue teams at risk, but if you set out in strong winds or get caught at sea by a gale there are various precautions that you must take.

The crew, fully dressed in foul-weather gear, must be organised into watches. These should be reduced to a minimum length so that nobody gets too tired, cold or wet and everybody has frequent periods down below where warmth, rest and nourishment are available. Hot snacks should be prepared and placed in flasks so that cooking is unnecessary. Seasickness tablets must be taken in advance as a precaution, and frequent light snacks eaten to help to fight off the symptoms. Not only must each crew member wear a lifejacket at all times, but they must each put on and secure their harness before entering the cockpit from below. Remember that crew failure is more likely than boat failure, and that it is the role of the skipper to ensure that the former does not happen.

The skipper should realise when the boat is overpressed: the leeward toerails will be constantly awash, and the helm will be forever spilling wind from the sail and will have difficulty holding a course. You should take action before you get to this stage. Once the boat is behaving like this, work on deck becomes very difficult and handling sails is almost impossible.

A skipper departing harbour in strong winds must ensure that the sails are reefed before departure. It is far easier to raise more sail if conditions prove to be lighter than expected than to attempt to reef in a near gale whilst trying to clear a harbour. All hatches and seacocks must be closed and all gear either stowed in lockers or lashed on deck. Make sure that no item, however small, will become loose down below. There is nothing more dispiriting than going below for a rest from the elements to be confronted by a mess

of food, charts, cushions and clothes lying on the floor. An emergency bag must be fully provisioned so that it is immediately available to go into the liferaft should that be necessary. Check that the bilge pumps are working and check the fastening of the washboards, which should only be opened for access.

Your passage planning must be thorough so that you do not have to spend much time at the chart table and so that all the information that you are likely to require is readily available. In a small boat the chart table is a very uncomfortable place at which to remain for any length of time in heavy weather.

The danger of heavy weather comes not so much from the wind as from the sea. To the experienced crew, large ocean waves are not a great danger unless a cross sea develops which is when swell from one direction has wind-driven waves superimposed upon it from another direction. This dangerous situation will occur either when there has been a shift in wind direction or where the wave form is interfered with by the seabed or current. Whatever the cause the danger comes from waves breaking over the boat. With large waves offshore the real danger occurs if the boat goes too fast so that it slews down and across the front of a wave with the risk of being rolled over, or where it buries its bow deeply into a wave and is turned stern over bow.

Closer to land the real danger occurs where the shallowing seabed or a strong tidal stream cause the waves to steepen and break over the boat. Such a situation is exacerbated when the wind is against the tide, as this produces extremely rough conditions. These will be especially pronounced during springs because of the greater strength of tidal streams at that time. The skipper who attempts to pass through a tidal race or overfall at such a time will be making a terrible mistake.

A boat riding out an increasingly violent storm at sea will eventually have to heave-to. The traditional method of doing this is to lower the mainsail, back the headsail and lash the tiller slightly to leeward. This works well with long keeled boats, but those with a fin keel may not lie so quietly. The easiest way to heave-to is to tack from close-hauled but leave the headsail on the original tack. With the boat almost through the wind the reefed mainsail is sheeted amidship and the helm lashed to leeward with elastic or shockcord. This allows a little movement of the rudder, reducing the likelihood of it being damaged as it is pounded by the waves.

Heaving-to with trysail and backed storm jib.

Should conditions allow, you could try heaving-to with the main eased rather than lowered. You need to know your boat's characteristics and to have practised heaving-to in order to find the best system. Hove-to, most boats will lie relatively quietly while making limited headway. Because the boat

When hove-to it is important that you have plenty of sea room and do not drift towards danger.

drift

land

drift

will continue to make some headway you must heave-to with plenty of sea room and must be heading away from the shore.

The head of most boats will be forced off the wind by the backed headsail, so they will end up sailing slowly along the troughs of the waves at about 50° to the wind. Ideally you should heave-to with a small storm jib and a trysail set. Too much sail area will put the rig under too much strain. If the wind continues to strengthen then you will find that even this sail arrangement creates too much pressure and will have to be reduced further.

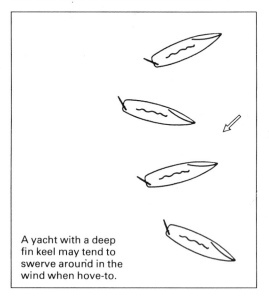

A yacht with a deep fin keel may tend to swerve around in the wind when hove-to.

As conditions worsen you should progressively lower all sails and lie beam-on to the wind. This is known as lying a-hull. The helm remains lashed to leeward. The boat will tend

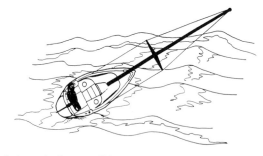

Lying a-hull as conditions worsen.

to lie beam-on to the wind and sea, which is very uncomfortable but not particularly dangerous because a slick is created to windward which interrupts the pattern of the breaking waves. The windage on the rig and hull will cause the boat to make some head-way as well as drifting at 1–2 knots to lee-ward. Adequate sea room is essential, as when hove-to.

Should conditions continue to worsen while the boat is lying a-hull there will be an increased danger of damage or capsize. This is the time to run with the storm, either with greatly reduced sail or under bare poles with warps streamed. The boat will continue to make headway, thus allowing it to be steered, which is vital because there are con-stant dangers. You must not let it go faster than the waves or it might accelerate down the front of a wave and then round up and broach in the trough, where it will be rolled over by the next wave. A further danger is that the boat might accelerate so fast down the front of one wave that it buries its bow deeply into the back of the next and is pitch-poled stern over bow. This inevitably leads to dismasting at the very least. You must also ensure that you do not go too slowly, other-wise you may be pooped, that is, engulfed by a wave breaking astern.

To avoid the danger of broaching or being pitchpoled you should stream warps to slow the boat. You will need to use these in any

Trailing warps to slow the boat when running before the wind.

event if you have limited sea room. Warps trailed correctly will slow the boat, keep the stern into the wind and quieten the seas astern. Warps should be as heavy as possible

and some 80–250m in length. More than one warp may be used, and knots can be tied to increase drag. Objects such as fenders or sail bags may be tied to the end of single warps, or a warp may be trailed as a loop. Each end of a loop, and the end of each single warp, must be attached to a point bolted through the hull because the strains will be enormous. It is possible to buy purpose-made sea anchors to stream from either the bow or the stern to assist the stability of the boat. You should realise that it is just as dangerous to slow the boat too much as it is to allow it to go too fast.

Poor visibility

One of the worst hazards that you will face at sea is poor visibility. Most skippers and their crews fear this far more than heavy weather because you lose sight of land and all other features, such as buoys. You must never set out in poor visibility and must plan your pas-sage very carefully if fog is a possibility later. The fog may be widespread or exist as banks or patches.

As the visibility decreases you must fix your position and update the log. Should you not be able to fix your position you must at least work out your EP (estimated position). The echo sounder must be switched on and a radar reflector hoisted high in the rigging. Without this the radar of a ship is unlikely to pick you up. Obviously if you have radar it must be switched on and monitored, al-though this does not obviate the need for a continuous lookout. The navigation lights should be switched on as soon as visibility deteriorates. The liferaft, flares and emergency bag must be readied and all crew must wear lifejackets (even if below) but not harnesses. Prepare hot snacks before you are enveloped in the fog so that no crew member is wasted below.

All crew must act as lookouts on deck in silence. One crew member should be as far forward as possible to be away from the noise of the engine if it is running. You should, if possible, sail rather than motor, to make listening easier. Without the engine running you might hear the sound of breakers before you run aground or you might hear the approaching bow wave of a vessel. Should you need to use the engine then you must reg-ularly put it into neutral to reduce the noise and so get a warning fractionally earlier.

You should make a sound signal to alert others of your whereabouts. For a vessel under sail this is one long and two short blasts at intervals of no more than two minutes. For a vessel under power it is one long blast made at the same time interval. Most cruisers carry the reed aerosol fog horn which tends to freeze in fog! You must therefore also carry a mouth horn. It is important that you know the sound signals likely to be made by other vessels and know how to react to them.

A major problem in fog is that sound waves are distorted to the extent that a sound apparently 40° on your starboard bow may actually come from abeam. Sound travels so badly upwind in fog that if you are to windward of a sound you may not hear it until you are almost upon the hazard.

Regulations require a vessel under 12 metres (40ft) to make an efficient sound signal at intervals of not more than two minutes.

The main dangers associated with poor visibility are being run down by a larger vessel or running aground. You should carefully revise your passage and decide if it is safe to continue. The choice lies between staying where you are, making for a port or heading for an anchorage. If you are in a shipping lane your first priority is to leave as quickly as possible. Exit the lane with your heading at a right angle to the traffic. Do not panic and do not go too fast. A slow to moderate speed will give you the time to react that you will not have at full throttle. If you are unfortunate enough to see a bow wave suddenly appear, then try to get end-on to it so that it pushes you clear.

From the chart, determine the nearest section of coastline away from the shipping lanes, and at a constant slow speed make for that. You should be looking for a safe anchorage or harbour, preferably with danger-free coast on at least one side. An attractive refuge would be one approached by smooth but positive contours. The existence of a fog horn close by would be an added attraction.

Having decided on the point you are aiming for you should have a definite plan of action. From your fix or EP, plot a course to miss the refuge by a good margin on the safe side. Use the charted depth at the entrance to the refuge and the tide tables to calculate the depth of water at the time you expect to arrive. When your echo sounder gives that depth then you are on the same contour as the entrance. This obviously only works where the contours roughly parallel the coastline. Having aimed very definitely for one side of the refuge you will know in which direction to head. Navigate along the contour until you reach the refuge.

There is a definite method to navigating along a contour like this. If the coast is to starboard then steer 15° to starboard if the water deepens and make a 40° course alteration to port as the water shoals to less than the desired depth. This course alteration, taking you 25° (40°–15°) from the contour line, helps to keep you on that line by counteracting the tendency to go too close to the shore.

Where both sides of a refuge are similar the advantage lies with the downtide section of coast. This is because you have more control over your speed when going against the tide.

You must take care not to let the echo sounder and your misjudgement lead you into a trap, as illustrated opposite. You should also take note of any forecast change in wind direction so that you do not find yourself anchored on a lee shore with improving visibility but strengthening wind.

Should there be no safe harbour or convenient anchorage close to the shore you will have to take the difficult decision to stay out. Keep calm and try to keep a safe balance between distance from a dangerous shoreline and distance from shipping lanes. Think carefully about what you are doing and remember that coastal shipping in particular tends to converge near headlands.

Collision

Collision may occur with a submerged object or with another vessel. If collision damage causes a leak your first priority should be to control the flooding by reducing the flow of water from the leak. All pumps must be put to use and the hole blocked with a sleeping bag or sail bag filled with clothes. Push part of the bag out through the hole and if possible pass a sail under the boat and secure it on deck so that it is pulled tight against the hole. If the hole is not too large then the combined effects of pumping water and blocking the hole should keep the boat afloat until it may be beached or help arrives. You may be able

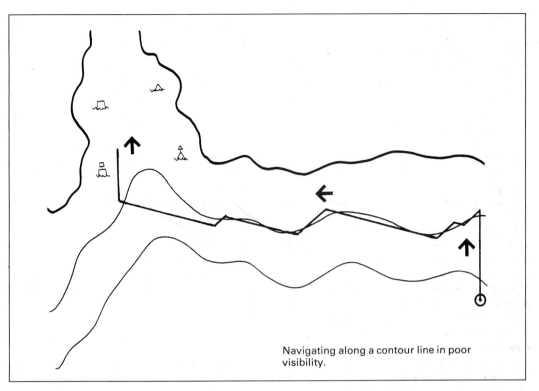

Navigating along a contour line in poor visibility.

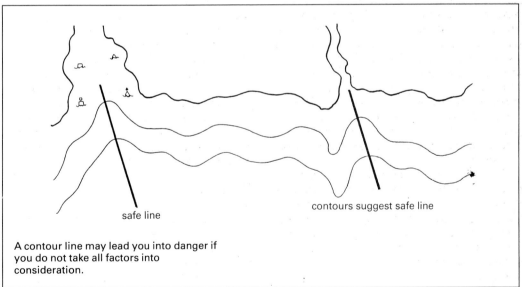

safe line

contours suggest safe line

A contour line may lead you into danger if you do not take all factors into consideration.

to seal a small hole with underwater filler. When the hole is close to the waterline you should either move all possible weight to the opposite side to lift it clear of the water or sail on the opposite tack.

Should your standard pumps not keep pace with the inflow of water then try other means of pumping. A pipe from the bilges into the toilet pan, with continual flushing of the toilet, will remove a large amount of water. You could also run the hose from the engine cooling system into the bilges so that the water is pumped overboard as the engine is run.

Fire

The fire hazard in boats is caused by the storage in close proximity of fuel and gas, and by the existence of these, an electrical system, a cooker and an engine all in the same confined space. Carelessness in the use of these systems will exacerbate the problem. Clearly you need effective maintenance of all such systems.

When you have finished using the cooker you must first turn off the gas supply at the bottle so that the remaining gas in the pipe is burnt. When the flame is extinguished you may turn the cooker off. The gas pipe to the cooker must have armoured flexible hosing. Liquid petroleum gas is heavier than air and will tend to sink down into the bilges if you are not careful. These and the engine compartment must be ventilated and kept very clean. The gas bottle must be stored in a lead free container in the cockpit with an overboard air drain to reduce the risk from a gas leak. A gas detector is a wise investment.

Do not smoke below deck and do not smoke anywhere when refuelling. Before refuelling stop the engine and turn off its fuel supply. You must also turn off all gas and electricity and ensure that the engine compartment is closed. Fuel tanks should be filled on deck, preferably in a way that directs spillage straight over the side. Spillage on the decks must be quickly hosed down. Any spare fuel should be carried in special containers stowed in lockers away from the engine and galley.

As standard equipment you must have a minimum of two multi-purpose fire extinguishers stowed in readily accessible positions. The best general purpose extinguishers are dry powder, which although messy are suitable for all fire types because they smother fire effectively and so prevent reignition. BCF (bromo-chloro-difluoromethane) extinguishers are equally good but are toxic and should not be used in confined spaces. Remember that it is best to aim an extinguisher at the seat of the fire and not at the flames. All crew must know where the extinguishers are stowed and how they work.

Ideally there should be one extinguisher at each hatch opening so that they may be reached from on deck away from the fire. There should also be a halon or BCF extinguisher attached to a remote control system in the engine compartment. This allows a fire in the area to be fought without letting air into the compartment. Fire blankets are very useful for smothering flames. There should be at least one on board, preferably to the side of the galley.

Fire is fed by heat, fuel and oxygen; it will go out if you remove any of these. Your prime objective should therefore be to smother the fire to deprive it of oxygen and to cool the surrounding area. A cooker fire must be smothered by a fire blanket. This should be applied away from you otherwise there is a danger of the flames being drawn onto your body. If a blanket is not available use a dry powder extinguisher. Do not attempt to carry the burning object in order to throw it over the side: you will probably drop it and spread the fire. Do not use water on an oil or engine fire or on cooking fat as, again, you risk spreading the fire. You must not use foam extinguishers on an electrical fire. Water may be used on fires such as those in bedding and clothes. These are liable to reignite so you should use plenty of it. Remember the importance of cooling adjacent areas, so if it is safe to do so cool these areas with water.

Opening the engine compartment in the event of an engine fire will let oxygen in to feed it, so if you do not have an automatic extinguisher fitted cut a small hole in the compartment and aim the extinguisher through that.

At the first sign of fire either drop the sails and stop if in a light wind or, in a strong wind, turn downwind to reduce the fanning effect. For the same reason close all hatches. Wet your clothes before tackling a serious fire. Any objects on fire which may be *safely* carried, such as cushions, should be thrown over the side. The engine and all gas and electrical systems must be turned off before you tackle the fire. If the fire is obviously extensive then preparations must be made to abandon the boat. This means launching the liferaft and putting lifejackets on. You must take care that the liferaft is not endangered by the fire.

If an individual crew member is engulfed in flames push them onto the floor so that the flames rise away from their face. Do not roll them over as that will spread the flames over their body. Smother the flames with a blanket or large cloth.

Man overboard

Should one of the crew go over the side someone should immediately shout 'man overboard'. At the same moment the lifebuoy or danbuoy must be thrown towards, and preferably upwind of, the casualty so that it will drift down to them. If you are under power then you must instantly turn the bow in their direction so that the stern, and therefore the propeller, is turned away from them. Someone must point continuously in the direction of the person in the water because at night or in rough weather they will be quickly lost from sight.

The boat must be returned as rapidly as possible to the casualty. The method of return depends on the sea and wind conditions, the type of boat and the remaining crew, who might be the one who is inexperienced or physically weak. For that reason alone it is important that the drill is practised frequently so that all crew know their exact role.

From the moment the casualty goes over the side the time elapsed and heading must be logged precisely. If you should then lose visual contact you can return on the reciprocal heading for the same time period with some confidence that you will regain contact.

Possibly the easiest method of return under sail is to head the boat onto a beam reach while the crew gets organised. When they are ready tack onto the opposite reach and return along the reciprocal heading. During the final approach turn the boat progressively towards the wind and let the sails fly as you reach the casualty.

Return to the man overboard on a beam reach and then turn head to wind when you reach the casualty.

The advantage of this method is that the boat is always under control. The disadvantage is that you will travel some distance before you tack and return, so that at night or in rough seas the casualty will soon be lost from sight.

Other possibilities include gybing or tacking immediately back to the position at which the crew member went over the side. This is quicker and lessens the possibility of the casualty being lost from sight, but it does require considerable skill and favourable conditions. You may, in this case, return so quickly that you reach the casualty before the boat and crew are organised for the pickup.

An inexperienced crew may find a return under engine much easier. In this case head the boat to wind, start the engine and drop the sails, having first made sure that there are no ropes in the water to foul the propeller. If short-handed it may be wise simply to let the headsail fly to avoid the risk of a lowered headsail going over the side. The engine must be stopped when the casualty is reached in order to avoid injury from the propeller.

Lifting casualties out of the water is a major problem. Their saturated clothes will have vastly increased their weight, the angle of lift will be inefficient, and they may be so exhausted that they are of no help. If there is just one crew member left on board then the problems will be readily seen. Once alongside secure the casualty to the boat so that he or she does not drift away. Bring the casualty alongside the cockpit where it is easier and safer to work. Cut the lifeline if it makes it easier to work; remember speed is of the essence. If the casualty is unconscious or injured another crew member, secured to the boat, may have to go into the water to give assistance. There are various methods of lifting someone from the water; none is easy and all need practice. One possibility is to secure a line to a winch and make a large bowline in the other end. This may be placed over the shoulders of the casualty, who is then winched aboard, or the casualty may use the loop of the bowline as a step and be winched upwards in stages. You could also try facing them away from the boat and putting your hands under their armpits in order to get some leverage.

Other alternatives include attaching a halyard to the casualty and then winching him or her up, or passing a headsail under her body and then using the winch. You could also use the mainsail in much the same way. To do this lower the boom into the cockpit and sheet hard in. Take the mainsail out of its mast track and put it over the side under the casualty. Haul up on the halyard and the casualty should come up in the folds of the sail. Try to use the roll of the boat to help this action. A further possibility is to roll the casualty into a half-inflated dinghy. This gets them closer to deck level and so reduces the distance they have to be lifted. A boarding ladder would make life easier for a casualty who has the strength to climb back on board, but make sure that the ladder is firmly secured.

Once you have recovered the casualty treat her for shock and hypothermia if she has been in the water for any length of time, or if she appears distressed.

Flares

Flares are used to attract attention when in distress or to warn of collision danger. You and your crew must learn thoroughly the various types of flare and how they are fired. The middle of an emergency is not the time to be reading the instructions. Learn how and when to use the various flares before setting out to sea. Never look directly at a flare, and never point it into the wind or you, the boat and any exposed lifesaving equipment will be covered with sparks.

Flares must be stowed so that they will not be affected by moisture and warmth, which hasten their deterioration. All flares deteriorate and have a useful life of about three years if the stowage recommendations on them are followed. Flares are marked by a date indicating the end of their working life, at which time they must be replaced. Out of date flares may be handed in either to the coastguard or police to ensure safe disposal. Alternatively you could keep your old flares as they usually work despite their age. Keep them clearly separate from your current flares and only use them as a last resort. Distress and collision flares must be stowed separately to avoid confusion. All crew must be familiar with the stowage of the flares so that the correct type may be found easily in an emergency.

Unlike some European countries the UK has no regulations requiring private pleasure

craft to carry flares. There are, however, clear recommendations set out by the RYA. The most important criteria is how far offshore you are passaging. At this stage you will probably come within Category 1 of these recommendations; with increased experience this will become Category 2.

CATEGORY 1
Yachts using sheltered waters during daylight only, within 3 miles of land or within sight of potential help, should carry the following:

> *2 hand-held red flares*
> *2 hand-held orange smoke signals*
> *4 hand-held white flares*

Use hand-held red flares to raise the alarm and later to pinpoint your position when within sight of land or another boat. These burn for 1 minute and have a visibility of 7 miles on a clear night. These red flares should be used in conditions of poor visibility, darkness or strong wind. In daylight with good visibility and light wind use the orange smokes. These produce a dense mass of orange smoke visible for 3 miles and burn for 50 seconds. They are particularly visible from the air.

CATEGORY 2
Yachts cruising day and night within 10 miles of the coast and about 4 hours from a safe harbour or refuge should carry the following:

> *4 hand-held red flares*
> *2 hand-held orange smoke signals*
> *2 red parachute rockets*
> *4 hand-held white flares*

More than 3 miles from land or another boat hand-held signals may not be seen as they are below the visible horizon. In this situation use the red parachute rockets. These project a very bright red flare suspended by a parachute up to an altitude of over 300m. On a clear night these are visible for some 28 miles and burn for 40 seconds. They should be projected vertically, except in strong wind when they should be fired 15° downwind, and in low cloud when they should be fired 45° downwind so that they deploy below the cloud base. The rockets should be separated by a 2 minute interval and followed by either hand-held red flares or orange smokes when rescuers are within visual range.

CATEGORY 3

Yachts cruising offshore making passages of between 50 and 500 miles between the British Isles and various parts of Europe should carry the following:

4 red hand-held flares
2 buoyant orange smoke signals
4 red parachute rockets
4 hand-held white flares

The buoyant orange smokes are ring-pull containers that should be put in the water to leeward of the boat. They burn for 3 minutes.

COLLISION

If a boat is on collision course at night use a hand-held white flare to draw attention to your position. These brilliant white flares burn for 50 seconds. They must never be used for distress and must be stowed within easy reach of the cockpit.

Other methods of signalling for help

1. S.O.S by sound or light
2. Slow raising and lowering of arms
3. Code flags NC
4. A square flag above or below a ball
5. Continuous sounding of a horn
6. Ensign hoisted high in the rigging

Liferafts

It is vital that there should be adequate means of abandoning a boat in case of foundering. The possibilities are rigid dinghies, cheap inflatables, more expensive genuine liferafts and recent 'Tinker' type development. There are Department of Transport recommendations on the type of raft to carry, however not all liferafts conform to these or to the manufacturing regulations.

For those going more than 3 miles out a traditional liferaft or Tinker must be considered essential. A liferaft is encapsulated in either a valise or a cannister, the latter being somewhat heavy and unwieldy and really only suitable for deck mounting. If a liferaft is not to be mounted on the deck it must be stowed in a locker that is easily accessible from the deck.

All crew must know how to inflate and board the liferaft. The painter attached to the liferaft has two roles. It helps to secure the liferaft to the deck and, when the liferaft is thrown into the sea with the painter still attached, it tightens and causes the liferaft to inflate. Clearly secure attachment of the painter is vital but it must also have a quick-release device so that there is no danger of a sinking boat taking a liferaft down with it. In fact most liferaft painters are designed so that the strain caused by a sinking boat will cause them to break. The painter should be arranged so that it will not snag on any part of the boat when the liferaft is thrown.

You are safer on the boat than in the water, so do not abandon until it is on the point of sinking or you are forced off by fire. Too many lives have been lost through premature abandonment. The danger of this was illustrated by the 1979 Fastnet tragedy when crew died having abandoned boats that were later recovered afloat.

Having reached the point at which abandonment is imperative launch the liferaft to leeward. Once it has inflated haul it alongside the boat and make it secure. If, as is possible, it turns upside down, the strongest member of the crew will have to get into the water to right it. The crew member doing this must be attached to the boat by a safety line to avoid being swept away. The strongest person should also be the first into the liferaft so as to stabilise it and to assist others. Your emergency bag (carried at all times and containing food, drink, flares, torch, first-aid kit and spare clothes) should be passed immediately into the liferaft. Before the crew leave the boat they should put on as much warm clothing as possible.

Once all the crew are in the liferaft cut the painter and paddle away. The advantage of inflating the liferaft on the leeward side is that the wind should carry it quickly from the boat. Bail any water that has collected inside and set the drogue anchor if it is necessary to restrict drift downwind. Check for leaks and seal any with the repair kit that should be part of the liferaft's equipment.

Unless you have a Tinker type raft, which you can sail and/or row, you will simply have to drift until rescued. As you are unlikely to be making offshore passages at this stage you should not have to wait long for rescue. In the meantime there are various problems to be avoided, such as seasickness, sunburn and hypothermia. You must take care not to puncture the raft, and must try to keep a continuous check on your estimated position.

A liferaft must be serviced annually by a service station which is approved by the manufacturer.

Air-sea rescue

If you see or hear a helicopter approaching at night do not fire a flare because that will cause its crew to lose their night vision. When one of the crew winches down to you do not touch the winch cable as you might get an electric shock and do not connect the cable to the boat. You must take to the water in lifejackets or launch the liferaft if so ordered.

First aid

This section gives a brief but life-saving outline of how to treat the injuries you are most likely to come across at sea. Whatever the level of experience of a boat's crew they must be able to render first aid so as to prevent, at the very least, worsening of an injury. Above all they must go on a first aid course.

BRUISE
Rest the injured part and apply a cold compress.

MINOR CUT
Apply gentle local pressure to the cut and wash the wound in running water. Dry the skin with cotton wool and apply a plaster or bandage.

SEVERE BLEEDING
At first apply direct pressure but if that fails to stem the flow you must apply indirect pressure to a pressure point. When the flow has stopped raise and support the injured part, if there is no break or dislocation, and then dress the wound.

INTERNAL BLEEDING
Signs of internal bleeding include blood issuing from the ears, nose or mouth or being passed in bowel movement. You must reassure the casualty, place them at rest with their legs slightly raised and loosen all tight clothing. Keep them warm and do not give anything by mouth.

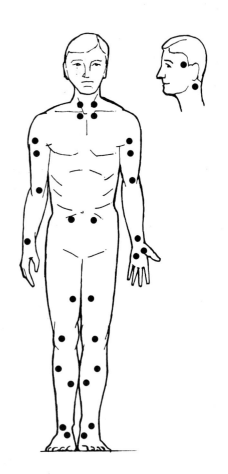

Pressure points where arteries pass over bones. Pressure on one of these on the heart side of the injury will stop serious bleeding.

SPRAIN OR STRAIN
Rest the injured part. Apply a cold compress to a sprain.

FRACTURE OR DISLOCATION
Immobilise the injured part by sling and bandages so that the injury is not aggravated by further movement. It is important to tie bandages firmly but not so tightly that they restrict the flow of blood.

BLOW TO THE HEAD
Refer casualty to a doctor as quickly as possible.

BURNS AND SCALDS
Either place the affected part in cool water or

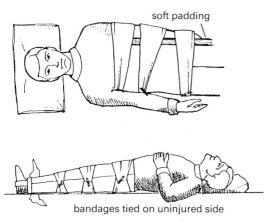

soft padding

bandages tied on uninjured side

A broken limb must be supported by a splint with a soft cloth between the splint and the injured limb.

run cool water over it. Loosen any restrictive clothing and lay the casualty down. Do not put any ointment or oil-based dressings on the wound but cover it with a clean cloth. If the casualty is conscious give them small cold drinks at frequent intervals.

SHOCK

Shock is likely to accompany all major injuries. The casualty in shock will have cold clammy skin, will perspire freely and have a tendency to vomit and to be thirsty. First deal with any serious injury and then lay the casualty down with the lower limbs raised and the head lowered and turned to one side. Loosen all tight clothing and keep the casualty warm. Moisten the lips lightly but do not give drinks.

UNCONSCIOUSNESS

Loosen all tight clothing and ensure that air passages are not blocked. Place the casualty in the recovery position with their head slightly lower than their feet. Their head must be pressed back and their lower jaw pushed forward so that their chin juts out, thus preventing their tongue from blocking the air passage. Keep the casualty warm but give no liquids while unconscious. Anybody who has been unconscious should see a doctor as soon as possible.

SEASICKNESS

Those suffering from seasickness should sit on deck in warm clothing and nibble on biscuits, boiled sweets and barley sugar. Unsweetened fruit juices will also help to settle the stomach. Keep them warm and in fresh air, not down below in a rolling cabin. However, if the vomiting is severe then they must lie down in a warm sleeping bag below deck having first removed all wet clothing. As they recover they should put on warm clothing and go on deck.

HYPOTHERMIA

Prolonged exposure to cold and damp will lower the deep body temperature and cause a severe lack of energy, extreme cramp, continuous shivering and lack of co-ordination. It is important to prevent further heat loss and to raise body temperature slowly. Place the casualty in a sheltered location in a warm sleeping bag with another crew member for added warmth. Sugar should be given in an easily digestible form such as condensed milk. Never give alcohol. Warming must be slow, otherwise the temperature of the body core will be dangerously lowered.

EMERGENCY RESUSCITATION

If a casualty has stopped breathing or has difficulty in breathing you must start immediate resuscitation, as when the brain is starved of oxygen for more than four minutes it is likely to be permanently damaged. The method is as follows:

1. Lay the casualty on his or her back and press the top of his head so that it tilts back pushing his chin upwards so that his tongue does not block the air passage.

Push the head back and the chin upwards to ensure that the airways are open.

2. Clear his mouth of any major obstructions to breathing.
3. Pinch his nostrils together and take a deep breath. Seal your lips around the casualty's mouth and breathe out until

you see his chest rise. If it fails to rise check for obstructions.

4. Immediately give four rapid inflations.
5. Continue with one inflation every five seconds until the casualty is able to breathe freely.
6. Place the casualty in the recovery position and continue to monitor breathing in case it should stop again.

Pinch the casualty's nostrils and seal your lips around the mouth.

With small children the method is as above except that the inflations are more rapid and more gentle. Seal your lips around the child's mouth and nostrils.

Refer to a doctor anybody who has stopped breathing, even if only for a short period.

The recovery position.

Questions

Answers are on page 223.

1. In poor visibility why should you not:
   a) Wear a harness?
   b) Pass close to a headland?
2. What sound signals do the following vessels make in poor visibility?
   a) A yacht sailing.
   b) A yacht motor-sailing.
   c) A power driven vessel underway.
   d) A vessel restricted in its ability to manoeuvre.
   e) A fishing vessel.
   f) A vessel over 100 metres (330ft) at anchor.
3. Where should you locate the following?
   a) A fire blanket.
   b) A multi-purpose dry powder fire extinguisher.
   c) An automatic halon or BCF extinguisher.
4. When would you use the following?
   a) Orange smokes.
   b) Red parachute rockets.
5. List five distress signals, apart from VHF and flares, that you could use in an emergency.
6. If a helicopter passes a weighted line down to you what action should you take?
7. If a crew member is bleeding from inside an ear is this serious enough to warrant a Mayday message? If so, why?

CHAPTER 7

International Regulations for Preventing Collisions at Sea

In 1972 the Inter-governmental Maritime Organisation (IMO) instituted a wide ranging revision of the International Regulations for Preventing Collisions at Sea, which had come into force in 1960. Further amendments were made in 1981 and came into force in 1983. These regulations, agreed by all maritime nations, apply to all vessels on the high seas and on rivers and estuaries navigable by seagoing vessels. You must know them: ignorance is no defence and in certain situations failure to comply could lead to prosecution.

The regulations are the maritime equivalent of the *Highway Code*. It is essential to have a thorough knowledge of the Steering and Sailing Rules (5, 7–10 and 12–19) so that you can act on them immediately. You also need to have a working knowledge of the other rules.

The Steering and Sailing Rules essentially refer to situations where boats are within sight of each other. Their importance is therefore obvious: they provide a means of avoiding collision.

It is sensible to keep clear of all commercial traffic whatever the rights and wrongs of a particular crossing situation. While you are there for pleasure they are there to earn a living, so it is for you to show courtesy and keep clear. You must realise that even on a clear day it is extremely difficult to see a small boat from the bridge of a large vessel. Remember that at the speed of today's merchant vessels one may suddenly be on top of you, although ten minutes earlier the horizon was clear.

Although the rules are clear their application is not always simple. At night it may be difficult to make sense of a cluster of lights crossing your path. You may be unsure of the size of the vessel and its heading. If the crossing angle is narrow it may be difficult to work out the situation, so you should start taking bearings at an early stage. Ultimately you have to decide whether to cross ahead of the vessel or to bear off and pass astern.

The specific action to be taken depends on the nature of the vessel (sailing, power or fishing), the relative tacks, and whether the situation is crossing or head-on. Whatever the action required, Rule 8 (emphasised by Rule 16) makes quite clear that the give-way vessel must take *early* and *substantial* avoiding action. The latter implies a course alteration of about 40°, preferably passing to the stern of the right-of-way vessel. This ensures that the vessel has altered course sufficiently to avoid a collision and that the avoiding action has been made clear to the right-of-way vessel. The latter should maintain her course and speed (Rule 17) so as not to confuse the give-way vessel. A series of minor course alterations by either vessel could cause confusion. If the give-way vessel fails to alter course, or fails to do so substantially, the right-of-way vessel must take avoiding action (Rule 17).

RULE 5: LOOKOUT

This emphasises that you must keep a continuous lookout, day and night, by sight and sound. You cannot do this if there is no one on deck. In view of the speed of modern ships it is not safe to look out only every half an hour, for example, especially in busy waters. The lookout *must* be continuous. It is the skipper's responsibility to ensure that whatever the weather conditions and regardless of the apparent absence of traffic a lookout is kept. On a cold night with the deck lashed with spray it is all too easy to huddle in the shelter of the sprayhood and not keep a lookout. The watch on deck must avoid bright lights that will destroy their night vision. Lights below must be kept to a minimum, and that above the chart table should be soft so that it may be used without causing a problem.

RULE 7: RISK OF COLLISION

Once a boat is sited on a converging course you must decide, before taking any action, if there is a collision risk. Using a hand-bearing compass take regular bearings on the target vessel. If the bearing does not change substantially as the vessel approaches then there is a definite risk of collision and you must take action according to whether you are the give-way or right-of-way vessel.

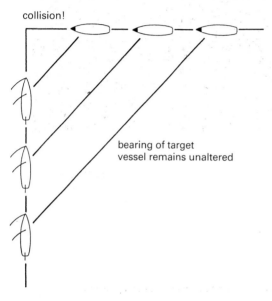

The target vessel is showing a constant bearing so you must alter course.

RULE 9: NARROW CHANNELS

As far as possible a vessel should keep to the starboard edge of a narrow channel. As some vessels can clearly only navigate within the channel because of their draught, other vessels, especially those of less than 20m (66ft) in length and all sailing vessels, must keep out of their way. Clearly, where possible, these small vessels should keep out of the channel. They should not anchor in the fairway or in a narrow channel unless forced to do so by circumstances. When approaching long and/or blind bends a vessel must sound one long warning blast and listen for a reply.

RULE 10: TRAFFIC SEPARATION SCHEMES

These schemes are found wherever there are congested waters around the UK. Through traffic is not only split into two streams going in opposite directions but is also separated from inshore traffic. The area between two traffic zones is called a separation zone. The latter may be entered only by fishing vessels, vessels crossing or vessels in a state of emergency. Traffic must proceed in the correct direction and must keep clear of the separation zones. Vessels should join or leave at the end of a traffic zone. If a vessel has to join at some other point then it should do so at as small an angle to the general traffic flow as is possible.

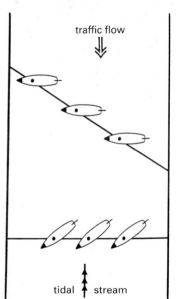

When crossing a shipping zone you must hold a course at a right angle to the flow of traffic.

Through traffic must not use an inshore zone, although this does not apply to vessels of less than 20m (66ft) in length or to sailing vessels.

You should avoid crossing a zone if at all possible. If you have to cross a zone then your heading must be as close as possible to a right angle to the general direction of flow. Sailing vessels are best advised to steer a course at a right angle to the flow so that a clear aspect is presented to the traffic. This is preferable to trying to keep the ground track at that angle to the traffic. If you attempt the latter you

fishing vessel entering Amble harbour with its aymark still raised.

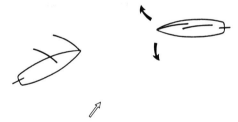

Rule 12: port tack gives way to starboard.

Rule 12: Windward vessel keeps clear when both vessels are on the same tack.

ill present a quarter aspect to the traffic and ill spend more time in the lane if fighting a ul tide.

.ULE 12: SAILING VESSELS MEETING

 coastal waters, harbours and estuaries you ·e likely to apply this rule frequently.

 i) The vessel that has the wind on the port side shall keep clear.

ii) The vessel to windward shall keep clear of the vessel to leeward when both have the wind on the same side.

iii) If a vessel with the wind on the port side sees a vessel to windward and cannot determine with certainty

97

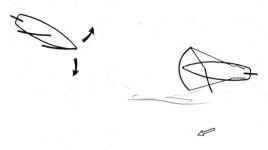

Rule 12: If in doubt as to the tack of a windward vessel a port tack vessel must keep clear.

whether the other vessel has the wind on port or starboard she shall keep out of the way of the other vessel.

RULE 13: OVERTAKING

The overtaking vessel must keep clear. A vessel is defined as overtaking when approaching from a direction greater than 22.5° abaft the beam of a vessel ahead. The responsibility to keep clear remains until it is well clear of the overtaken vessel.

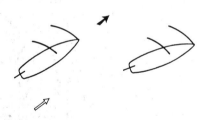

Rule 13: Overtaking vessel must keep clear.

RULE 14: POWER DRIVEN VESSELS MEETING HEAD-ON

Each vessel must alter course to starboard. This refers not only to power vessels but also sailing vessels using their auxiliary with the sails hoisted.

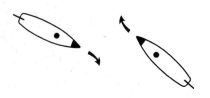

Rule 14: Power vessels meeting head-on must alter course to starboard.

RULE 15: TWO POWER DRIVEN VESSELS CROSSING WITH RISK OF COLLISION

The vessel which has the other on her starboard side must keep out of the way and, where possible, pass astern of the other. The alternative to altering course is to reduce speed to allow the other vessel to pass safely ahead.

Rule 15: A power vessel which has another power vessel on her starboard side must give way.

RULE 18: RESPONSIBILITIES BETWEEN VESSELS

a) Sailing or power vessels when under way must keep out of the way of a vessel engaged in fishing and all three must keep out of the way of:
   i) vessels not under command;
   ii) vessels restricted in their ability to manoeuvre.
b) Power vessels when under way must keep out of the way of sailing vessels.
c) Any vessel other than one not under command or one restricted in its ability to manoeuvre should keep out of the way of a vessel constrained by its draught.

RULE 19: RESTRICTED VISIBILITY

This rule emphasises that in restricted visibility vessels must reduce their speed so that they can stop within the distance that they can see. If a fog signal is heard forward of the beam a vessel must reduce its speed to the minimum sufficient to maintain manoeuvrability until the danger has passed.

LIGHTS
The regulations set out the specific light requirements for various types of vessel in all possible situations, as well as various light

Cumulus clouds indicating an unstable atmosphere.

Cirrus clouds indicating the approach of a depression.

Sudden squalls create specific problems.

Southampton to Cowes hydrofoil.

signals. These are given in the illustration opposite. p 199

SOUND SIGNALS
Large commercial vessels manoeuvring in the vicinity of other craft are likely to use a variety of sound signals the meaning of which you must be aware. These signals are not generally used by family cruisers. In the following table, which gives the most important sound signals, short blasts (1 second duration) are represented by a dot, and long blasts (5 seconds duration) by a dash.

.   I am altering course to starboard

. .   I am altering course to port

. . .   My engines are going astern (the vessel may not yet have sternway on)

– – .   I intend overtaking on your starboard side

– – . .   I intend overtaking on your port side

– . – .   I agree to your wish to overtake me (a reply to the two previous signals)

–   Warning signal by vessel approaching bend or obstruction

. . . . .   I am in doubt regarding your intentions

Questions

Answers are on page 223–24.

1. In what way do the rules make a single-handed passage difficult?
2. What day shapes should the following display?
   a) A vessel sailing and using power.
   b) A vessel aground.
   c) A vessel minesweeping.
3. What do the following day-shapes indicate?

a

b

c

4. Which lights should a 10m (33ft) yacht show in the following situations?
   a) At anchor in a fairway.
   b) Under sail.
   c) Motor sailing.
   d) Under engine only.

5. Identify the following vessels and state whether they are underway or not and which aspect is in view.

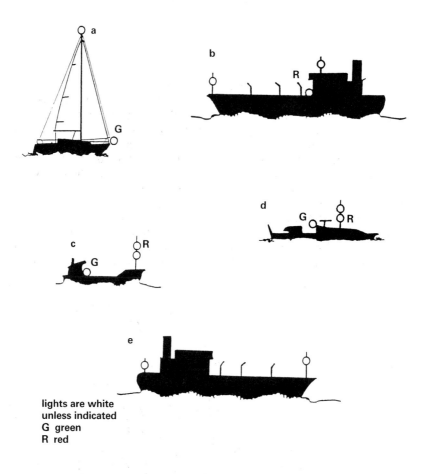

lights are white
unless indicated
G green
R red

6. How can you determine if a risk of collision exists?
7. What action must the right-of-way vessel take, according to the rules?
8. What do you understand by the following sound signals?

a) . .   b) – – .   c) –

CHAPTER 8

Meteorology

Weather plays a major role in boating because it provides the motive power for sailing and affects our level of comfort and enjoyment. It presents challenges to the experienced crew and dangers to the unwary.

Those aspects of weather that most concern the boat owner are wind and fog. Light air may lead to a delayed passage and the forced use of the auxiliary engine, while heavy weather will bring the need to reef and possibly to seek shelter. Wind direction is also important, because if the boat is headed by the wind the passage is likely to be much longer, wetter and generally less comfortable. Precipitation and temperature will also be of interest because whilst they do not directly affect safety they do affect your comfort and feeling of well being.

To the navigator wind is associated with four major weather phenomena:
- *depressions;*
- *anticyclones;*
- *land and sea breezes;*
- *cumulus development.*

Fog is even less predictable than the wind. Its location, depth and horizontal extent are

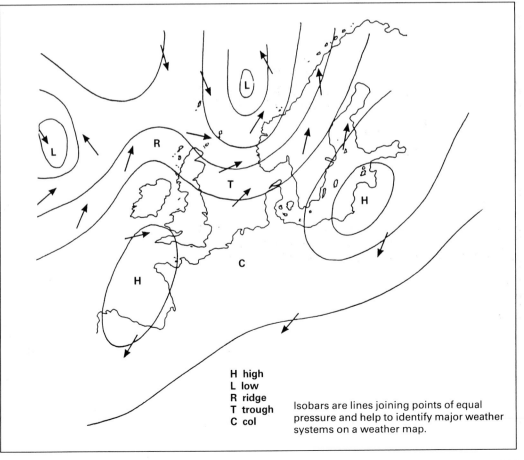

H high
L low
R ridge
T trough
C col

Isobars are lines joining points of equal pressure and help to identify major weather systems on a weather map.

variable and constantly changing. With it comes the danger of being run down by a larger vessel or of running aground. Fog may completely disorientate the unwary which places special demands upon the navigator.

The weather we experience in the British Isles is invariably related to travelling weather systems such as depressions and anticyclones. These are best understood in terms of the movement of vast masses of air both horizontally and vertically.

Air moves across the surface of the earth because of imbalances in surface atmospheric pressure. This pressure is the weight of the atmosphere pressing down on the earth. It is measured in millibars (mb), 1,000mb being equal to a mercury reading of 29.53in. The latter is still used in barometers but the weather forecasts only use millibars. Centres of low pressure crossing the British Isles typically have a central pressure of 970–980mb while anticyclones have pressures of 1,020–1,030mb. Both sets of figures serve only as a general guide. On a meteorological map pressure is shown by isobars. These are lines that join points of equal pressure. The isobar interval on any one map is constant, with 4mb being the most frequently used.

Atmospheric pressure is important to the skipper because horizontal variations in pressure generate the movement of air over the earth's surface. Between adjacent areas of differing pressure there is a pressure gradient down which the air flows from higher to lower pressure, never the reverse. However, it does not flow directly from high to low because of the deflection caused by the earth's rotation. In the northern hemisphere this causes the air to curve to the right of its path; in the southern hemisphere the curvature is to the left. This explains why air tends to flow around areas of high and low pressure rather than flowing directly between them.

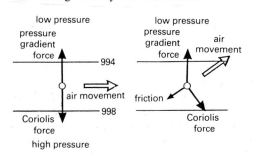

The forces that act upon moving air.

The strength of the pressure gradient controls the speed of air movement and therefore wind strength. It follows that when the isobars are closer together the pressure gradient is steeper and therefore the winds are stronger. The reverse holds for widely spaced isobars.

The pattern of the isobars will help you to identify the major weather systems and to determine wind strength and direction.

The only complication to add to all this is the position of fronts. These are imaginary lines drawn on a map to separate air masses of differing characteristics. Air masses, like oil and water, do not mix. In the atmosphere there will therefore be a distinct frontal zone where two air masses meet. It follows that as the air masses move so too do the fronts. These frontal zones are marked by distinct weather characteristics which obviously also move. A meteorologist picks out the location of a front by finding those areas where there is a pronounced change in curvature of the isobars. For the beginner this is virtually impossible to do accurately. Fortunately all published meteorological maps appear with the fronts already drawn. There are three types of front each with its own symbol.

The movement of frontal systems probably has greater significance for the crew of a boat in north European waters than any other meteorological phenomenon.

Depressions

Depressions bring the bulk of our rapidly changing cloudy and wet weather. The summers of 1976 and 1989 were so fine because these depressions tracked further north, the jet stream lying to the north of the British Isles. These low pressure systems, with their steep pressure gradients, are commonly associated with moderate to strong wind, cloud, periods of rain and poor visibility. They tend to be most intense in winter, as a result of steeper pressure gradients. At that time of the year they frequently bring gales and often develop storm-force winds.

A depression (or cyclone) is a massive whirl of air moving in three dimensions: anticlockwise, inwards and upwards. The formation of depressions is related to vast troughs in the upper westerlies that flow at the top of the troposphere. These feed on the temperature contrasts produced by warm and cold air

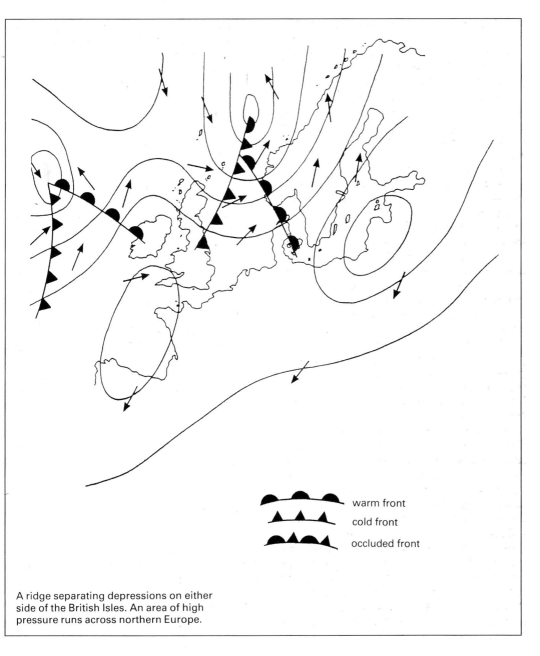

◖▬◖▬	warm front
▲▲▲	cold front
◖▲◖▲	occluded front

A ridge separating depressions on either side of the British Isles. An area of high pressure runs across northern Europe.

masses meeting over the North Atlantic along the Polar Front. These temperature contrasts produce the abrupt pressure changes that are marked by fronts. In terms of wind strength and direction it is the movement of the whole feature and the associated fronts that the navigator needs to appreciate.

The movement of these fronts may be followed by studying weather charts and by producing your own synoptic chart from the shipping forecasts. The easiest way to under-stand and to forecast the weather associated with them is to memorise the diagrams on page 107.

Surface depressions invariably move west to east because the waves in the upper atmosphere that control their movement always move in that direction. As a depression travels at up to 70kn you may assume that the whole feature will pass over you, as shown in the diagram, if you are directly in its path. It is important always to remember that no two

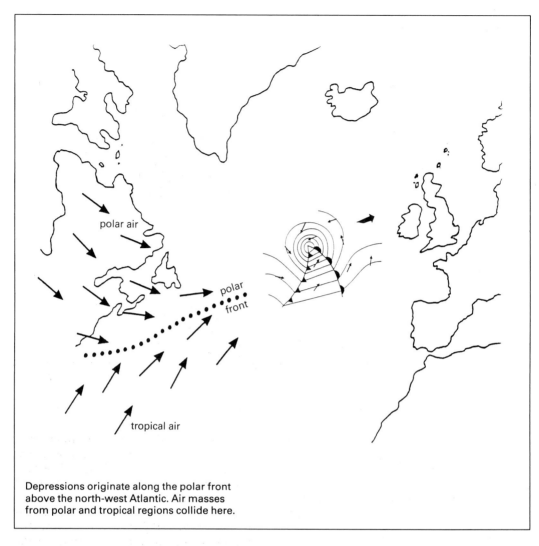

Depressions originate along the polar front
above the north-west Atlantic. Air masses
from polar and tropical regions collide here.

depressions are alike and that the intensity of
the wind depends on the central pressure; the
lower that pressure the greater the wind
strength.

As the warm front approaches an observer
directly in the path of a depression the
weather will change from the west. At first
the skies will be relatively clear with scattered fair-weather cumulus, good visibility
and light to moderate winds. High cloud
(cirrus) will then approach from the north-
west followed some hours later by lower
cloud (stratus) from the south-west. The sky
will become progressively overcast and the
temperature will fall as the sun disappears
beneath an ever-deepening mass of cloud.
The pressure will fall steadily and the wind
will slowly strengthen as it backs slightly to

the south. The visibility will decrease from
good to poor.

Some 6 to 8 hours before the arrival of the
warm front, intermittent light rain will become continuous and increase in intensity
from dark masses of deep nimbostratus. As
the front clears the cloud will lighten to a low
amorphous mass of grey stratus which is
likely to give prolonged drizzle. The temperature will rise and conditions may well feel
muggy. Visibility will be poor, with a likelihood of fog. The wind will veer to the south-
west and is likely to be moderate in strength
and steady in direction.

The approach of the cold front is heralded
by the development of massive cumulus and
cumulonimbus. During the passage of the
front these will give torrential rain for one to

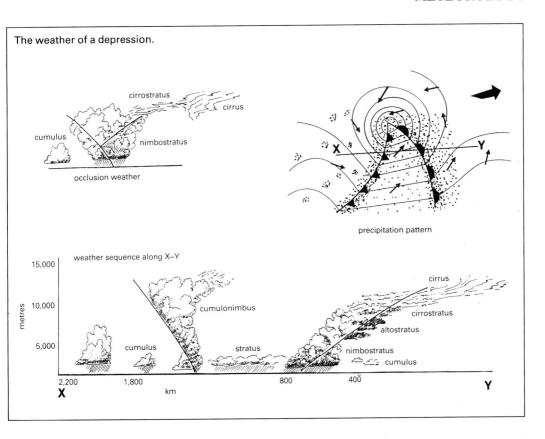

The weather of a depression.

cirrostratus

cirrus

cumulus

nimbostratus

occlusion weather

precipitation pattern

weather sequence along X–Y

15,000

metres

10,000

cirrus

cumulonimbus

cirrostratus

altostratus

5,000

cumulus

stratus

nimbostratus

cumulus

2,200   1,800   800   400

X   km   Y

two hours. They may also give rise to thunder storms accompanied by lightning and hail. The wind will veer abruptly to the north-west and will decrease for a short time. As the front passes, the cloud cover will break into scattered cumulus which in time will lead to

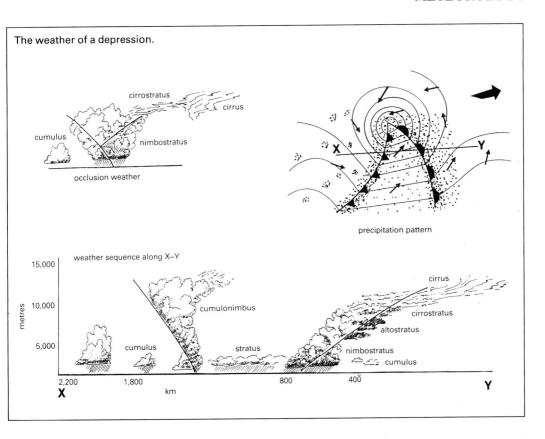

The weather sequence of an approaching depression will vary according to your position in relation to the low pressure centre and fronts.

heavy showers and squalls. The latter may be very violent and associated with gusts possibly reaching gale force. Visibility will be very good except in the showers. The pressure will rise steadily in this cool air mass.

The sequence of events within a depression is so important that we will go through it once more, this time concentrating on the wind. You must first note your position relative to the oncoming depression. If you are at X in the diagram the winds may back to the south briefly but will soon intensify and veer to the south-south-west. As the warm front passes there may be short-lived squalls which will be replaced by a steady west or south-west wind in the warm sector. At the cold front very squally conditions may be experienced and the wind will veer violently to the north-west. The wind is likely to stay in that sector for some time, depending on the nature of the following system.

If you are further north, at Y, the depression centre will pass to the south and the frontal changes will not be experienced. The wind will tend to strengthen and back from a southerly to a northerly quarter.

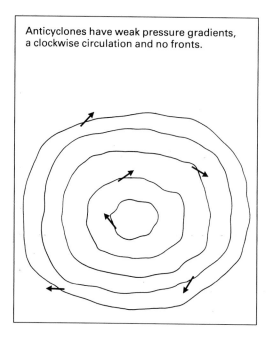

Anticyclones have weak pressure gradients, a clockwise circulation and no fronts.

Anticyclones

Slow moving areas of high pressure, anticyclones consist of a downward clockwise movement of air in the lower atmosphere, with the air spiralling outwards from the centre. The usually weak pressure gradients lead to light winds which are variable in direction, although no two anticyclones are identical. The descending air within an anticyclone becomes drier and tends to bring clear skies, although a specific high pressure system may bring cloud and wind depending on the precise position of the centre. The direction and strength of the wind affecting your boat will depend on your position and distance from the anticyclonic centre. The air rotating in an anticyclonic direction around the centre tends to increase in velocity away from the centre and to move in a less anticyclonic manner.

Once formed, anticyclones may persist for several days, giving little or no change in the weather. If they do remain stationary over the British Isles or western Europe they will force depressions either to the north or south of their normal track so that the variable weather associated with depressions will not be received.

An elongated area of higher pressure extending away from a larger high pressure centre is known as a ridge. Ridges frequently occur between two depressions, building soon after the passage of the cold front. They are associated with brief periods of fair weather with light winds. Occurring as they do between depressions, which bring stronger winds, they are often referred to as windows in the weather. Should you be stuck in port they provide a 'window of opportunity' which may allow you to continue your passage.

An elongated area of lower pressure extending away from a larger low pressure centre is known as a trough. Troughs are frequently associated with fronts. Even if not frontal they bring wind, cloud and rain.

Ridges and troughs are distinctive on a meteorological map because of their elongated shape and the absence of a definite centre with an enclosed isobar.

Land and sea breezes

Most parts of the world experience local winds. In the British Isles these are pronounced along the coastlines where, in summer, a strong breeze may flow from the sea to the shore during the day and then reverse at night.

These breezes are most likely to occur when the country is dominated by quiet anticyclonic weather with a weak pressure-gradient wind. If the latter is in excess of 10kn, as is usually the case with depressions, then neither breeze will develop.

The breezes are driven by the temperature contrast between land and sea, and as this is at its maximum in May and June these are the months when they are most likely. With the clear days of a summer high pressure the land temperature rises rapidly, while that of the sea rises only very slowly. The air over the land therefore expands and rises producing pressure that is locally lower than that over the adjacent sea. As a result, during the late morning the air begins to flow from the high pressure over the sea to the low pressure over the land as a sea breeze. This reaches its maximum intensity by mid-afternoon when the temperature, and therefore the pressure gradient, is at its greatest. The breeze is usually about force 3 but may reach force 5 as the source of the wind moves some 5–10 miles offshore during the afternoon.

At night conditions are reversed. With clear skies the land rapidly cools while the sea

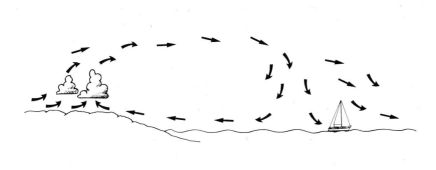

A sea breeze flows from the sea to the land
between late morning and late afternoon.

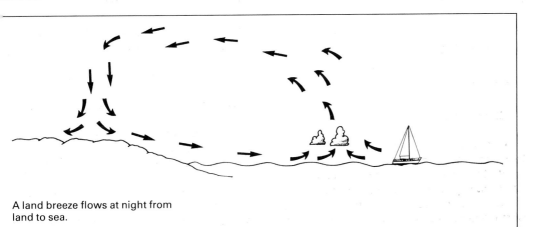

A land breeze flows at night from
land to sea.

retains its heat for longer. High pressure
therefore develops over the land, causing a
land breeze to flow out over the sea to the
relatively lower pressure. This breeze
reaches force 3–4 and may reach 5–10 miles
offshore before dying out at dawn.

Cumulus development

Intense squalls with violently variable gusts
frequently accompany the larger cumulus
and cumulonimbus. These clouds are associated with unstable air such as occurs when a
cool air stream from the north passes over a
warmer sea, or when convection clouds produced over the land drift out to sea. Such in-
stability also occurs behind the cold front of a
depression. There may be absolute calm as a
convection cloud approaches, but with its
arrival a light variable breeze of 10–12kn is
instantly replaced by gusts averaging 30–
35kn and reaching a maximum of up to 60kn.

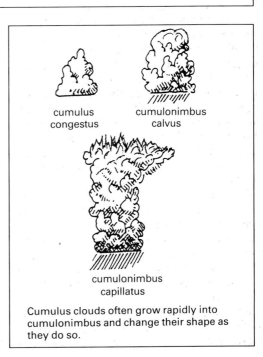

cumulus   cumulonimbus
congestus   calvus

cumulonimbus
capillatus

Cumulus clouds often grow rapidly into
cumulonimbus and change their shape as
they do so.

The suddenness of the arrival of such squalls is as harmful as the actual wind strength. They are obviously very dangerous to the over-canvassed, unprepared sailing boat. The danger is increased by the fact that the gusts will veer by up to 30° from the previous breeze. Such squalls associated with individual clouds last for only a minute or two but when these clouds merge the squally conditions may last for 15 to 20 minutes.

Fog

When minute droplets of water suspended in the lower atmosphere reduce the visibility to

The effects of fog.

1,000–2,000m this is described as mist; when the visibility falls below 1,000m it is fog.

Advection fog, which is the type that most frequently affects sea areas, results from the passage of warm moist air over a body of water whose temperature is below the dew-point temperature of the air. When this occurs the sea lowers the temperature of the surface layer of air to its dew point, at which stage condensation produces the droplets that are the fog.

Ideal conditions for the formation of fog in

he English Channel are the passage of a tropical maritime air mass from the south-west across the Western Approaches and into the Channel. Along the east coast a polar continental air mass from Europe will pick up moisture whilst also being cooled by its passage across the North Sea in early summer. This leads to fog formation along the east coast.

The patchy nature of fog is due to the great variation in sea temperature over a relatively small area. It is only where the water temperature is actually below the dew point temperature of the air that fog will develop. This explains the reference to fog patches and fog banks in the shipping forecasts.

Forecasting

There is no valid excuse for being caught out by strong winds or fog because warnings will probably have been broadcast in local forecasts as well as in the shipping forecast.

The navigator must be able not only to understand the weather forecasts but to use the signs that are in the sky and water to supple-ment this knowledge. This will allow individual judgement of the conditions likely to be experienced in the vicinity of the boat. It is important to remember that forecasts present a general picture of what will probably happen over a large area. It is up to the navigator to use this in conjunction with the visual signs to produce a forecast of the weather that will directly affect the boat in question. Part of the skipper's role is to ensure that barometric pressure, wind strength and direction and any other possible clues as to likely changes in the weather are regularly recorded. Such records may be made either in the navigator's log or in a special weather log.

The signs of an approaching depression will be seen towards the western horizon. High cirrus to the north-west developing into a total cover of cirrostratus and then alto-stratus from the west is a sure sign of a warm front 6–8 hours away. If this is accompanied by falling pressure and low level stratus building from the south-west then you may be certain that a warm front is rapidly approaching. The general rule is that the

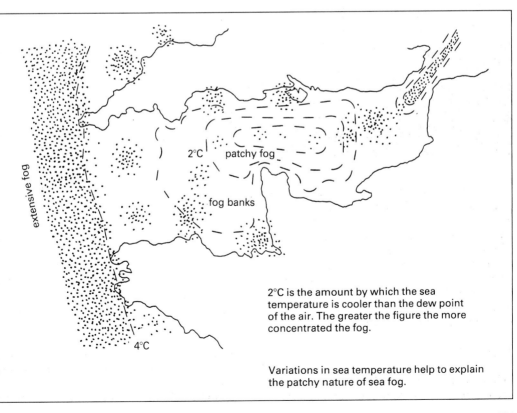

2°C is the amount by which the sea temperature is cooler than the dew point of the air. The greater the figure the more concentrated the fog.

Variations in sea temperature help to explain the patchy nature of sea fog.

faster and further the pressure falls the greater the probability of a gale, although one will not always occur. Swell out of proportion to the local wind is clear evidence of strong winds in the distance. You will of course have to look at other signs to determine if the stronger wind is coming towards or going away from you.

The subsequent clearance of a cold front with its clearly defined edge of dark clouds will herald a period of greater visibility alternating with squally showers from the northwest.

You should never be caught unaware by a squall because there are plenty of warning signs. Cumulus becoming progressively deeper with associated heavy showers in the distance during a period of relatively light gradient wind is a clear indicator of squally conditions close by. The immediate approach of a squall is likely to be heralded by light and variable winds with the first gusts being preceded by cat's-paws on the water.

The approach of fog is often stealthy, but the alert crew should be able to interpret the warning signs. If a light breeze feels muggy and the sea is cool to touch then fog is likely to develop. Once you are close to developing fog the sun will begin to take on the appearance of a blurred yellow ball while at night the moon will appear watery and lights will have an indistinct, fuzzy appearance.

Weather forecasts

It is essential that you never depart from harbour without a recent detailed weather forecast. While on passage you must have an efficient means of updating that forecast regularly. Before departure spend several days familiarising yourself with the prevailing weather pattern. There are various sources of data for this. Newspapers such as the *Guardian* and *Daily Telegraph* carry detailed forecasts and weather maps of the British Isles and Atlantic. These are very useful for observing the long-term trends. The forecasts after the major news programmes on BBC1 provide the same information. A video is very useful for recording these.

A telephone call to the Meteorological Office Marinecall Service will give you a forecast for one of fifteen specific coastal areas. There is a different telephone number for each area. These forecasts are available 24 hours a day, every day, and are updated at least twice each day.

The depression that was forecast to pass over the British Isles on 1 August 1990 was quite intense for the time of year. Strong winds were forecast for all coastal areas, with gales expected in some. These would certainly not have been ideal conditions for an inexperienced crew. If, for example, you were based on the east coast and expected to go sailing on that day you should certainly have delayed your plans for 24 hours. The warm front was about to cross the east coast to be followed a few hours later by the cold front. During that time the wind would be continuously strong and gale force for a time as the fronts passed through. Squalls would be likely after the passage of the cold front. The weather would be cloudy, cool and wet with periods of poor visibility.

Some 6–12 hours after the passage of the cold front would have been an ideal time to go sailing. As the ridge built from the west the cloudy wet weather would have cleared and the wind would have moderated and steadied in direction.

Once at sea there are various ways of keeping up to date with the forecasts. An ordinary radio will provide much useful information. The most detailed forecasts are the shipping forecasts issued by Radio 4 on 1515m (198kHz). These are transmitted daily at 0033, 0555, 1355 and 1750 local time and as such do not need to be altered for British Summer Time. The 0033 forecast is followed by an inshore forecast, the 1750 by a land area forecast. These forecasts indicate the movement of pressure systems and give 24 hour forecasts for all major sea areas as well as reports from coast stations. They also give gale warnings, which are first broadcast at the first programme break after their issue by the Meteorological Office. They are then repeated after each news bulletin until the warning is no longer in effect. There is also an inshore forecast on Radio 3 at 0655. This is issued for a 24 hour period and applies to areas within 12 miles of the UK coastline, as does the Radio 4 inshore forecast. The many local radio stations around the coastline issue regular inshore forecasts as well as other information such as times of tides and shipping movements. It is now possible to receive continuously updated forecasts through an onboard Navtex teleprinter.

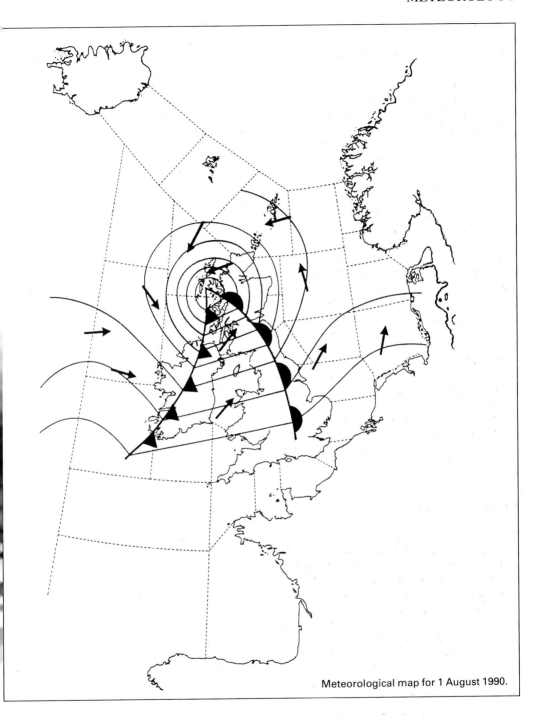

Meteorological map for 1 August 1990.

Coastguard rescue centres issue forecasts every four hours (every two hours when winds of force 6 and above are expected). In order to receive these you need a marine radio-telephone. The first announcement is on channel 16 and then the forecast is broadcast on channel 67.

Coast radio stations give the general synopsis and local information on the local marine band and rebroadcast the shipping forecast for the local area at 0803 or 0833 and 2003 or 2033 GMT.

The various nautical almanacs give information on how to obtain weather forecasts

113

from the above sources. It is important to remember that commercial and BBC local radio stations provide much valuable up-to-date weather data for the navigator. You will also find such information on the noticeboards of harbour offices, marinas and yacht clubs.

The terminology used in these forecasts is easy to follow, although there are a few terms that may be unfamiliar at first.

The shipping forecasts follow a set pattern, broadcasting information in the following order:

1. Gale warning, if any.
2. General synopsis: the location and forecast movement of the major weather systems affecting the British Isles.
3. Sea area forecasts for the next 24 hours:
   a) wind direction and strength;
   b) present weather – rain, thunder, fog, haze, etc;
   c) visibility – good, moderate or poor.
4. Coast station reports (actual weather a few hours before the broadcast):
   a) wind direction and strength;
   b) significant weather;
   c) visibility;
   d) pressure in millibars and pressure tendency.

The various meteorological terms used in shipping forecasts are given below.

TERMS DESCRIBING WIND

Storm	mean wind speed expected to increase to force 10 or more, or gusts of 61kn and above expected
Severe gale	wind expected to increase to force 9 or more, or gusts of 52kn and above expected
Gale	Mean wind speed expected to increase to force 8 or more, or gusts of 43kn and above expected

TERMS DESCRIBING PRESSURE CHANGE

Pressure is rarely static for long. The rate and direction of change are important clues to forthcoming weather changes.

The following expressions all indicate the amount and direction of change in millibars over the previous 3 hours:

Steady	less than 0.1mb
Rising or falling slowly	0.1–1.5mb
Rising or falling	1.6–3.5mb
Rising or falling quickly	3.6–6.0mb
Rising or falling very rapidly	more than 6.0mb
Now falling (or rising)	change from one tendency to the other in the last 3 hours

TERMS DESCRIBING MOVEMENT

These refer to the rate at which the positions of fronts, low pressure systems, troughs, ridges and high pressure systems are changing.

Slowly	less than 15kn
Steadily	15–25kn
Rather quickly	25–35kn
Rapidly	35–45kn
Very rapidly	more than 45kn

TERMS DESCRIBING TIMING

These refer to predicted weather changes or passage of weather systems from the time of issue of the warning.

Imminent	within 6 hours
Soon	6–12 hours
Later	12–24 hours

TERMS DESCRIBING VISIBILITY

These self-explanatory terms have set limits:

Good	5–30 nautical miles
Moderate	2–5 nautical miles
Poor	1,000m – 2 nautical miles
Mist or haze	1,000–2,000m
Fog	less than 1,000m

BEAUFORT SCALE

The Beaufort scale is a method of relating the state of the sea, or conditions on land, to a scale of numbers from 0–12. Each Beaufort number covers a given wind speed. As wind strengths given on weather forecasts are invariably in Beaufort numbers it is easy to judge conditions.

Beaufort number

0	Wind description	calm
	Wind speed	less than 1kn
	Probable sea state	sea like a mirror.
1	Wind description	light air
	Wind speed	1–3kn
	Probable sea state	ripples with the appearance of scales, but without foam crests.
2	Wind description	light breeze
	Wind speed	4–6kn
	Probable sea state	small wavelets, still short but more pronounced. Crests have a glassy appearance and do not break.
3	Wind description	gentle breeze
	Wind speed	7–10kn
	Probable sea state	large wavelets, crests begin to break. Foam of glassy appearance, perhaps scattered white horses.
4	Wind description	moderate breeze
	Wind speed	11–16kn
	Probable sea state	small waves becoming longer. Fairly frequent white horses.
5	Wind description	fresh breeze
	Wind speed	17–21kn
	Probable sea state	moderate waves taking a more pronounced long form. Many white horses, chance of some spray.
6	Wind description	strong breeze
	Wind speed	22–27kn
	Probable sea state	large waves begin to form. White foam crests are more extensive, probability of some spray.
7	Wind description	near gale
	Wind speed	28–33kn
	Probable sea state	sea heaps up and white foam from breaking waves begins to be blown in streaks in the direction of the wind.
8	Wind description	gale
	Wind speed	34–40kn
	Probable sea state	moderately high waves of greater length, edges of crests begin to break into spindrift. The foam is blown in well-marked streaks in the direction of the wind.

Beaufort number

9	Wind description	severe gale
	Wind speed	41–47kn
	Probable sea state	high waves with dense streaks of foam in the direction of the wind. Wave crests begin to topple, tumble and roll over. Spray may affect visibility.

10	Wind description	storm
	Wind speed	48–55kn
	Probable sea state	very high waves with long overhanging crests. The resulting foam is blown in dense white streaks in the direction of the wind. The general appearance of the sea is white. Tumbling action of the sea becomes heavy and shocklike. Visibility likely to be poor.

11	Wind description	violent storm
	Wind speed	56–63kn
	Probable sea state	exceptionally high waves so that small and medium sized ships are for a time lost to view. The sea is completely covered with large white patches of foam in the direction of the wind.

12	Wind description	hurricane
	Wind speed	63kn and above
	Probable sea state	the air is filled with foam and spray. As a result the sea appears completely white and visibility is very poor.

Questions

Answers are on page 224.

1. a) What are isobars?
   b) Which unit is used for measuring pressure?
   c) Why does air not flow directly from high to low pressure?
2. a) Name the pressure systems marked at A, B and C.
   b) Describe, in general terms, the wind strength at Q.
3. a) What is the approximate wind direction at each of the points: S, T, U, V and W?
   b) If the high pressure persists in summer what is the danger to shipping in the northern half of the North Sea?

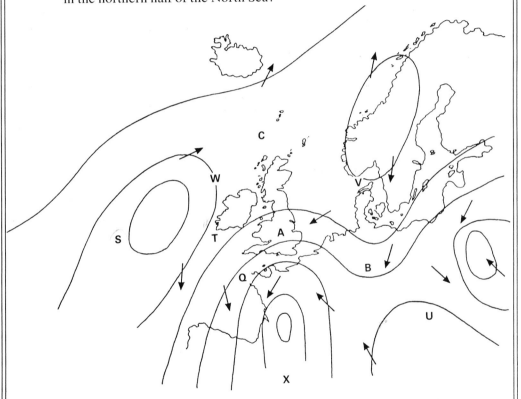

4. a) On which frequency is the shipping forecast broadcast?
   b) What is the time of the forecast closest to midday?
   c) Which shipping forecast is followed by an inshore forecast?
5. If you have VHF what other forecasts might you listen to?
6. What is the meaning of the following terms used in the shipping forecast?
   a) Rising or falling slowly.
   b) Steadily.
   c) Imminent.
   d) Poor.
7. What is the Beaufort wind strength if wave crests are just beginning to break?
8. If the wind is forecast to be force 6 what is the likely sea state?

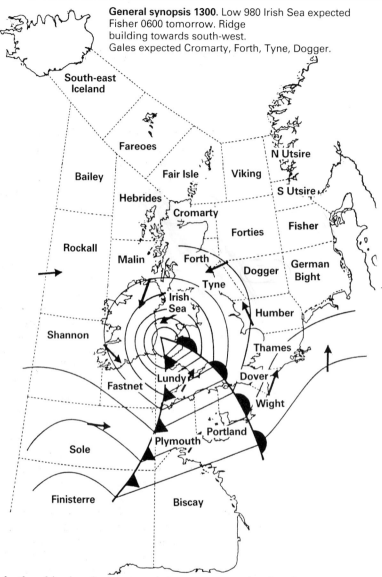

General synopsis 1300. Low 980 Irish Sea expected Fisher 0600 tomorrow. Ridge building towards south-west. Gales expected Cromarty, Forth, Tyne, Dogger.

9. Study the shipping forecast and the met. map that has been prepared from that forecast.
   a) Why on the afternoon of this day would you be unwise to go far offshore in the English Channel?
   b) Compare the relative merits of Dover and Boulogne outer harbours for shelter over the next 24 hours.
   c) Does the forecast suggest that conditions might improve in the near future?
10. To gain more experience you have joined the crew of a boat going across the Channel. The plan is to passage from Rye to Etaples and then to return to Rye via Boulogne and Folkestone. The intention is to depart during the late afternoon of 21 June and to return about 72 hours later. Looking at the chart above explain why you believe it would be wiser to go first to Folkestone and then cross the Channel.

CHAPTER 9

VHF Radio Operation

A VHF radio works in very much the same way as the domestic telephone, although the range of direct communication is very much less. The set must be situated where it is easy to use and where it will be dry. The latter point explains why the set is invariably located in the cabin of a cruiser. A useful addition to your equipment would therefore be a waterproof extension located in the cockpit. The whole crew must not only be familiar with the general working of VHF but must be able to use it to summon help whatever the situation.

As with all radio, VHF operates in frequencies, ie in cycles per second. One cycle is the equivalent of one hertz (1Hz) so, for example, the shipping forecast is broadcast on BBC Radio 4, 198 kHz. The entire range of radio frequencies is divided into a number of bands determined by a frequency range. Marine VHF exists within the VHF band, which is between 30MHz and 300MHz. Within this band the International Maritime Mobile (IMM) is found between 156MHz and 162MHz. You may realise that this is the same VHF band as the BBC. The reason why you do not pick up BBC on your VHF radio (or ships on your domestic radio) is that the IMM is in a different part of the VHF band.

For convenience the range 156–162MHz is divided into a series of channels. A glance at your set will show that these channels are indicated by whole numbers ranging from 00 to 88, and not by frequencies. The latter, usually given to three decimal places, are of academic interest to the day skipper, who does not need to learn them. Instead of referring to a frequency of 156.850MHz, for instance, we refer to channel 17. Each channel in the IMM band is dedicated for a specific use; some are dedicated exclusively. For example, 08 is for inter-ship communication only, while others, such as 17 (inter-ship and port operations), are shared.

While safety demands that you have a VHF set fitted the law requires you to have a ship radio licence if you do. Issued by the DTI, this licence is renewable annually and must be kept on board ready for inspection along with an operator's certificate and copy of Section 11 of the Post Office (Protection) Act, 1884. The latter is supplied with the licence. The DTI, holding the power to confiscate and prosecute, does make random checks.

There must be at least one person on the boat who has an operator's certificate. These are gained by passing a written and oral examination conducted by, or on behalf of, the RYA at various colleges and sailing schools. This simple examination for the 'Restricted Certificate of Competence in Radiotelephony (VHF only)' is also held at various boat shows. The certificate is only valid for ship radiotelephones operating in the VHF maritime band. Anyone who does not hold the certificate may use the VHF as long as it is controlled by an authorised operator. The authority to operate will be granted by the DTI to a holder of a certificate of competence provided that they are at least 16 years old.

The 'VHF only' examination consists of a fifteen-question written paper that lasts about 30 minutes, a few oral questions and a practical test. The RYA booklet *G 26* gives the full syllabus and the list of questions from which the examination papers are compiled.

The regulations also stipulate that you must carry and keep up to date a radiotelephone log. This should record all messages sent and received. It should include the general content of the message, the identity of the sender and recipient, the channel used and the time of the message (GMT). Where a message is transmitted via the public correspondence service the log entry should be restricted to the time and the serial number of the message.

Reed's Nautical Almanac or *The Macmillan and Silk Cut Nautical Almanac* are very useful because they contain detail on radio communications, including the frequencies of coast radio stations and the port operations for individual harbour authorities.

Between channels 08 and 17 each channel has just one frequency for both ship and shore station. This means that if you are talking to a harbourmaster on channel 15 you will both be speaking on 156.750MHz. At the relative extremes of the frequency band each channel has two frequencies, one for the ship and one for the shore station. You can see this in channels 1–5, 7 and 18–28 which are primarily for public correspondence. Should you call Cullercoats Radio on channel 26 your transmission will be made on 157.300MHz which is the channel on which Cullercoats listens and will hear you. However, Cullercoats will transmit to you on a completely different frequency, 161.900MHz. To receive their transmission your receiver will therefore need to be tuned to 161.900MHz. You will not have to change channels in order to achieve this because your set will automatically separate the different transmit and receive frequencies while on the one channel.

On two-frequency channels you may only talk to the appropriate shore station. It is impossible to talk to another vessel because all VHF sets are programmed so that on these channels the vessel will transmit on one frequency but receive on another. For instance, if you attempted to communicate with another vessel on channel 02 this would not work because you would transmit on 156.100MHz while the other vessel was trying to receive on 160.700MHZ.

The apparent anomaly of the standard 55 channel marine VHF set whose display indicates channels numbered up to 88 needs to be explained. The original 28 channels had become so congested by the early 1970s that more needed to be found. The IMM band limits could not be extended so the width of each existing channel was reduced from 50kHz to 25kHz. This created a 25kHz gap between each of the original channels and so immediately doubled the number of channels. It would have created chaos to renumber the existing channels so these were left unchanged. The new channels could not start at 29 because channels 29–59 were allocated to other services so they had to start at 60. These new channels are known as interleaved channels.

There are a number of channels that you should not use although it is technically possible to do so. For inter-ship communication you should stick exclusively to channels 06, 08, 72 and 77. Channel 10 should be avoided because it is used for pollution control activities while channels 11, 12 and 14 must be avoided because they are for the exclusive use of harbour authorities. Channel 9 is used by pilot vessels and tugs so you must certainly not use that when close to a port, and you must not use channel 13 in the Clyde, Plymouth, Portsmouth or Weymouth areas as these are used by the Queen's Harbourmaster to talk to warships.

Each government is permitted to designate some of its channels as private channels and allocate them to those who need a private and exclusive channel, such as ferry and salvage companies. Three such channels are of particular interest to the boat owner in the UK. The first, channel M, on 157.850MHz, was allocated to British yacht clubs to be shared with marinas. With the increased use of this channel the government released channel M2, 161.425MHz, as the working channel for yacht clubs and channel 80 for British marinas.

Most of the VHF sets found in small boats operate in what is described as simplex mode. In this system the transmitter is connected to the microphone and the receiver to the ear-piece. Both use the same power supply (usually a 12V battery) and both use the same aerial, but they do not use the aerial simultaneously. Thus, unlike the domestic telephone, it is possible to transmit or receive but not simultaneously. For the set to receive, the aerial must be connected to the receiver, and to transmit it must be connected to the transmitter. This switching from receive to transmit is achieved automatically by a power switch on the handset (or on the microphone). Depress the switch and the aerial is connected to the transmitter: release the switch and it is connected to the receiver.

The more complicated duplex mode allows transmission simultaneously in both directions. Unless you have a special electrical switching device you will need two widely separated aerials, which is why you rarely find this mode on small boats. With this mode you may have a two way conversation in the exact manner that you would on a domestic telephone.

The range of transmission is perhaps more limited than you would expect. The curvature of the earth is the significant restricting factor because VHF radio waves travel in straight lines. It is therefore the height of the respective aerials that determines the aerial-to-aerial range. Meteorological conditions are also likely to affect the range. Higher atmospheric pressure and higher humidity may both produce a higher range while rough seas will reduce the range as the aerial sways on top of the mast. You may expect a ship to shore range of 30–50 miles and ship to ship range of 10 miles depending on the aerial heights and the weather conditions.

The permitted maximum power output for a VHF set on a small boat is 25W. All sets have a low power (1W) facility that you should use on most occasions. Using the 25W output will interfere with other stations without producing any significant benefit to you unless you are making a distress call or making a telephone call via a coast radio station. The higher output simply gives you a greater range. For short-range inter-ship communication, or for communication with a marina or port authority, it is of no value and would simply lead to interference with more distant stations.

If you are close to the station you are calling you should get a very clear signal because VHF uses frequency modulation (FM). That is to say if several signals are being received at once the receiver will lock on to the strongest one, so you will not get the blurring of signals that you sometimes hear on domestic radio.

Dual watch, a useful facility found on many sets, will allow the operator to monitor two stations at the same time without manually switching from one to the other. You select which stations you wish to monitor; these will usually be channel 16 and one other. The receiver will continuously scan from one to the other, spending less time on channel 16. When a transmission is received on 16 the receiver will lock on to that but will continue to scan if a transmission is received on the other selected channel. Despite this you will still pick up 90% of that other transmission. You must remember to switch off dual watch before transmitting.

Between transmissions the set will pick up an irritatingly large amount of background noise. To cure this turn the squelch control fully off and then turn it in the opposite direction so that the noise just stops. As soon as a transmission is picked up the set will override the muting system so that the signal can be heard.

The VHF system is used by the boat owner for communicating with a wide range of stations. You may call other vessels, though not just for idle chatter. The transmission must relate to safety, navigation or general ship's business. You may contact the coastguard on matters relating to safety and you may talk to harbourmasters on matters related to port entry and traffic movement. You may contact a coast radio station if you wish to make a telephone link call. Apart from inter-ship the most frequent use of your set is likely to be with marinas and yacht clubs.

Transmitting a message is very straightforward. Before transmitting listen for at least 30 seconds to ensure that nobody else is using your intended channel. You must not waste airtime, so start transmitting as soon as you press the transmit button. If you are inexperienced or nervous write out the intended message before you begin to transmit.

Phonetic Alphabet

The internationally recognised phonetic alphabet must be used to avoid confusion between like-sounding letters such as B,C,D and E. It may be that you need to emphasise a particular part of a message or the spelling of a particular word in a message. The difficulty of distinguishing between letters such as B and P or M and N may be avoided by spelling out the word letter by letter with a clearly different word for each letter. This must be learnt so that speaking BRAHvoh, CHARlee, DELLtah, ECKoh . . . becomes second nature. The part of the word that is in capitals must be stressed.

Letter	Code word	Pronunciation
A	Alfa	ALfah
B	Bravo	BRAHvoh
C	Charlie	CHARlee
D	Delta	DELLtah
E	Echo	ECKoh
F	Foxtrot	FOKStrot
G	Golf	Golf
H	Hotel	HohTELL
I	India	INdeeah
J	Juliett	JEWleeETT

K	Kilo	KEYloh
L	Lima	LEEmah
M	Mike	MIKE
N	November	NoVEMber
O	Oscar	OSScah
P	Papa	PahPAH
Q	Quebec	KehBECK
R	Romeo	ROWmeoh
S	Sierra	SeeAIRrah
T	Tango	TANgo
U	Uniform	YOUneeform
V	Victor	VIKtah
W	Whisky	WISSkey
X	X-ray	ECKSray
Y	Yankee	YANGkee
Z	Zulu	ZOOloo

As numbers may also be confused there is an internationally accepted form of pronunciation, shown below.

Figure	Word	Pronunciation guide
0	Zero	
1	Wun	Emphasis on n
2	Too	Long oo
3	Thuh-ree	Long e

4	Fower	Long o as in foe
5	Five	Emphasis on f with long i
6	Six	Emphasis on x
7	Sev-en	Two distinct syllables
8	Ate	Long a
9	Ni-ner	Emphasise each n, long i
Point	Day-see-mal	

It is obviously important that your speech is very clear when using VHF. The pitch of your voice must be maintained at a level slightly higher than that used for normal conversation and you must avoid the tendency to lower the pitch at the end of a word or phrase. The volume of your voice should be the same as for normal conversation, with the microphone held a few inches in front of your mouth. Speech must be slower than normal because the receiver may have to write down the message. Do not speak word by word but have pauses where you would have them in normal conversation. Where a word has particularly weak syllables, as does 'weather', then it must be emphasised. Sounds such as 'er', 'ah' and 'um' should be avoided as they lead to confusion.

Procedural words

These single words or short phrases have very specific meanings and are in constant use in radiotelephone communication.

Words	Meaning
Affirmative	Yes, or, permission granted.
Negative	No, or, permission not granted, or, that is not correct.
All after/before	Used to identify part of a message and used in conjunction with other words or phrases.
Correct	You are correct (confirmation that a message has been repeated correctly).
Correction	Cancel the last word or phrase sent. This should be followed by I say again.
Read back	To request the other station to repeat a message, or, the following is my response to your instruction to read back.
Say again	Request to repeat a message. May be combined with all after/before to indicate part of message to be repeated.
I say again	Response to the above or simply to emphasise, or when conditions for reception are bad.
I spell	Used to spell a word for clarity.
Over	Used when transmission is finished and a reply is expected.
Out	End of message (reply not expected).
Roger	Message received and understood.
Received	Message received and understood.
Wrong	Message has been incorrectly repeated.

Guidelines for use

The increasing and sometimes indiscriminate use of VHF radiotelephone, and channel 16 in particular, has prompted the coastguard to issue guidelines to minimise problems. These are:

1. Where possible routine calls to the coastguard should be made by telephone when in harbour or by radio–telephone link call through the appropriate coast radio station when at sea. If you have a message for the coastguard which cannot be passed by other means you should make the initial contact on channel 16 and expect to be directed to a working channel, usually channel 67. The first contact has to be on channel 16 because the coastguard cannot keep a constant watch on channel 67.
2. Test calls must not be made on channel 16 unless you are offshore and doubt the working of your set. Repeated transmissions may block distress traffic so if you do not receive a reply do not make repeated calls. Inshore test calls must be made on the relevant frequency to the local harbour office or port authority.
3. Routine messages should be passed via the normal public correspondence frequencies used for ship-to-shore communication and not via channels 16 and 17. These messages should be brief and must not develop into prolonged discussions.
4. Once you have set out, passage details should not be passed to the coastguard unless there is some element of risk, in which case you must send either a safety, urgency or distress message.
5. Only in exceptional circumstances should you ask the coastguard for a weather forecast. All main coastguard stations broadcast weather forecasts every 4 hours; every 2 hours if there is a gale or strong wind warning in force.

Channel 16 priority scale

All communication on channel 16 must follow the accepted scale of priorities. The importance of the channel for distress working means that this must be given first priority. Radio silence must be maintained at all times by vessels not involved in the distress. The station controlling the distress communication will announce when either restricted or normal working is permitted to recommence.

The second communication on the scale of priorities is an urgency call. Radio silence must be observed during the message and for 3 minutes after. Requests for medical assistance have the same priority.

The third priority is safety traffic communications, which are normally transmitted by coastguard and coast radio stations, although on occasions a small boat may need to make such a call.

Any communication other than the above should not exceed one minute on this channel.

Controlling station

When the communication is between two vessels then it is the called vessel that controls the communication. When the communication is ship-to-shore, between a vessel and a coast radio station, it is the latter that is the controlling station, except in some instances of distress, urgency or safety.

Procedure cards

Procedure cards are obligatory where a ship or fishing vessel is required by law to have a radiotelephone installed. Family cruisers are not obliged to install VHF and are not required to display procedure cards. However, the wise owner will have, immediately next to the set, a card detailing the distress procedure so that if an inexperienced crew member has to send a distress message they can simply read through the information on the card and add the relevant detail. A specimen procedure card is given below.

Yacht's name   *Red Devil*
Callsign   Delta Whisky Tango November

TO SEND DISTRESS SIGNAL
CHECK – Main battery switch ON
Set switched ON
Power switch set to HIGH (25W)
Switch to channel 16
To speak – PRESS microphone switch
Transmit SLOWLY and CLEARLY
'Mayday, Mayday, Mayday
This is yacht *Red Devil*, yacht *Red Devil*, yacht *Red Devil*
Mayday, yacht *Red Devil*

My position is . . .' (latitude and longitude or bearing and distance FROM a conspicuous charted feature)

Now describe the nature of the distress, eg 'I am sinking', followed by any other relevant information

Now say 'Over' and RELEASE the microphone switch

If there is not an IMMEDIATE reply repeat the above checks and try again

Distress call

The sending of a distress call is only justified when there is grave and imminent danger to a vessel or person and immediate assistance is required. Some find it difficult to decide whether a given situation warrants a Mayday call. The simple answer is that if you or another person are likely to die within a few minutes without assistance then it is a distress situation and you send a Mayday. Should your engine fail within about 1,000m of a lee shore during a gale then you will be shipwrecked in a matter of minutes and must send a distress message. If the engine fails on a sunny summer's day 3 miles from the coast in light winds then it is clearly not a distress situation. The man overboard situation is more difficult. In heavy weather if you do not make a rapid recovery of the person overboard then they are likely to be quickly lost from view. Clearly, therefore, they are in grave and imminent danger and you must send a distress message. If someone breaks an arm there is no immediate threat to life and you do not send a Mayday but a request for medical assistance, if you need it. An accident which leads to suspected internal injuries and/or bleeding is very different. When the visual signs suggest that this is the case then you must send a distress message because internal injuries and bleeding are invariably fatal if not treated quickly.

Channel 16 is the international distress, safety and calling frequency on VHF. It is for this reason that all coastguard stations, and all UK and most foreign coast radio stations, keep a continuous watch on channel 16. Your watch on this channel should be as continuous as possible. Effectively this means that when on passage you must have the set switched on and tuned to channel 16 except when you are using another channel.

You must know the precise procedure

should you have to make a distress transmission. When you require immediate assistance, in other words when you are making a distress call, the procedure is as follows: switch on the set, select high power and channel 16 and push the transmit button. First send the distress call and then the distress message. The 'call' alerts other stations to the imminent transmission of the distress message.

DISTRESS CALL
Distress signal 'Mayday, Mayday, Mayday'.
'This is', followed by the callsign of the vessel in distress, three times.

DISTRESS MESSAGE
Distress signal 'Mayday', once.
Callsign of the vessel in distress, once.
Position (a).
Nature of distress (b).
Assistance required.
Amplifying information (c).
'Over.'

(a) Position must be given as latitude and longitude or as a true bearing and distance of the vessel from a well-defined point. If you are close to an identifiable geographical position such as a headland or are aground on a named rock or shoal then you should give a geographical location.
(b) The nature of the distress must be concise and succinct, eg 'holed and sinking rapidly', or, 'on fire and taking to liferaft'.
(c) Amplifying information includes the number of people on board, whether you have a liferaft, flares, EPIRB, etc.

A distress message is illustrated by the following example, in which the yacht *Firefox* has hit an underwater object 5 miles south-east of Coquet Island and is sinking rapidly.

'Mayday, Mayday, Mayday.
This is yacht *Firefox*, yacht *Firefox*, yacht *Firefox*.
Mayday, yacht *Firefox*.
One three five from Coquet Island, hit submerged object, sinking rapidly.
Require immediate assistance.
Total crew three on auxiliary cruiser, taking

to liferaft with flares and EPIRB.
Over.'

You can expect an immediate reply or acknowledgement from the coastguard, coast radio station or a ship. If such is not forthcoming then check the equipment and repeat the transmission at regular intervals.

All vessels, whatever their size or purpose, are obliged to acknowledge receipt of a distress message. This is made very clear in the International Rules which state: 'The obligation to accept distress calls and messages is absolute in the case of every station without distinction, and such messages must be accepted with priority over all other messages; they must be answered and the necessary steps must immediately be taken to give effect to them.'

Should you hear a distress call that is not acknowledged you must take action. First you must decide if you can render physical assistance to the vessel in distress. This will depend on the size of the vessel and its distance from your position. You should have obtained this information from the distress message. If the vessel concerned is obviously a large commercial vessel then there is not much help that you can give. Neither are you likely to be able to give much help if the vessel is several hours away from you. Whatever the situation you must make a written record of the message in case you are the only station to receive it and in case the distressed vessel does not have the chance to send a further message.

Having decided that you *are* in a position to help you must acknowledge the distress message. The procedure is as follows (remember that any transmission concerned with giving direct assistance to the distressed vessel must be prefixed by the distress signal 'Mayday'):

Distress signal 'Mayday'.
Callsign of the station in distress, three times.
'This is', followed by callsign of acknowledging station, three times.
'Received Mayday.'

This is illustrated in the following example in which *Red Devil* is responding to the distress message of *Firefox*.

'Mayday yacht *Firefox, Firefox, Firefox*.
This is yacht *Red Devil*, yacht *Red Devil*, yacht *Red Devil*.
Received Mayday.'

As quickly as possible you must work out your course to the distressed vessel and your ETA at its location. Then send the following message:

Distress signal 'Mayday'.
Callsign of the station in distress, three times.
'This is', followed by callsign of acknowledging station, three times.
Your position.
Your speed in a direction towards the distressed vessel.
Your ETA.

This is illustrated below, where *Red Devil* sends a message to *Firefox*.

'Mayday *Firefox, Firefox, Firefox*.
This is *Red Devil, Red Devil, Red Devil*.
My position is zero six five from Flamborough Head 2 miles.
Speed 5 knots.
ETA your position one six three zero.
Over.'

If the crew of *Firefox* are in a position to reply they should do so as follows:

'Mayday *Red Devil*.
This is yacht *Firefox*.
Message understood.
Will fire flares at intervals from one five three zero.'

MAYDAY RELAY
You must attempt to contact a coast radio station, the coastguard or another vessel and advise them of the distress in the following situations:

– when the vessel in distress cannot transmit a message;
– when further help is required;
– when you have heard an unacknowledged distress message and are not in a position to help directly.

Follow the Mayday relay procedure:
The signal 'Mayday Relay', three times.

'This is', followed by callsign of the station making the transmission, three times.
The signal 'Mayday' followed by the callsign of the vessel in distress, once.

If *Red Devil* hears the unacknowledged distress message of *Firefox* she relays it as follows:

'Mayday Relay, Mayday Relay, Mayday Relay.
This is yacht *Red Devil*, yacht *Red Devil*, yacht *Red Devil*.
Mayday yacht *Firefox*.
Zero six five from Start Point, 3 miles, hit submerged object, sinking rapidly.
Requires immediate assistance.
Crew of three on auxiliary cruiser has taken to liferaft with flares and EPIRB.
Over.'

You should not acknowledge a distress message transmitted as a Mayday relay by a coast radio station unless you are in a position to assist.

All transmission concerning the distress, for the duration of the distress, will be controlled either by a coast radio station or coastguard, by the station in distress or by the station sending a Mayday relay. In most circumstances it is best if either the coast radio station or coastguard takes control as they have the better radio facilities. The controlling station has responsibility for imposing radio silence during the distress. Should there be interference the station will transmit as follows:

'Mayday.
Seelonce Mayday, Seelonce Mayday, Seelonce Mayday.
This is Cullercoats Radio, Cullercoats Radio.
Out.'

No other station is permitted to transmit 'seelonce Mayday'. If another station believes that such a transmission is necessary then it must use the expression 'seelonce distress' as follows:

'Mayday.
Seelonce Distress, Seelonce Distress, Seelonce Distress.
This is *Red Devil*, *Red Devil*.
Out.'

When the controlling station decides that complete silence is no longer necessary it will transmit as follows:

'Mayday.
Hello all stations, hello all stations, hello all stations.
This is Cullercoats Radio, Cullercoats Radio.
Time one seven three five.
Yacht *Firefox*.
Pru-donce.
Out.'

This message indicates to other stations that they may begin restricted working. Effectively this means if you need to transmit you may do so, although it is not the time to be contacting your friends in another boat.

When distress traffic has completely finished the controlling station will advise all other stations by transmitting the above message with the phrase 'seelonce feenee' replacing the word 'pru-donce'.

Urgency message

An urgency message should be used when there is no imminent danger to a vessel or person. It has priority over all other messages except distress and is transmitted as follows:

Urgency signal 'Pan Pan, Pan Pan, Pan Pan'.
'Hello all stations', three times.
'This is', followed by callsign of the station sending the message, three times.
Position.
Nature of the urgency.
Assistance required.
'Over.'

In the following situation the yacht *Firefox* has had engine failure and is drifting 2 miles east of Whitby.

'Pan Pan, Pan Pan, Pan Pan.
Hello all stations, hello all stations, hello all stations.
This is yacht *Firefox*, yacht *Firefox*, yacht *Firefox*.
One three five from Whitby harbour entrance, 2 miles.
Total engine failure, drifting south-west at 1 knot. Require urgent tow.
Over.'

Medical emergencies

In cases of serious illness or injury send an urgency signal and urgency call on channel 16. Make sure that you make clear in the initial call that you wish to transmit a long medical message on a working frequency. The communication would be as follows:

'Pan Pan Medico, Pan Pan Medico, Pan Pan Medico.
Cullercoats Radio, Cullercoats Radio.
This is yacht *Firefox*, yacht *Firefox*.
Have a long urgency message for you.
Channels 26 or 28?
Over.'

Cullercoats Radio would inform you which channel to use and would then link you with a hospital.

Ship-to-ship

The initial contact will be made on channel 16 unless you have arranged to communicate at a set time on a given frequency. The initial call should be as brief as possible so that you do not transmit on channel 16 for longer than is necessary.
Proceed as follows:

'*Solitaire*, this is *Red Devil, Red Devil*.
Channel 6 or channel 8?
Over.'

(If your message is expected then you need state your yacht's name once only.)
The reply from *Solitaire* should be as follows:

'*Red Devil*, this is *Solitaire*.
Channel 6.
Over.'

Red Devil would then confirm:

'*Solitaire*, this is *Red Devil*.
Channel 6.
Over.'

Both boats then switch to channel 06. It is the called boat, *Solitaire* in this case, that controls the communication. After ensuring that channel 06 is not in use *Solitaire* continues the communication:

'*Red Devil*, this is *Solitaire*.
Over.'

Red Devil continues:

'*Solitaire*, this is *Red Devil*.
Where do you intend to anchor tonight?
Over.'

Solitaire replies:

'*Red Devil*, this is *Solitaire*.
Helford river.
Over.'

The communication will probably then continue with the exchange of the usual pleasantries about the passage and the weather. Conversation on this channel may be longer than that on channel 16, but still must not be too long because the air waves are becoming increasingly overcrowded and others will wish to use the channel. Remember that the radio is for discussing matters relating to navigation, it is not for prolonged general chatter.
The above communication would then be ended as follows:

'This is *Red Devil*.
Out.'

'This is *Solitaire*.
Out.'

Both vessels must then switch back to channel 16 to maintain their continuous watch on that frequency.
Channel 06 is the primary inter-ship frequency. It and channels 08, 72 and 77 are exclusively for inter-ship traffic and must be used in preference to others. The other inter-ship channels are 09, 10, 13, 67, 69 and 73. The higher numbered channels are used least, so if you and the ship you are calling can use these you are less likely to be interrupted.

Calling harbour authorities

Today harbour authorities invariably listen on channel 16 and on their working channel. You may therefore contact them either via channel 16 or directly on a working channel. Some do prefer to be called on one channel rather than the other. You need to consult an almanac or the *Admiralty List of Radio Signals* to ascertain which. Only major ports operate a twenty-four hour radio watch. This information will be found in the same texts. The calling procedure is as follows:

'Ramsgate Harbour Radio.
This is yacht *Red Devil*, yacht *Red Devil*.
On channel 14.
Over.'

Communication on port operations frequencies must be restricted to traffic related to the movement of ships, entry to and exit from the harbour and safety where persons are at risk. At some harbours, such as Dover, you may enter or leave harbour only after gaining permission from the authorities via the VHF radio. There are also strict regulations governing the use of VHF in port. Inter-ship traffic is permissible only when it relates to matters of safety. Otherwise the radiotelephone may be used only for communications related to the operations of the port, the exchange of traffic through a coast radio station or if using a private channel such as M.

Calling a marina

The procedure is exactly the same as for calling a harbour except that you do not need to state the frequency on which you are calling. (You do this when calling a harbour because they are monitoring more than one channel, so if they are not actually looking at their set they will not know the frequency on which they have been called unless it is stated in the message.)

Calling the coastguard

Channel 67 is the channel designated for the exchange of safety traffic between the coastguard and small boats. The coastguard has a chain of strategically located stations. These regularly broadcast weather forecasts, strong wind warnings and local navigational warnings. Such information is broadcast on channel 67 after an initial broadcast on channel 16. You may talk to the coastguard on any matter concerning safety, although during a short routine passage it is an abuse of the system to be constantly passing information to the coastguard. On a longer passage it is quite acceptable to pass occasional information. You may, for instance, use channel 67 to advise the coastguard of your intention to change your passage plan or you may ask for a weather forecast in deteriorating weather. In both cases you should make the first con-

tact on channel 16 and state that you hav safety traffic.

Red Devil, on passage from the Solent t Fowey, may be forced to alter course and pu into Falmouth because of deterioratin, weather. To avoid the danger of search an rescue services being launched because o her non-arrival at Fowey she should contac the coastguard as follows:

'Falmouth coastguard.
This is yacht *Red Devil*, yacht *Red Devil*.
Safety message, channel 67.
Over.'

To which the reply would be:

'*Red Devil*.
This is Falmouth coastguard. Channel 6'
and stand by.
Over.'

Red Devil and the coastguard then switch tc channel 67. It is the latter who begins the communication on channel 67:

'*Red Devil*.
This is Falmouth coastguard. What do you have for me?
Over.'

Red Devil then passes on the information:

'Falmouth coastguard.
This is *Red Devil*, on passage Solent to Fowey.
Intend mooring overnight in Falmouth.
Solent coastguard holds my safety scheme card.
Over.'

The coastguard then acknowledges this message:

'*Red Devil*.
This is Falmouth coastguard.
Message understood.
Over.'

The communication is then completed by the two stations:

'Falmouth coastguard.
This is *Red Devil*. Thank you very much for your help.

Out.'

The coastguard signs off:

'Red Devil.
This is Falmouth coastguard.
Out.'

Radio check

In the absence of any other convenient shore station you can always ask a coastguard (with the exception of Solent coastguard) to verify that your transmitter is working correctly. The procedure is as follows:

'Yarmouth coastguard.
This is *Red Devil*, callsign Delta Whisky Tango November.
Radio check please.
Over.'

The reply would be along the lines of:

'Red Devil.
This is Yarmouth coastguard.
Loud and clear.
Over.'

Red Devil would then complete the communication:

'Yarmouth coastguard.
This is *Red Devil*.
Loud and clear.
Thank you very much.
Out.'

Calling a coast radio station

Coast radio stations connect vessels with the global telephone system and are managed by the telephone company of that country. Although they maintain a continuous watch on channel 16 you should contact them on one of their working channels, which you will find in either the *Admiralty List of Radio Signals* or an almanac.

The precise wording of your message will depend on how you intend to pay for the call. You do not pay for the initial transmission to the station but for the successful connection to a land line. Unlike the domestic telephone there is just one standard charge with no peak or cheap rate. Having established communications with the station you must first indicate the method by which you intend to pay.

There are two payment methods. When you first applied for your ship radio licence you would have been asked on part of the application form to appoint an authorised accounts company to deal with the boat's radio accounts. The owner of a British boat is advised to appoint British Telecom International plc, whose account code is GB 14. When making a call via a coast radio station anywhere in the world if you give that code British Telecom will send a bill to the name and address given on the ship's licence. This method is slightly more expensive, because a handling charge is included in the account.

The alternative method is YTD (Yacht Telephone Debit). In this case the cost of the call is directly debited to the number that you 'nominate' in your call (this is not necessarily the number that you are calling). The net cost of the call will appear in the next quarterly British Telecom account for that number. This method may only be used when the call is being made to a British telephone from a British boat via a British coast radio station. If this is not the case then the caller will have to give an international account code number.

You may also make a transferred charge call, although the charge will be the actual cost plus 2 minutes.

It is a good idea to write down your initial messages to the coast radio station so that neither party gets the numbers mixed up. Select the working frequency and listen for 5 to 10 seconds to ensure that it is free. (Should it not be free then you will either hear a voice or a series of pips.) Having ascertained that the channel is free make your initial call, which must be no less than 3 seconds in duration because it takes that length of time for your call to switch on the automatic monitoring equipment at the coast radio station and for it to register your call. For this reason you should repeat the name of the coast radio station and your own callsign twice. You should then hear the 'channel engaged' signal, which means that you have activated the answering equipment and that the operator will contact you as soon as possible. Remember that such stations are very busy and there may be a short delay before the operator gets back to you. If you do not hear the answering pips then your set may be at fault. In any event you must wait at least 3 minutes before attempting again.

Your transmission should start as follows:

'Cullercoats Radio, Cullercoats Radio.
This is Delta Whisky Tango November.
One YTD telephone call please.
Over.'

To which the reply would be:

'Delta Whisky Tango November.
This is Cullercoats Radio.
What do you have for me?
Over.'

You should then continue:

'Cullercoats Radio.
This is Delta Whisky Tango November.
My ship's name is *Red Devil*.
I spell – romeo echo delta, delta echo
victor india lima.
I have a call for zero nine one two four
seven one one.
My account code is YTD zero six seven
zero two seven one four one zero one.
Over.'

The coast radio station would then acknowledge:

'*Red Devil*.
This is Cullercoats Radio.
Stand by please.
Over.'

You then confirm:

'Cullercoats Radio.
This is *Red Devil*.
Standing by.
Over.'

When the number you have dialled answers,
the coast radio station will inform you in the
following manner:

'*Red Devil*.
This is Cullercoats Radio.
You are connected. Go ahead now.
Over.'

If, as is very likely, you have a simplex set you
must remember to release the microphone
switch when you stop speaking. It helps if the
person you are talking to understands the
system and says 'over' when they stop speaking. If you have a duplex system then you
may keep the switch continuously depressed
and communicate as you would in a normal
domestic telephone conversation.

It is the called person who terminates the
communication, because when they replace
their handset the clock in the coast radio station which records the duration of the call is
stopped. This is the basis on which you will be
charged. You must not switch back to channel 16 until the operator has informed you of
the duration of the call.

Traffic lists

It is equally possible to contact a ship from
the shore. Dialling Freephone 0800 37838
gets Portishead Radio, which co-ordinates all
shore-to-ship calls via coast radio stations in
the UK. The caller will be asked to give information such as the ship's name and callsign,
passage details and the method of payment.
The radio officer will then ask the caller to
ring-off and wait to be contacted when a
coast radio station has contacted the ship.

Each coast radio station makes up a 'traffic
list' of the names or callsigns of all the ships
for whom it is holding traffic. Such lists are
transmitted on the working frequency of the
station at times that you will find stated in
almanacs. The intention to broadcast a traffic
list is transmitted on channel 16 as follows:

'Hello all ships.
This is Buchan Radio, Buchan Radio.
Listen for my traffic list on channel 25.
Out.'

If you were expecting traffic you would then
switch to channel 25 and listen.

'Hello all ships.
This is Buchan Radio, Buchan Radio.
I have traffic for the following ships:
Solitaire, Firefox and *Red Devil.*'

Having heard your name or callsign you
would then contact the coast radio station on
its working frequency, asking what traffic it
had for you. When a coast radio station has to
contact a ship between traffic list times it will
call on channel 16.

Questions

Answers are on page 224.

1. Who nominates the channel to be used in:
   a) Ship-to-shore communication?
   b) Inter-ship communication?
2. On which channel are most inter-ship calls initiated?
3. Which is the primary inter-ship channel?
4. Apart from distress working what is the time limit for communication on channel 16 before changing to a working channel?
5. Why should you use only 1W power for short range inter-ship communication?
6. For what reason would you use channel M?
7. Is inter-ship communication by VHF allowed in harbour?
8. In harbour you are permitted to communicate with just one coast radio station – which?
9. If you heard 'pips' on a coast radio station frequency what would you do?
10. What does 'out' mean?
11. What are the times of the channel 16 silence periods?
12. Which signals would you send in the following situations?
    a) Signs of internal bleeding.
    b) Engine failure on a calm day 3 miles offshore.
    c) Crew overboard and lost from sight.
    d) A broken arm.
13. On passage towards Portsmouth in your yacht *Bluebird* you are 1 mile from the Nab Tower which bears 320°T. You have hit a submerged object and are sinking rapidly. You have a crew of three, liferaft and EPIRB. What VHF message should you send?

CHAPTER 10

Charts, Publications and Plotting Instruments

Charts and publications

In the simplest situation, where you can see your destination and there are no tides or obstacles, you could argue that a chart is unnecessary. However, this is rarely the case, and now that you have invested in a boat or have joined a boat as a crew member you will undoubtedly have recourse to charts and other publications. Indeed, you will soon consider these to be essential.

There are many easily obtainable publications that are an important part of a navigator's library. These include:

- an almanac such as *Reed's Nautical Almanac* or the *Macmillan and Silk Cut Nautical Almanac;*
- various charts such as:
    Admiralty 2045 Isle of Wight;
    Imray C8 Start Point to Lizard Point;
    Stanford 9 English Channel – Goodwins to Selsey Bill;
- Chart 5011 (abbreviations/symbols found on Admiralty charts);
- tide tables;
- tidal stream atlas;
- pilots such as that produced by the Royal Northumberland Yacht Club for the sea area between Rattray Head and the Humber;
- *Admiralty Sailing Directions* (pilots);
- *Admiralty Lists of Lights and Fog Signals;*
- *Admiralty Lists of Radio Signals.*

Some navigators may consider that the last three are not essential because much of the information is reproduced in various almanacs.

The Admiralty publishes charts for the whole world. There are two commercial producers: Imray and Stanford.

The Admiralty charts are the most detailed, although those published by the two commercial companies are excellent fo small boat navigation. Hydrographicall they are less detailed than those of th Admiralty but tend to be easier to follow an include abundant information such as cours lines with bearings and distances betwee significant points such as headlands. On th reverse side of the commercial charts and th new edition Admiralty charts there is info mation on harbour and port facilities.

The main disadvantages of the tradition Admiralty charts are that you will need mor of them for a particular passage because o their generally larger scale, and you will hav to thumb through an almanac constantly t find information that would readily be avail able on an Imray or Stanford chart. If yo were relying on Admiralty charts for a pas sage along the English Channel, for instance you would need a separate chart for eac harbour you wished to visit. The Imray an Stanford, on the other hand, contain inse 'chartlets' of harbours and ports. The smal scale Stanford passage chart 'The Eas Coast', for example, has several suc chartlets, including that of Southwold. Th larger size of the traditional Admiralty chart also makes them unwieldy on the small char table of a family cruiser. A further dis advantage is that they do not fold, unlike th Imray and Stanford.

The Admiralty are responding to criticisn of their charts with the growing series o 'Small Craft Editions'. These charts hav been modified from selected Admiralt charts to meet the specific needs of the smal craft user. They are easy to use and stow be cause they fold to a convenient 215mm b 355mm. On the reverse side they include mass of supplementary information obtaine from Admiralty nautical publications.

Charts are the basis of navigation an passage making. As the maritime equivalen of Ordnance Survey maps they allow you t plot your position and to shape your course. They tell much about the nature of the coastline as well as the nature and depth of the seabed. They warn of hazards and indicate navigational aids as well as safe anchorages. All this is achieved by the use of symbols that are detailed in Chart 5011, a booklet providing a key to the symbols and abbreviations used on Admiralty charts.

A glance at any chart will show the mass of information presented:

– major land (relief) features;
– major constructions useful for navigation, eg towers, chimneys and masts;
– lighthouses, buoys and beacons;
– harbours and ports;
– anchorages;
– navigable rivers;
– depth of water;
– nature of the seabed;
– shoals;
– rocks;
– wrecks;
– prohibited areas;
– tidal information;
– distance.

The coastal waters of the British Isles are divided into sections in much the same way that the land is divided into Ordnance Survey sheets. The Stanford chart 12 'English Channel' covers that area of water from The Needles to Start Point while chart 13 'English Channel' extends from Start Point to Land's End and Padstow. Both these are small-scale charts showing relatively large coastal areas with the more significant features and marks indicated. They are vital for passage planning but are of less use when approaching a harbour or anchorage. Chart 18 'The Solent' and chart 10 'Chichester and Langstone Har-

bours' are of progressively larger scales showing smaller areas in very much greater detail. Whereas chart 5055 has a scale of 1:150,000, chart 5061 is 1:37,500 and therefore shows much more detail.

On most charts you will see that apart from the main coastal area charted there are larger scale inset charts showing harbour and river entrances. This is illustrated by the plans for Rye (1:25,000) on chart 5055 and Ramsgate (1:5,000) on chart 5061. On the chart you will find a key to the more important symbols as well as details of radio beacons. Tidal information is given in a series of chartlets based on Dover high water, with a table showing the time to be either added to or subtracted from Dover high water to obtain the time of high water are various locations on the main chart. Admiralty charts, however, use a system of diamonds scattered across the chart, each diamond being related to a specific column in a table that gives direction and rate of tidal streams.

Below a chart's heading you are informed that it is metric and that all soundings and drying heights are given in metres and decimetres.

Charts used for navigation must be kept up-to-date. The date of publication is given outside the margin in the middle of the bottom edge of the chart. If there is a second date, to the right, that will refer to the new edition. An Admiralty chart bought from an Admiralty chart agent will be corrected to the date of purchase. Corrections are issued daily as *Admiralty Notices to Mariners* by the Hydrographic Department. They are published in weekly editions which may be obtained from various sources such as Admiralty chart agents, harbour offices, customs offices and chandlers. The Admiralty now publishes quarterly a *Small Craft*

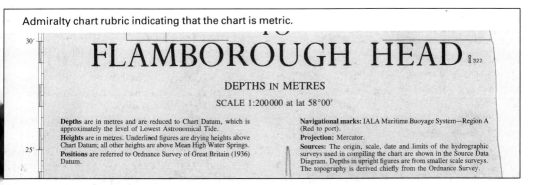

Admiralty chart rubric indicating that the chart is metric.

The last correction to this chart was number 696, 1990.

Small corrections 1988-*2890-3105-3636 3637 3708*-**1989**-*3374-3610*: **1990**: 696:

Edition of the *Notices for Home Waters Only.* Each Notice lists all the charts and publications affected and states the number of the Notice with the last correction. Detail in these Notices is varied, and may include a change in the position of a buoy, a change in the characteristics of a light, or a new hazard to navigation such as a wreck. Temporary and Preliminary Notices are prefixed T and P respectively. These should be marked on the chart in pencil until confirmed or cancelled. Some of these remain in force for years but are not marked by chart agents. To find them you need to look through the annual summary of *Notices to Mariners*. Permanent corrections must be indicated on the chart in waterproof magenta ink using the correct abbreviations. Where the chart has already been corrected by the publisher this will be indicated by the year and number of the Notice in the bottom left-hand corner. Any future corrections that you make to the chart should be noted in the same corner, again with the year and number of the correction. With each successive Notice showing the number of the last correction to that chart it is easy to check if any have been missed. If you send your Admiralty chart to the chart agent they will correct it for you for a fee.

One example of a *Notice to Mariners* (to week 38, 28 September 1991) included the following change:

'2605. Scotland, west coast, Firth of Clyde, Ayr Bay:

'DZ' special conical light buoy at 55°27'.25N 04°44'.70W – deleted.'

This correction indicates that the buoy in question has been removed and not replaced.

Corrections to the *Admiralty Lists of Lights and Radio Signals* are notified in the same way as are corrections to charts. Before setting out on a passage you should check through the latest corrections to see if there have been any changes.

Admiralty Sailing Directions (pilots) are for the larger vessel and are of limited use to the small boat navigator although they do have harbour entry signals.

The Admiralty produces a wide range of other publications. These include a list of lights, tidal stream atlases and instructional charts such as those used by the RYA in its courses.

Nautical almanacs such as *Reed's* contain a vast amount of useful information. Apart from tide tables for every standard port in the British Isles, *Reed's* has sections ranging from navigational techniques to emergency childbirth.

There are a variety of 'Yachtsmen's Sailing Directions' produced by cruising clubs and commercial publishers. These have a wealth of information on harbours and anchorages, with detail on shore facilities. They make entry into harbour very much easier by giving detail on leading lines, dangers and signals. An excellent example of such a publication is the *Humber to Rattray Head Sailing Directions* published by the Royal Northumberland Yacht Club.

LATITUDE AND LONGITUDE

Although you are unlikely, as yet, to be making passages involving a significant change of latitude and longitude it is more than useful to have an understanding of these terms. Positions are frequently given in latitude and longitude, corrections in *Notices to Mariners* being one example, while the latitude scale is in constant use for measuring distance. Navigation systems such as Decca and SATNAV also give positions using latitude and longitude.

Latitude and longitude co-ordinates provide a global grid whereby any point on the surface of the earth may be pinpointed with

Latitude is measured in degrees north and south of the equator.

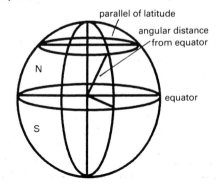

reference to this two dimensional system. The north–south reference lines are longitude; the east–west are latitude.

Lines of latitude (known as parallels) are drawn east to west parallel to the equator and to each other. Although these parallels are equidistant on the surface of the earth they are not equidistant on a chart: this has significance for the navigator. Each line of latitude is defined by its angular distance north or south of the equator measured at the centre of the earth. The poles, being the equivalent of a quarter of a circle away from the equator (0° latitude), have an angular distance of 90° from the equator. These two points therefore have the highest latitude and areas close to them are described as being in the high latitudes. Areas close to the equator are described as being in the low latitudes. It goes without saying that the British Isles lie in the mid-latitudes. A latitude is described as north or south depending on its direction from the equator. The latitude of London is therefore given as approximately 51°N, while that of Cape Town is approximately 34°S.

Longitude is measured in degrees east and west of the Greenwich meridian.

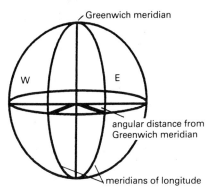

Lines of longitude (meridians) run from pole to pole. Unlike parallels they are not parallel to one another on the surface of the earth and are not equidistant. On some charts they will be drawn as parallel and equidistant because of the method of chart projection used. The prime meridian (Greenwich meridian) from which all other meridians are measured runs from pole to pole through Greenwich in London. Each meridian is defined by the angular distance between it and the prime meridian, measured from the centre of the earth along a parallel of latitude. Clearly you will travel

The International Date Line deviates around land so as to avoid confusion.

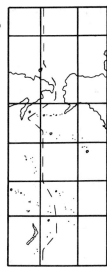

halfway around the world in a westerly direction from the prime meridian before meeting someone who has travelled the same distance east from that meridian. The meeting point is therefore 180° from the prime meridian. Longitude is therefore measured to 180° east and 180° west, with the position named east or west according to the direction from the prime meridian. The 180° line running through the Pacific Ocean is both east and west and is followed for most of its length by the International Dateline. The day of the week changes as you cross the Dateline.

Degrees of latitude and longitude are further divided to make possible more accurate map drawing and navigation. There are 60′ (minutes) in one degree and 60″ (seconds) in one minute. In general navigation, latitude and longitude are given accurate to one-tenth of one minute. The position of Beachy Head would therefore be given as 50°44′.00N 00°14′.60E, but if extreme accuracy were required you would give the position to the nearest second. In the case of the Eddystone lighthouse this would be 50°10′48″N 04° 15′52″W.

Plotting instruments

The plotting instruments that you require for coastal navigation are:

– *parallel rule;*
– *Douglas protractor;*
– *dividers;*
– *drawing compass;*

– pencils (2B);
– soft rubber.

A parallel rule consists of a pair of perspex rules of equal length joined near each end by swivels. These allow one of the rules to be moved parallel to the other which remains stationary. In this way they are used for laying off a course or bearing on a chart. Rules come in a variety of sizes, the larger sizes being easy to use only if you have a large chart table and spacious navigation area. You will probably find that on a small cruiser the 15in rules are the best size. It is essential that rules are looked after so that they do not warp or develop rough edges. Do not be tempted to buy the rolling rules that you may see in some chandlers. These are fine on the kitchen table but useless on a rolling yacht.

There are various nautical versions of the standard protractor which are a useful alternative to the parallel rule on a small chart table in heavy weather. One such is the Douglas protractor which combines the function of parallel rule and protractor. It is a square of transparent perspex graduated around the edge from 0° to 360°. A grid of horizontal and vertical lines on the face allow you to align it accurately with the chart. Breton and Hurst plotters are similar but may be pre-set for variation.

Dividers are used for either plotting position or measuring distance. The best type are the bow-shaped brass dividers sold in chandlers. These are easy to grasp, one-handed if necessary, and, unlike the standard geometrical types, do not rust.

Drawing compasses are useful for drawing range circles and for general construction on the chart, such as marking off a distance along a line.

Pencils and rubbers should be soft to avoid damaging the chart material. A modern propelling pencil has the advantage of not requiring a pencil sharpener.

FINDING LATITUDE AND LONGITUDE

To find the latitude and longitude of the buoy in the river mouth you need to use a parallel rule and/or a pair of dividers. If you decide to use a rule, lay it beneath the nearest parallel of latitude to the buoy, then 'walk' it to the buoy. This you do by first moving the lower half as far down the chart as it will go while keeping the upper half firmly in position. Next you keep the lower half firmly in position while you move the upper half downwards so that you close the rule. Although you have moved the rule down the chart it remains parallel to the parallel of latitude. In effect you have moved this line down the chart while keeping parallel with the original position. The process is repeated carefully until you have walked the rule to such a position that one edge of it passes through the buoy. You then walk the rule sideways to the near edge of the chart until it intersects the latitude scale. The figure on the scale at that point is the latitude of the buoy. (In other situations you might move the parallel rule up rather than down the chart.)

Longitude is found in exactly the same way except that you start with the rule along a meridian of longitude and walk it to the buoy and then to the nearest longitude scale. Note that latitude is always given before longitude.

Dividers may be used in much the same way. First place one point of the dividers on the buoy and the other on the longitude meridian nearest to that position. Then transfer the dividers to the nearer longitude scale, taking care to keep them the same distance apart. Place one point on the same meridian and the other on the longitude scale, either to the east or west. The latter point will be the required longitude. Latitude will be found in the same way, using the latitude scale.

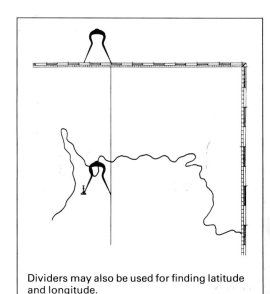

Dividers may also be used for finding latitude and longitude.

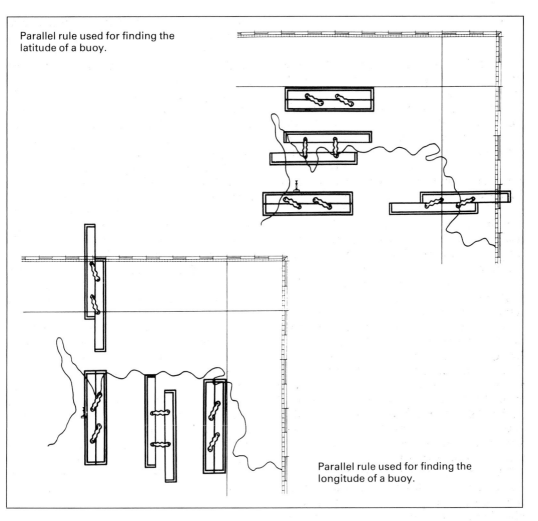

Parallel rule used for finding the latitude of a buoy.

Parallel rule used for finding the longitude of a buoy.

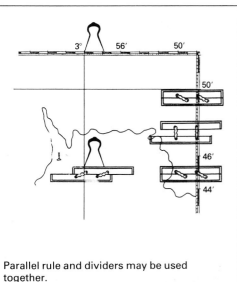

Parallel rule and dividers may be used together.

In practice parallel rules and dividers may be used together, one to find the latitude and the other to find the longitude. That the dividers are more restricted in the span of the chart they can cover clearly limits their use for position finding to within reach of the nearest meridian or parallel.

The same two instruments may also be used to plot a position. Say the position you wish to plot is 49°45′.40N 02°57′.80W. Place the rule along the parallel nearest to 49°45′.40 and then walk it down the chart until it intersects 45′.40 on the latitude scale. Then walk the rule across the chart to the approximate longitude that you are plotting. Use the dividers to plot the longitude while keeping the rule firmly in position. Place the dividers on the longitude scale with one point on 02°57′.80 and the other on the nearest meridian. Keeping that distance set on the dividers move them

137

to the rule so that one point is on the meridian and the other indicates 02°57′.8.

FINDING BEARINGS

Bearings and headings (the direction in which the boat is being steered) are determined by reference to the nearest compass rose. There are three such roses on Stanford chart 12. Each rose consists of two circles. For the moment we only need to consider the outer circle. You will see that it is labelled from 0° to 360° in a clockwise direction. If your vessel was at the centre of the rose and you looked towards the headland you would see the headland in the direction of 075°. That is therefore its bearing from you. A line drawn from the headland through your position and extended beyond would pass through 255° on the outer circle. That is the reciprocal bearing and always differs by 180°. The buoy at the river mouth bears 322° from the boat. If the boat was moving towards the entrance to the cove its heading would be 035°.

Once you have plotted your position you may use the parallel rule to find the bearing between that position and any other point. Imagine that you wish to find the bearing of the buoy from your previously plotted position. First place the rule so that one edge goes through both the boat and the buoy. You

may then walk the rule towards the nearest compass rose until one edge passes through the centre of that rose. The edge of the rose is intersected twice by the rule, at points separated by 180°. The point on the side towards the buoy is the bearing of the buoy from the boat while the reciprocal is given by the other point. The bearing of the buoy is said to be 322°, while that of the boat from the buoy is 142°.

When you have taken the bearing of an object and wish to lay that off on the chart the procedure is effectively reversed. Lay the rule on the rose so that it passes through the relevant bearing, the centre of the rose and the reciprocal. Then walk the rule across the chart until it passes through the object on which you took the bearing. You may then draw the line from that object in the correct direction using the edge of the rule.

On Stanford charts you will find straight red lines marked between major navigational points. Such a line represents the magnetic bearing between the two points, the relevant figure being printed along the line.

MEASURING DISTANCE

As a result of the curvature of the earth the meridians of longitude converge towards the poles so that the linear distance of a degree of longitude varies with the latitude. This figure

Bearings are taken
from a compass rose.

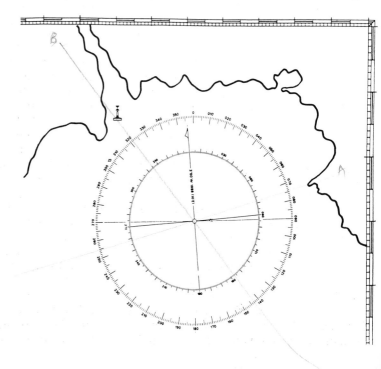

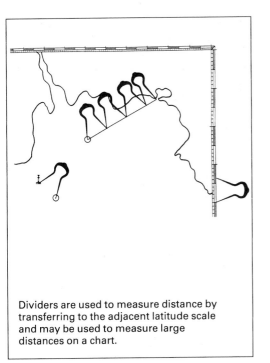

Dividers are used to measure distance by transferring to the adjacent latitude scale and may be used to measure large distances on a chart.

than at the equator in order to represent the globe on a flat surface. In order to maintain the correct shape of the land and also to maintain correct angular relationships the latitude scale must also increase polewards in order to balance the increase in east–west distortion in that direction. So in the northern hemisphere 1 sea mile will be a larger measurement at the top of the chart than at the bottom. For this reason it is vital that when measuring distance on this projection you use the part of the latitude scale immediately adjacent to the part of the chart where you are plotting.

The great advantage of the Mercator is that the rhumb line (straight line) between two points on this projection will cut all the meridians at the same angle and so give the navigator a constant course to follow.

Dividers are used to measure distance on a chart. To find the distance between the buoy and the boat open out the dividers and place one point on the boat and the other on the buoy. Transfer the dividers to the latitude scale adjacent to this sea area and read off the distance. (Remember that 1′ of latitude equals 1 sea mile.) Accuracy should be to within 0.1 or 0.05 of mile, depending on the scale of the chart.

If you wish to know the distance between the boat and the entrance to the cove the theory is the same, although the dividers obviously cannot span that distance. Using the latitude scale open the dividers up to a convenient distance and walk them from one point to the next, either along the edge of a parallel rule or along a straight line that you have drawn. It is unlikely that your chosen span multiplied a few times will bring you exactly to the destination point. When you are less than a whole span from that point adjust the dividers to bridge the remaining distance and measure that off the latitude scale.

When you wish to plot a specific distance from a known point open the dividers to that distance, using the latitude scale, and place one point of the dividers on the known point and the other in the required direction. This allows you to plot where you expect to be within a given time period. The navigator of a boat making 4kn and assuming a constant speed and heading would open the dividers to 4′ on the latitude scale and then place them along the course line to find where the boat is likely to be in an hour's time.

obviously declines polewards. We therefore cannot use longitude for measuring distance. Instead we use the sea mile, which is equal in feet to the distance measured along a meridian separating two places whose latitude differs by 1′ of arc. Again because of the curvature of the earth this figure varies, but the standard figure in use is 6,080ft.

There are several methods of projecting the spherical earth onto a plane surface, whether chart or map. The method used will be stated at the top of the chart. Although most charts used by the coastal navigator are, like 5055, based on the Mercator projection some harbour plans are based on the gnomonic. Chart 5061 is a transverse Mercator, unlike its predecessor 5043 which is gnomonic.

You will note that on the traditional Mercator projection the meridians which curve towards the poles on the earth's surface are produced as straight lines, each making a right angle with the parallels that it crosses. A comparison of a rectangular map of the world and a globe will emphasise that in order to straighten the meridians they and the surface of the earth have been pulled apart in an east-west direction. The distortion that this produces increases polewards because the radius of the earth decreases in that direction, so that more distortion is needed at the poles

Questions

Answers are on page 224.

1. On Admiralty chart 5055 find the latitude and longitude of the following to the nearest 0′.1:
   a) Vergoyer West buoy.
   b) Colbart North buoy.
   c) Rye fairway buoy (red and white).
   d) Sandgate buoy.
   e) North East Varne Buoy

2. On Admiralty chart 5061 find the latitude and longitude of the following to the nearest 0′.05:
   a) South East Margate buoy.
   b) North Goodwin buoy.
   c) South Goodwin buoy.
   d) Light on Deal pier.
   e) South East Goodwin buoy.

3. On chart 5055 find the distance between the following points to the nearest 0.1 mile:
   a) Vergoyer North buoy and Ridens South East buoy.
   b) Rye fairway buoy (red and white) and CS 3 buoy.
   c) Ruytingen South West buoy and Ruytingen North West buoy.
   d) Folkestone light and Dungeness light.
   e) Vergoyer East buoy and Vergoyer West buoy.

4. On chart 5061 find the distance between the following points to the nearest 0.05 mile:
   a) Downs buoy and North West Goodwin buoy.
   b) North East Goodwin buoy and Broadstairs Knoll buoy.
   c) Ramsgate harbour entrance and B2 buoy.
   d) North Goodwin buoy and Gull Stream buoy.
   e) East Brake buoy and Gull buoy.

5. a) What is the latitude and longitude of the Greenwich lanby in the south-west corner of chart 5055?
   b) Why is it prefixed by Greenwich?

6. What is the latitude and longitude of the flashing yellow light 3.6 miles south-east of Dungeness on chart 5055?

7. What do the areas coloured green indicate on an Admiralty chart?

8. Which line are drying heights and soundings measured from?

9. a) On chart 5055 what colours does Dungeness light show?
   b) What is the charted drying height 2.1 miles north of Dungeness?

10. a) What is the nature of the seabed immediately to the south-south-west of the Greenwich lanby on chart 5055?
    b) What is the charted sounding immediately to the south-south-east?
    c) How close is the nearest charted wreck?

11. a) On chart 5055 what is the true bearing of the Royal Sovereign light from the Greenwich lanby?
    b) What is the distance between the two?
    c) What is the range of the Royal Sovereign light?
    d) What is the latitude and longitude of that light?
    e) How far is it from Beachy Head light?
    f) What is the true bearing of Beachy Head light from the Royal Sovereign light?

12. What is indicated by the (purple) area running through Le Colbart and The Ridge?

CHAPTER 11

Using the Compass

To passage between two points we need a course to steer. On the chart we may draw a line between Folkestone and the East Road port lateral. We obviously cannot mark this line on the sea so we need some method of relating it to the direction we are going to head in across the water. The link between the line on the chart and the direction across the water is provided by the compass and compass rose.

The course, whether on the chart or water, is always stated as a degree of a circle in three figure notation. For centuries the compass was divided into the traditional thirty-two points that most people will be familiar with. Although these are still used in shipping forecasts and general conversation they have little value for course shaping. When a course is required it is given as a degree of a circle because that is more definite and so leads to greater accuracy.

Variation

The earth behaves as a large magnet, producing a magnetic field with north and south magnetic poles. Charts (and maps) are constructed so as to be aligned between the geographical (true) poles, but a compass needle points towards the magnetic poles. There is therefore an error produced. This error is known as variation.

A compass rose on a chart consists of two concentric circles graduated from 0° to 360°. North on the outer circle points exactly to the top of the chart while on the inner it points a little to the left or right, that is west or east, of a line running straight from the top to the bottom of the chart. The outer circle points to geographical north and so indicates true north, while the inner circle points to the magnetic north pole.

Variation is the angle between the geographical north pole and the magnetic north pole. As a result of the constant movement of

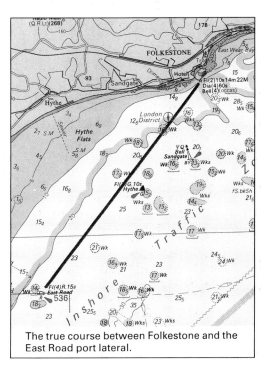

The true course between Folkestone and the East Road port lateral.

The earth behaves as a bar magnet with fields of force flowing between the magnetic poles.

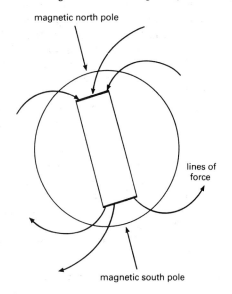

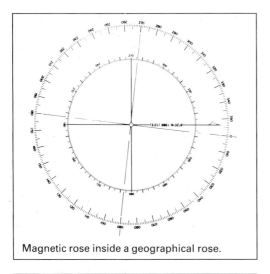

Magnetic rose inside a geographical rose.

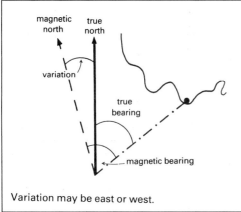

Variation may be east or west.

the magnetic poles, the north pole at present being in the Canadian Arctic, the actual variation changes from place to place and over a period of time, both in its magnitude and whether it is an east or a west variation. The Mercator Atlantic chart of 1981 shows the great change in variation across that ocean:

25°W off Newfoundland
15°W off Bermuda
10°W off the Canaries

The amount and direction of this change is indicated on a chart's compass rose. If there is more than one rose on the chart they will show the change in variation from place to place as well as the trend.

The Stanford (1979) chart of that section of the Channel between Start Point and the Needles has three roses as follows:

1. Lyme Bay with variation 07°40'W decreasing about 5' annually.

2. South of Portland Bill with variation 07°20'W decreasing about 5' annually.
3. South-west of the Isle of Wight with variation of 06°45'W decreasing about 4' annually.

With the above trends the respective variation figures for 1993 are:

1. 06°30'W
2. 06°10'W
3. 05°49'W

At present around the coastline of the British Isles all charts show a variation of about 3°–6°W, decreasing at about 8' annually. Charts 5055 and 5061 also have three roses each. You will realise from the above that when plotting on these charts you will need to use 3°W variation.

The differences between the multiple roses on a chart are not normally significant unless passages of more than 200 miles are being considered, because navigators usually convert variation to the nearest whole degree.

Deviation

A steering compass that was perfectly accurate would always point to magnetic north. That they do not usually point precisely in that direction is due to deviation.

Deviation is the difference between magnetic north and the line along which the

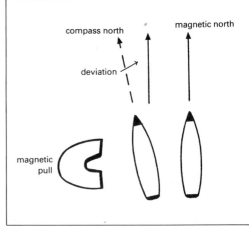

Locally generated magnetic fields on the boat will pull the compass needle away from true north.

north pointer of the compass actually lies. It does not point directly to magnetic north because small locally generated fields of magnetic force (on the boat) cause it to deviate

Such local fields are produced by a variety of objects containing a strong metallic or electrical component. These include engines, radios, light meters, beer cans, tool boxes and batteries. This has obvious implications for the positioning of the steering compass, and these objects should obviously be stowed as far away from it as possible.

The deviation should be small in GRP and wooden boats if you site the compass carefully and take care where you stow electrical and metallic objects. Steel hulled boats are a greater problem because they may become magnetised by the earth's magnetic field. This will almost certainly happen if they are laid up facing in one direction for any period of time.

The position of the compass card does not change as the heading of the boat is changed because its position is only affected by magnetic fields. What does change with the heading is the position of deviation-producing objects in relation to the north pointer.

For as long as the compass and the deviation-producing objects retain their relative positions the deviation of the compass on a particular heading will remain constant.

Whereas the variation to be applied to the true bearing is given on the chart the deviation is unique not only to every single boat but also to every single heading that is followed by that boat. As deviation may be considerable it would be courting disaster to ignore it. The navigator therefore needs to prepare a deviation card for the boat for various headings. This is simple to do using

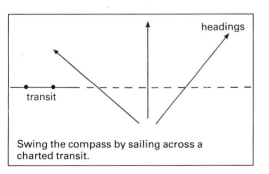

Swing the compass by sailing across a charted transit.

the transit method. If your steering compass does not have an azimuth ring you will need a hand-bearing compass. Find two clearly identifiable objects on the chart which can be lined up so that they appear as one from the boat. When they are so aligned they are de-

scribed as being in transit. Find the true bearing of the transit from the chart. You then sail on various headings across that transit, noting the heading of the boat and the compass bearing of the transit by using either the steering compass or a hand-bearing compass. The deviation for each heading is the difference between the compass bearing of the transit and magnetic bearing, the latter being found by applying variation to the true bearing obtained from the chart. A card giving the deviations for the various headings should be placed next to the steering compass so that the helm may clearly read it.

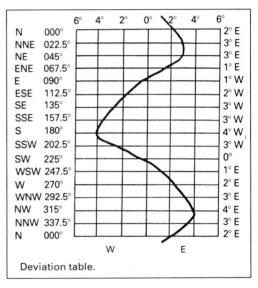

		6°	4°	2°	0°	2°	4°	6°	
N	000°								2° E
NNE	022.5°								3° E
NE	045°								3° E
ENE	067.5°								1° E
E	090°								1° W
ESE	112.5°								2° W
SE	135°								3° W
SSE	157.5°								3° W
S	180°								4° W
SSW	202.5°								3° W
SW	225°								0°
WSW	247.5°								1° E
W	270°								2° E
WNW	292.5°								3° E
NW	315°								4° E
NNW	337.5°								3° E
N	000°								2° E

W   E

Deviation table.

This 'swinging' of the compass should be carried out at the beginning of each season and whenever you add new electrical and/or metallic equipment. It is worthwhile employing a professional compass adjuster to do it for you. The adjuster will check the accuracy of the compass and, where necessary, will either adjust the tiny magnets built into the compass or fix small compensating magnets to the boat close to the compass.

You may also use the sun to check deviation. Almanacs such as *Reed's* tabulate the true bearing of the sun at sunrise and sunset in different latitudes for particular days. The difference between the compass bearing of the sun at sunrise or sunset and the tabulated bearing is the amplitude and is named either east or west according to whether the sun is rising or setting. The difference between the tabulated bearing with variation applied and the compass bearing is the deviation.

Compass correction

When working out a course on a chart the bearing obtained will be an angle from true north, for example 316°T. In order to make good this course, variation and deviation have to be added to, or subtracted from, the true bearing to give the compass bearing by which the helm steers. This is worked as follows:

TRUE	TRUE
add if	subtract if
west variation	east variation
MAGNETIC	MAGNETIC
add if	subtract if
west deviation	east deviation
COMPASS	COMPASS

If a compass bearing has been taken on a shore object, for example, the following procedure needs to be followed in order to plot it on a chart:

COMPASS	COMPASS
subtract if	add if
west deviation	east deviation
MAGNETIC	MAGNETIC
subtract if	add if
west variation	east variation
TRUE	TRUE

This gives the direction of the object from the boat, on the chart. In order to produce a position line the reciprocal of the true bearing must be found and drawn from the object. If the object has a true bearing of 330°T the re-ciprocal will be 150°T. A reciprocal is found by adding 180° to a bearing between 0° and 180° and subtracting 180° from a bearing between 180° and 360°. Therefore a line drawn 150°T from the object will be the position line of the boat.

You will see that when variation is west the magnetic course will be greater than the true course and that when it is east the magnetic course will be the lesser of the two.

The variation and deviation combined give the compass error. Take the smaller from the larger and name east or west according to the larger. If they are of the same name then they are added. For example:

$$\text{Variation} = 5°\text{W}$$
$$\text{Deviation} = 4°\text{E}$$
$$\overline{}$$
$$\text{Compass error} = 1°\text{W}$$

If the true course was 087° and the compass error was 2°W then the compass course (the course to steer) would be:

$$\text{True course} = 087°\text{T}$$
$$\text{Compass error} = 2°\text{W}$$
$$\overline{}$$
$$\text{Course to steer} = 089°\text{C}$$

You must use the T, M or C suffix after each heading or you will find yourself on the wrong and possibly dangerous course.

It needs to be remembered that while the true bearing of an object will remain constant from a given position the magnetic bearing will change as the variation changes.

Taking a bearing

On larger boats the steering compass has an azimuth ring which enables you to sight along the top of the compass and so use it to take accurate bearings. Space restrictions in the cockpit of the smaller cruiser mean that the compass is either mounted in a bulkhead, so that this is clearly not possible, or is mounted low down, in which case sighting over it gives you no view of the horizon.

The alternative in the smaller boat is to use a hand-bearing compass. This is used primarily to obtain bearings of conspicuous objects on the coastline or offshore. Such a compass is not permanently fixed to the boat so it cannot be corrected for deviation. If you use it

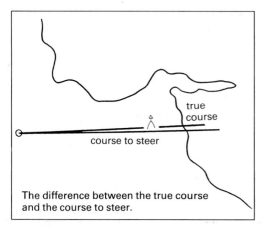

true course

course to steer

The difference between the true course and the course to steer.

well away from any object likely to cause deviation then it will not present a problem. A good position to stand in is with one arm around the backstay because that is stainless steel, and therefore not magnetic, and will also give you some support as you try to take a bearing. Having obtained a bearing, correct it for variation in order to obtain the true bearing. A reciprocal of that will give the bearing of the boat from the object and therefore a position line.

If you are unsure of the accuracy of the steering compass you may use a hand-bearing compass to check it. With the boat on a steady heading line up the hand compass with the fore–aft line, then compare the two compasses.

In any kind of sea the movement of the boat will make it impossible to obtain a steady bearing on an object with a hand-bearing compass. You must therefore take several bearings and use the average of these, ignoring those that are clearly inaccurate.

Stowage of the hand-bearing compass is very important. You must make sure that it is kept well away from electrical or metallic objects otherwise it will become affected by deviation.

Questions

Answers are on page 225.

Use 4°W variation and the deviation table on page 143 unless stated otherwise.

1. What are the following in three figure notation?
   a) North-west.
   b) South-west.
   c) South-south-west.
   d) East-north-east.
2. Convert the following magnetic bearings to true bearings.
   a) 260°M Var 3°W
   b) 242°M Var 2°E
   c) 018°M Var 4°W
   d) 351°M Var 1°W
   e) 017°M Var 3°E
3. Convert the following true bearings to magnetic bearings.
   a) 014°T Var 1°E
   b) 167°T Var 2°W
   c) 321°T Var 4°W
   d) 142°T Var 3°E
   e) 084°T Var 2°W

4. The navigator of a boat steering a course of 245°C takes the following bearings using the steering compass. Convert the bearings to true so that they may be plotted on a chart.

Beacon	132°C
Flagstaff	265°C
Church tower	324°C

5. Complete the following table.

T	Var	M	Dev	C
046°				044°
	5°W	134°		
156°	3°E			
	5°W	157°		
295°		299°		
320°	4°E			
045°	3°W			

6. If the charted course between two points is 135°T and the variation is 3°E what is the compass course to steer?
7. If a boat is steering a course of 185°C and variation is 4°W what is her true course?
8. In 1993 you are using a chart on which the nearest compass rose shows a variation of 6°15′ (1979) decreasing 8′ annually. What is the variation to convert magnetic bearings to true bearings?

Use chart 5061 for questions 9–11. Take variation from the chart.
9. A navigator in the red sector of the North Foreland light has a transit on the Longnose port lateral and Northdown church tower. The steering compass reads 207° along the transit.
   a) What is the true bearing of this transit?
   b) What is the magnetic bearing?
   c) What is the compass error on this heading?
   (all bearings are from the boat)
10. A boat is alongside the Gull Stream buoy, 51°18′.10N 01°30′.E. What are the magnetic bearings of the following from the boat?
   a) The North Foreland light.
   b) The entrance to Ramsgate harbour.
   c) The North Goodwin buoy.
11. Find the compass course to steer between the following positions:
   a) South West Goodwin buoy to the South Goodwin buoy.
   b) South East Goodwin buoy to South Goodwin buoy.
   c) Elbow buoy to the North East Goodwin buoy.
   d) Broadstairs Knoll buoy to the Longnose port lateral.
   e) South Goodwin light vessel to the Deal Bank buoy.
12. Find the compass course to steer between the following positions (using chart 5055).
   a) Royal Sovereign light to Beachy Head light.
   b) Hythe buoy to the South Varne buoy.
   c) Ruytingen South West buoy to Abbeville buoy.
   d) Bullock Bank buoy to the Ridens South East buoy.
   e) Vergoyer West buoy to the Vergoyer South West buoy.

CHAPTER 12

Tides

Tides are produced by the gravitational pull of the moon and sun. The former being so much closer to the earth produces tidal generating forces that are more than twice those of the sun. The general effect of these forces is to cause the water level in the oceans to rise and fall, which in turn produces the tides and tidal streams familiar to us. The lunar gravitational pull creates high-water bulges on opposite sides of the world, so as the earth rotates once in a 24 hour period any point on its surface will have two occasions each day when the tidal generating forces are at their maximum. This is why many but not all parts of the world have semi-diurnal tides, that is two high and two low waters each day. The period of 6 hours when the tide is rising to high water is described as the 'flood' while the 6 hours of falling tide are the 'ebb'. Although tides around Britain are generally semi-diurnal the Solent is one area where this is not the case, as we shall see.

Spring and neap tides are produced by the varying phases of the moon.

The lunar gravitational pull creates two high waters on opposite sides of the earth.

The effects of this tidal movement are not noticeable in mid-ocean but become pronounced in coastal waters where the tidal surge causes the water to pile up. This may be seen in its extreme in the Bristol Channel where the rise in tide may be as much as 15m.

When the earth, moon and sun are in line the tidal generating forces are at their greatest, producing spring tides. This term is not related to the season but to the Norse word meaning big. Springs, having a greater high water height and high to low water range than other tides, coincide with each new and full moon, so they occur twice a month. Neaps, on the other hand, with a lower than average height at high water and a smaller high to low water range, occur when the earth, moon and sun make a right angle, in other words when they are in quadrature. As with springs, neaps occur twice a month, in the first and last quarters. The tidal generating forces are at their weakest at these times. The tide will usually stay at a spring or neap level for two to three days. The rise in range up to a spring and the subsequent decline to a neap is a gradual change which leads to the slight change in time and depth of high and low water on successive days. The times are usually some 50 minutes later each day, because while the earth rotates in 24 hours the

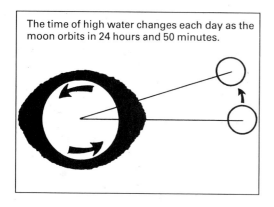

The time of high water changes each day as the moon orbits in 24 hours and 50 minutes.

period of rotation for the moon is 24 hours and 50 minutes.

Equinoctal spring tides occur close to the equinoxes, on 21 March and 23 September, when the sun is directly over the equator with zero declination so that the tidal generating forces are at their greatest.

Meteorological conditions may also affect the height of tide. An onshore wind may raise the level by up to 0.4m, while an offshore wind may have the opposite effect. High pressure persisting for several days may lower the level by up to 0.3m.

Tidal streams are horizontal movements of water produced by the vertical movement of the tide level. As with tides their magnitude in northern and western Europe (including the British Isles) varies with the lunar phases: the strongest streams occur at springs, the weakest at neaps.

Streams around the British Isles vary

.remendously in speed. Often 2–3kn, they exceed 5kn in several places such as the Pentland Firth. Tending to run either clockwise or anticlockwise they are usually either with you or against you when you are passaging along the coast.

Tide tables

Tide tables give the times and heights above chart datum of high and low water each day throughout the year for standard ports. (These are usually the large ports used by commercial shipping.) It is impossible to give predictions for every port in the UK, so time and height differences have to be applied to the predictions for the nearest standard port in order to obtain the prediction for a secondary port. It is because these tables only give the height of the tide at high and low water that we need to use tidal curves (see page 154ff) in order to find the height at intermediate times.

Tide tables are found in nautical almanacs and small booklets obtainable from chandlers, harbourmasters and marinas. While an almanac such as *Reed's* gives the times and heights of high and low water for every day of the year for every standard port in the country a booklet gives the same information for just one particular port. It is very important to remember that all almanacs give times in GMT, so during the period of BST you must add one hour to the tabulated times.

Most charts are in metric and so, there-

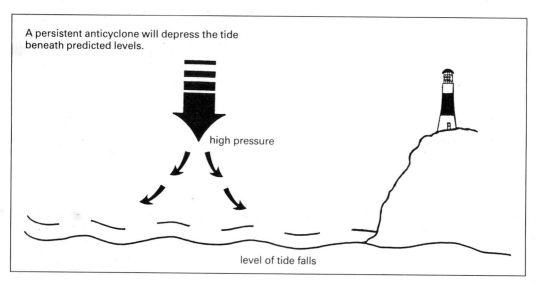

A persistent anticyclone will depress the tide beneath predicted levels.

high pressure

level of tide falls

fore, are the depths they show. All depths are measured from a line known as chart datum. The depth of the seabed is given by submarine contour lines, which also help to give an impression of the topography of the seabed. The contour interval is relatively small close to the coast and increases as deeper water is reached. On chart 5055 the 0m and 5m contours are shown, but the lines are drawn at 10m intervals after the 10m contour. The lines are supplemented at regular intervals by figures. These show either the depth of water (sounding) measured below chart datum or the height to which a part of the seabed will dry out (drying height) measured above chart datum. Drying heights are underlined to distinguish them from soundings. Areas that dry are shown in green. Both soundings and drying heights are given in metres and decimetres. To find the actual depth of water at a particular location at a specific time you have to apply worked tidal calculations to the charted sounding or drying height.

At the entrance to Plymouth Sound a sounding of 3.7m is shown on the chart. If you wished to know the depth of water at that point at high water on a given day you would have to look up the height of high water in the tide tables for Plymouth and work as follows:

Height of HW from the tide table	4.3m
Charted sounding	3.7m
Depth of water at HW	8.0m

In Whitsand Bay, near Plymouth, a drying height of 2.0m is indicated on the chart. If you wished to know the depth of water at that point at high and low water on the same day you would have to find the heights of high and low water in the Plymouth tide tables and work as follows:

Height of HW from tide table	4.3m
Charted drying height	2.0m
Depth of water at HW	2.3m
Height of LW from tide table	2.1m
Charted drying height	2.0m
Depth of water at LW	0.1m

Tidal stream predictions

When passage planning it is vital to use tidal streams where possible. Much time and energy will be lost going against a tidal stream, especially where it is strong. The information for these predictions comes not from the tide tables but from the *Admiralty Tidal Stream Atlas* and from chartlets in *Reed's* and other publications. For each of the 6 hours before and after high water at a specified standard port, frequently Dover, a chartlet gives an impression of the tidal stream for that hour and that sea area. Direction is given by arrows while the rate of drift is given by two numbers. The larger figure represents springs, the lower neaps. You should bear in mind that the decimal point is missed out from these figures in order to reduce the detail on the chartlet and so make it easier to read. The small size of the arrows, however, does make it difficult to measure the set (direction) accurately. Unlike the wind, the direction of a tidal stream is always referred to in terms of the compass point that it is going towards. A north-easterly stream, therefore, would be going towards the north-east.

When the day in question is between springs and neaps you will have to interpolate between the two figures given on the chartlet. This may be done either by eye, by straightforward arithmetic or by using the clearly explained table on the inside front cover of the *Admiralty Tidal Stream Atlas*.

The tidal stream tables and diamonds found on Admiralty charts give the most useful data. The magenta coloured diamonds enclose a letter and are scattered across the chart. On chart 5061, for example, diamond K is just to the west of the Goodwin Fork buoy. The letter in the diamond relates to the same letter in the tidal stream table found on the chart. The figures beneath that letter give the set and rate (for that position on the chart) at the time of high water at a standard port and for the 6 hours before and after high water. The tables gives both spring and neap figures. In order to use the diamonds you need to know the time of high water at the standard port, the time at present, and whether the tidal phase is spring or neap. If the phase is between the two some interpolation will be necessary.

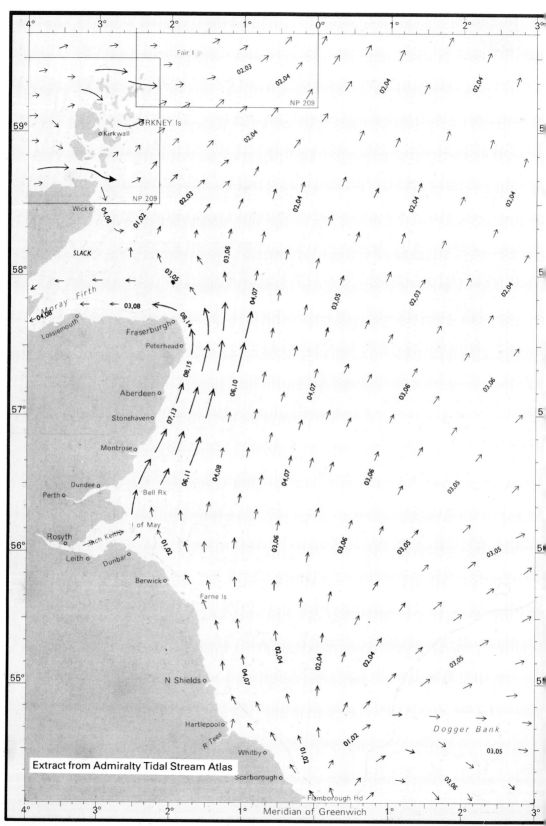

Extract from Admiralty Tidal Stream Atlas

Tidal diamond table from Admiralty chart.

Tidal Streams referred to HW at RIVER TEES ENTRANCE

Geographical positions (Directions of streams in degrees; Rates at spring tides / Rates at neap tides in knots):

- A: 55°04·5N 1 16·9W
- B: 54°58·1N 1 13·3W
- C: 55°01·0N 1 03·0W
- D: 54°38·0N 0 58·0W
- E: 54°41·8N 0 27·6W
- F: 54°27·0N 0 06·0W
- G: 54°09·8N 0 01·0E
- H: 55°10·0N 0 02·0E

Hours	A dir	A sp	A np	B dir	B sp	B np	C dir	C sp	C np	D dir	D sp	D np	E dir	E sp	E np	F dir	F sp	F np	G dir	G sp	G np	H dir	H sp	H np
−6	340	0·5	0·3	339	0·7	0·3	325	0·7	0·4	303	0·8	0·4	317	1·3	0·6	318	1·4	0·8	326	2·2	1·2	330	0·9	0·5
−5	317	0·1	0·0	340	0·3	0·1	320	0·4	0·2	303	0·4	0·2	322	0·9	0·4	318	1·2	0·7	329	2·1	1·2	317	0·6	0·3
−4	188	0·3	0·2	142	0·3	0·1	255	0·1	0·1		0·0	0·0	333	0·4	0·2	314	0·7	0·4	323	1·4	0·8	285	0·3	0·2
−3	180	0·5	0·2	152	0·5	0·2	172	0·4	0·2	111	0·8	0·4	118	0·3	0·1	255	0·2	0·1	317	0·6	0·3	182	0·3	0·2
−2	171	0·7	0·3	157	0·7	0·3	167	1·1	0·6	112	1·3	0·7	134	1·1	0·5	150	0·7	0·4	154	0·6	0·3	168	0·8	0·4
−1	161	0·8	0·4	165	0·9	0·4	155	1·1	0·6	109	1·1	0·6	134	1·4	0·6	141	1·2	0·7	140	1·9	1·1	156	1·0	0·5
0	158	0·6	0·3	172	0·7	0·3	145	0·9	0·5	107	0·9	0·5	132	1·5	0·7	137	1·4	0·8	148	2·5	1·4	141	0·8	0·4
+1	144	0·1	0·1	178	0·4	0·2	135	0·4	0·2	110	0·7	0·3	130	1·1	0·5	148	1·2	0·7	148	2·2	1·2	133	0·7	0·4
+2	358	0·2	0·1	220	0·1	0·0	035	0·1	0·1	097	0·2	0·1	149	0·5	0·2	132	0·8	0·4	143	1·8	1·0	110	0·4	0·2
+3	352	0·5	0·3	345	0·4	0·2	345	0·5	0·3	278	0·2	0·1	290	0·3	0·1	326	0·5	0·3	036	0·3	0·2	036	0·3	0·2
+4	348	0·8	0·4	347	0·8	0·4	341	0·8	0·4	288	0·7	0·4	311	0·9	0·4	331	1·4	0·8	327	0·3	0·2	356	0·6	0·3
+5	342	0·8	0·4	344	1·0	0·5	335	0·9	0·5	291	1·2	0·6	321	1·0	0·6	319	1·4	0·8	331	1·4	0·8	345	0·9	0·5
+6	340	0·6	0·3	340	0·8	0·4	330	0·8	0·4	296	1·1	0·6	312	1·4	0·6	319	1·4	0·8	326	2·1	1·2	334	0·9	0·5

Geographical positions:

- J: 53°59·9N 0 17·4E
- K: 54°16·8N 0 20·7E
- L: 54°30·0N 0 30·0E
- M: 54°13·5N 0 36·0E
- N: 55°10·0N 0 42·0E
- P: 54°24·4N 0 51·4E
- Q: 54°20·4N 1 03·8E
- R: 54°00·3N 1 06·1E
- S: 54°30·0N 1 26·0E

Hours	J dir	J sp	J np	K dir	K sp	K np	L dir	L sp	L np	M dir	M sp	M np	N dir	N sp	N np	P dir	P sp	P np	Q dir	Q sp	Q np	R dir	R sp	R np	S dir	S sp	S np
−6	330	1·7	1·0	356	1·4	0·7	332	1·3	0·8	331	1·4	0·7	334	0·9	0·5	339	0·7	0·4	332	0·9	0·5	324	1·0	0·5	328	0·8	0·4
−5	333	1·6	0·9	359	1·5	0·7	331	1·1	0·6	327	1·2	0·6	308	0·6	0·3	331	0·8	0·4	320	1·1	0·6	317	1·4	0·8	314	1·0	0·5
−4	326	1·0	0·6	342	0·9	0·4	315	0·8	0·4	321	0·8	0·4	275	0·4	0·2	317	0·7	0·4	313	1·0	0·6	311	1·4	0·8	305	1·0	0·5
−3	300	0·3	0·2	318	0·3	0·1		0·0	0·0	297	0·2	0·1	205	0·4	0·2	315	0·5	0·3	307	0·7	0·4	303	1·0	0·6	296	0·4	0·2
−2	169	0·8	0·5	175	0·3	0·2	165	0·7	0·4	168	0·5	0·3	183	0·7	0·4	303	0·2	0·1	240	0·3	0·1	271	0·4	0·2	194	0·6	0·3
−1	154	1·5	0·8	174	1·0	0·5	157	1·2	0·7	162	1·1	0·6	169	1·0	0·5	153	0·2	0·1	153	0·7	0·4	169	0·5	0·3	163	0·8	0·5
0	153	1·7	1·0	173	1·5	0·7	151	1·4	0·8	159	1·4	0·7	152	0·9	0·5	142	0·6	0·3	145	1·0	0·5	145	1·0	0·6	146	1·0	0·5
+1	151	1·8	1·0	167	1·3	0·6	150	1·1	0·6	149	1·5	0·7	140	0·7	0·4	147	1·1	0·5	141	1·2	0·7	137	1·4	0·8	138	1·0	0·5
+2	150	1·2	0·7	162	1·0	0·5	143	0·8	0·4	145	1·1	0·6	120	0·4	0·2	152	1·2	0·7	145	1·2	0·7	132	1·3	0·7	136	0·7	0·4
+3	139	0·4	0·2	148	0·2	0·1	096	0·3	0·1	135	0·4	0·2	048	0·3	0·2	152	0·6	0·3	142	0·7	0·4	128	1·1	0·6	112	0·4	0·2
+4	005	0·5	0·3	330	0·3	0·1	347	0·5	0·3	350	0·4	0·2	006	0·5	0·3	356	0·1	0·1	087	0·2	0·1	115	0·7	0·4	053	0·4	0·2
+5	348	1·1	0·6	347	0·9	0·5	348	1·0	0·6	338	1·0	0·5	350	0·8	0·4	345	0·4	0·2	003	0·6	0·3	047	0·3	0·2	050	0·5	0·3
+6	333	1·6	0·9	355	1·4	0·7	338	1·4	0·8	334	1·4	0·7	341	0·9	0·5	341	0·6	0·3	336	0·9	0·5	331	0·7	0·4	340	0·7	0·4

The effects of tidal streams must be considered very carefully. Where they flow very fast, near headlands or through very restricted channels such as the Solent, they may result in very confused seas, especially if the wind is against the tide. Off headlands they produce significant areas of disturbed water, such as the race off Portland Bill. The over-falls off Beachy Head are clearly shown on chart 5055. In heavy weather such areas are very dangerous to the small boat. Streams tend to move more slowly in shallow water but may still cause problems. They tend to be set into a bay, so the unwary navigator passaging between headlands may well find the boat taken deep into the bay, making for a very much longer passage and the possibility of grounding in shallow water. This could well happen between Beachy Head and Dungeness (chart 5055). A bar such as that at the entrance to Chichester or that outside Salcombe may create potentially dangerous standing waves downstream of it.

When navigating in the upper parts of estuaries, such as the river Stour on chart 5061, it is important to bear in mind the nature of flow around a meander (river bend). The flow is very much faster and the water deeper on the outside of the meander.

The alert navigator will be able to detect the set of the stream by looking at the water motion near moored boats and buoys. Boats, depending on the wind, tend to point into the tidal stream, while heavy buoys lean downstream and light buoys upstream. Downtide of a large heavy buoy there will be a marked disturbance of the water.

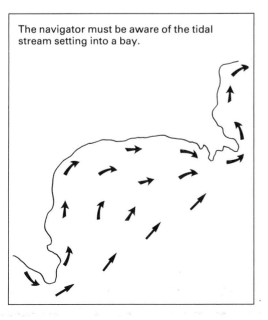

The navigator must be aware of the tidal stream setting into a bay.

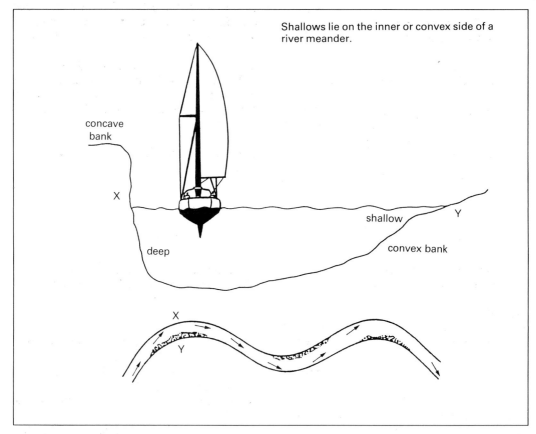

Shallows lie on the inner or convex side of a river meander.

concave bank

X

deep

shallow

Y

convex bank

X

Y

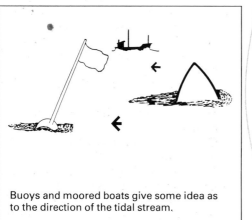

Buoys and moored boats give some idea as to the direction of the tidal stream.

The information in a tidal atlas or chartlet tells you what the stream is doing at a particular time, in terms of its rate and set. However, the rate and set are constantly changing between one hour and the next. To avoid unnecessarily time-consuming arithmetic the stream is considered to remain constant in rate and set between one hour and the next. You must not make the mistake of thinking that a chartlet referring to, say, 3 hours after high water means precisely that. Should high water be at 1200, and the relevant chartlet be designated as 3 hours after, it does *not* mean that the chartlet relates to the period between 1400 and 1500. It in fact refers to the period between 1430 and 1530. Failure to appreciate this very important point may lead to a significant navigational error. A detailed explanation therefore follows.

ALL hourly predictions given in tidal stream atlases and tidal diamonds refer to the MIDDLE of the period in question.
Example: HW 1630 BST

	1400	
1430		− 2
	1500	
1530		− 1
	1600	
1630		high water
	1700	
1730		+ 1
	1800	
1830		+ 2
	1900	

(− prefixes hours before high water:
+ prefixes hours after high water)

1745 would therefore be during the period + 1

If, with high water at 1630, your passage started at 1430 and you expected to reach your destination in 90 minutes you would plot the tidal streams as:

1430
     − 2 (for 30 minutes)
1500
     − 1 (for 60 minutes)
1600

You must interpolate between springs and neaps in order to find the correct rate.

Example:
Mean spring range standard port = 5.9
Mean neap range standard port = 3.3
            ——
        Difference = 2.6

Suppose that range at standard port on day in question = 4.2

$4.2 − 3.3 = 0.9$ above neaps

$$= \frac{0.9}{2.6} \times 100 = 35\% \text{ above neaps}$$

If spring rate = 2.6 and neap rate = 1.1
then rate on day = 2.6 −1.1 = 1.5

$$= \frac{1.5}{100} \times 35 = 0.525$$

$$= 1.1 + 0.525 = 1.625$$

The required rate is therefore 1.625

Reduction to soundings

The operation of finding the height of the tide above chart datum at a time other than high or low water is called reduction to soundings. You would perhaps do this to determine whether there is enough water to enter a harbour or whether you will remain afloat at low water in a shallow anchorage. You will require a tide table and the tidal curve (the graph that shows the rise and fall of the tide)

for the port in question. You will also need the time and height differences if you are doing the calculations for a secondary port. All of these are published by the Admiralty and also appear in almanacs such as *Reed's*.

To find what the predicted height of the tide at North Shields (River Tyne) was at 1854 BST on 16 August 1989 work as follows:

Tide table extract for that day (all times are GMT)

16	0223	4.7
W	0901	1.0
	1503	4.7
	2111	1.1

1. Convert all times to BST.
2. Find the times of high and low water that straddle the required time:
        1603
        2211
3. Find the height of high and low water:
    HW = 4.7m   LW = 1.1m
4. Find the range for the day: 3.6m
5. Time required: 1854.
6. Find the interval between HW and the time required:
        2 hours 51 minutes
7. In the time scale beneath the tidal curve write the time of HW and the time interval before or after HW as required.
8. On the top height scale mark the HW height (4.7m).
On the lower height scale mark the LW height (1.1m).
Draw the range line between these points.
9. On the time scale mark a point equal to HW + the interval (ie 1603 + 0251 = 1854). From that point draw a vertical line to intersect one of the tidal curves. The solid line is the spring line while the pecked line is the neap line. To the top right of the diagram there is a small box containing the spring and neap ranges for the port. If the tide in question has a range close to the spring range then draw your vertical line to the solid curve. If closer to the neap range draw the line to the pecked curve. Should you be halfway between the two ranges then your line should go to a point half way between the two curves.

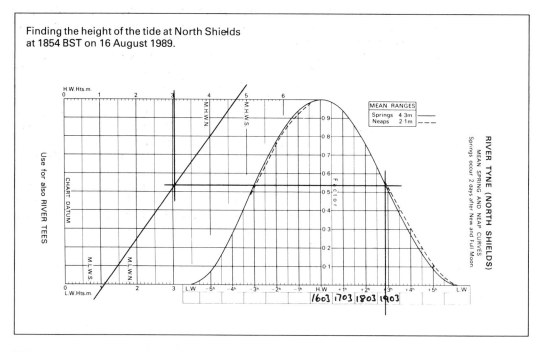

Finding the height of the tide at North Shields at 1854 BST on 16 August 1989.

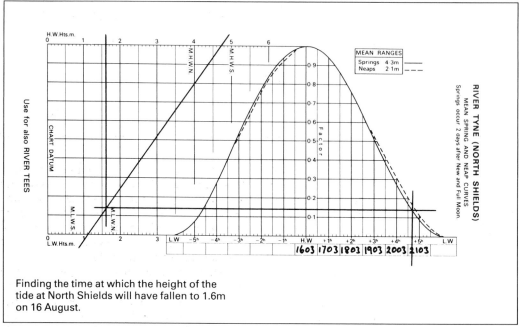

Finding the time at which the height of the tide at North Shields will have fallen to 1.6m on 16 August.

10. From the point of intersection on the curve draw a horizontal line to intersect the range line.
11. From the last intersection draw a line vertically upwards to the height scale. The height required is read off from the point on the height scale where the two lines meet.

The Answer is found to be 3.05m.

We may now consider a different problem, how to find the time at which a certain height of tide will be reached. Using the extract of 16 August 1989 you wish to find the time at which the height of the tide fell to 1.6m.

Start by working through steps 1–8 of the previous example. Then:

9. On the top height scale mark the height of tide required (1.6m) and from that draw a line vertically to the range line.
10. From the intersection on the range line draw a horizontal line to cut the falling curve if working from a time after high water and the rising curve if before high water. You may need to interpolate between springs and neaps.
11. From the point of intersection on the curve draw a line down to the time scale and read off the interval:

$$1603 \text{ (HW)} + 0440 = 2043$$

Tidal predictions at secondary ports

There is not enough space in an almanac to publish tide tables for all ports. Most smaller harbours are considered to be secondary ports for the purpose of giving tidal information. All such ports are related to a standard port for which tables are available. The almanac will give the differences to be applied to standard port times and heights of high and low water in order to determine the times and heights for the secondary port.

The procedure is exactly the same as for standard ports except that the differences first have to be applied to the standard port tide times and heights. The application of these differences is relatively simple but to ensure you avoid error you should use the Admiralty calculation form NP 204.

Say you need to find the height of tide at Deal on 8 August 1989, at 1827 BST.
First you look up the tidal differences at Deal:

Time differences				*Height differences*			
Dover	HW		LW	MHWS	MHWN	MLWN	MLWS
	0000	0600	0100	0700	6.7	5.3	2.0	0.8
	&	&	&	&				
	1200	1800	1300	1900				
Deal	+ 0010	+ 0020	+ 0010	+ 0005	−0.6	−0.3	0.0	0.0

The above information, found in the *RYA Practice Navigation Tables* (PNT), has been taken from *The Macmillan and Silk Cut Nautical Almanac*. Above the data in the almanac it makes it clear that the standard port for Deal is Dover, while an arrow indicates that the Dover tide tables are found further on in the almanac. The differences show four times of high water and four times of low water. These refer to times at Dover and are necessary because the time difference between the two ports varies according to the time of high water at Dover. From the table you will see that if high water is 0000 or 1200 at Dover then it is 10 minutes later at Deal. At 0600 or 1800 it will be 20 minutes later. More often than not high water will not be at one of the four stated times and you will have to interpolate between them. For instance if high water at Dover was 0300 then the differ-

ence to apply would be 15 minutes because 0300 is halfway between 0000 and 0600 and 15 is halfway between 10 and 20. The same working is used for low water times. Although it is usually sufficient to interpolate by eye you should be able to work out the difference precisely, as explained below.

In the height section of the above table you will see four columns. From these it is clear that if high water at Dover on the day in question is 6.7m then at Deal it is 6.7m − 0.6m = 6.1m. If the range on the day is neither springs nor neaps then you will have to interpolate.

Tide table extract for the day in question:

8	0230	5.9
Tu	0941	1.6
	1447	6.0
	2207	1.6

The height difference (X) to be applied for high water clearly lies between −0.6 and −0.3. To find this figure you must solve it as a simple proportion of how far the range of the day is above the neap range.

Range on the day in question = 4.4

$$\begin{array}{r} \text{Dover MHWS} = 6.7 \\ \text{Dover MHWN} = \underline{5.3} \\ 1.4 \end{array}$$

$$\begin{array}{r} \text{HW on day in question} = 6.0 \\ \text{MHWN} = \underline{5.3} \\ 0.7 \end{array}$$

$$\left.\begin{array}{l} \text{Deal spring} \\ \text{difference} \quad = 0.6 \\ \text{Deal neap} \\ \text{difference} \quad = \underline{0.3} \\ \qquad\qquad 0.3 \end{array}\right\} \begin{array}{l} \text{X must be between} \\ \text{these figures} \end{array}$$

therefore $X = \dfrac{0.7}{1.4} = \dfrac{X}{0.3}$

or, $X = \dfrac{0.7}{1.4} \times 0.3$

$$= 0.15$$

From NP 204 it will be seen that the height correction is:
$$0.3 + 0.15 = 0.45$$

The same result will be obtained by graphical solution. It may well be argued that a very similar result could be obtained by mental arithmetic because the range has risen by close to 50% from neaps. There is no reason why you should not interpolate by eye, especially if you require only an approximate depth.

There will be times when the figures are not as convenient as in this example. When in

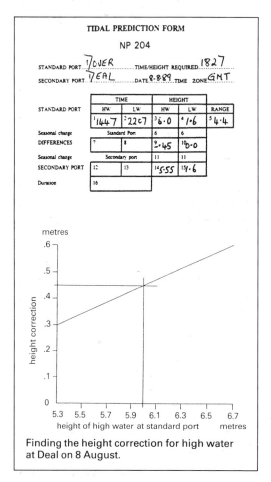

Finding the height correction for high water at Deal on 8 August.

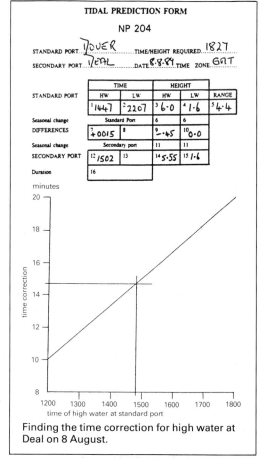

Finding the time correction for high water at Deal on 8 August.

doubt, or if circumstances dictate the need for a high level of accuracy, you must either graph the answer or go through the whole interpolation procedure.

Note that there is no correction to apply to the low water depth because the difference is zero whatever the low water range at Dover.

You now need to find the time of high water at Deal in order to use the tidal curve. Again you must interpolate.

Standard port times	1200
	1800

Difference	6

Standard port HW on day	1447
	1200

	0247 = 2.78 hours

Secondary port
correction

$\left.\begin{array}{l} 0010 \\ 0020 \\ \hline 10 \end{array}\right\}$ X must be between these figures

therefore $X = \dfrac{2.78}{6} = \dfrac{X}{10}$

or, $X = \dfrac{2.78}{6} \times 10$

$= 4.63$ minutes

$\begin{array}{r} 0010 \\ 4.63 \\ \hline \end{array}$

$0014.63 = 15$ minutes

	HW time	Height
Dover	1447	6.0
Deal difference +	0015	−0.45
	1502	5.55
+ 1 hour BST =	1602	

Times are converted to BST at the end of these calculations because the time differences at a secondary port are related to the times of high and low water that are given in GMT.

The height of the tide at Deal at 1827 BST.

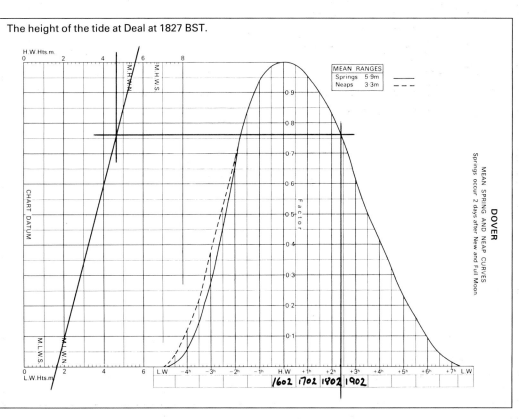

MEAN RANGES
Springs 5·9m
Neaps 3·3m

DOVER
MEAN SPRING AND NEAP CURVES
Springs occur 2 days after New and Full Moon

1602 1702 1802 1902

The tidal curve for the standard port is now used to work out the required time or depth in this example, but you must remember to enter the secondary port times and heights on the curve.

In this case the height of the tide at Deal on 8 August 1989, at 1827, was 4.65m.

The differences worked out for Deal are small but they are not insignificant. In your navigation you must always strive for pin-point accuracy, and that includes the working out of tides and tidal streams.

Solent ports

Most navigators will realise that because of the effect of the Isle of Wight on tidal streams the tidal curves for the Solent do not fit into the normal pattern. At Southampton, for example, there are two separate high waters at springs, separated by an interval of about 2 hours. At neaps there is a prolonged stand at high water. Such tidal anomalies exist not just in Southampton Water but along that part of the coastline from Swanage to Selsey. Within these complex tides there are small variations between individual ports. At some there may be a stand of the tide at high water when the tide remains at a constant level for up to 2 hours. The rising tide at others may reach a relatively high level and then fall back only to rise again to produce a second high water. It therefore becomes very difficult to predict the time of high water with any accuracy. This variability of the tidal characteristics is even more pronounced in secondary ports. For this reason the secondary ports of the area are grouped together so that each particular group has its own tidal curve. These curves are set out and used in the same way as other curves except that low water is used as the datum, so it is the time of low water not high water that becomes the key factor. On the time scale at the base of the curve you therefore enter the time of low water.

Clearances

Tidal height calculations have a variety of applications. These include determining whether it is safe to cross a bar into a harbour, determining whether a boat may safely berth alongside a harbour wall, and navigating your way through shoal waters.

By knowing:
– the draught of your boat;
– the sounding or drying height at the location;
– the clearance you require;

it is easy to work out the required height of tide. This height is equal to either:

draught + clearance − sounding;

or draught + clearance + drying height.

The wise navigator will always seek a minimum clearance of 0.5m. Many would

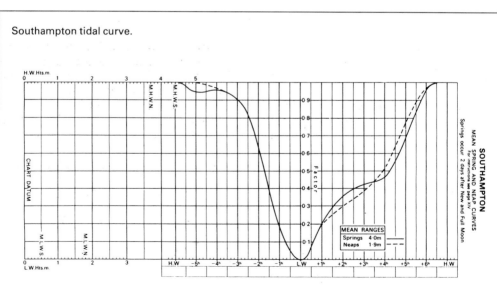

Southampton tidal curve.

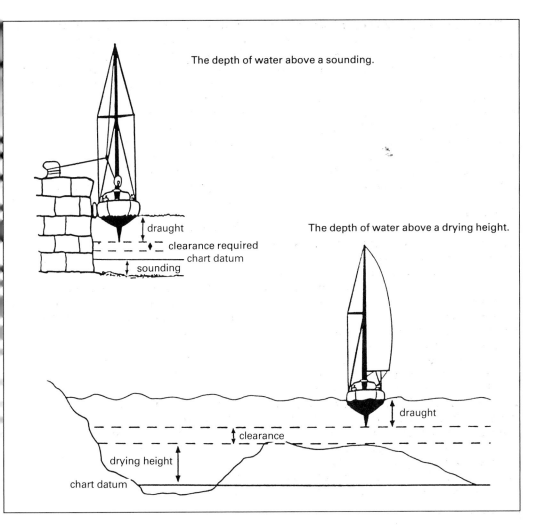

The depth of water above a sounding.

draught
clearance required
chart datum
sounding

The depth of water above a drying height.

draught

clearance

drying height

chart datum

argue that a figure equal to half your draught would be more realistic.

For example, your boat, with a draught of 1.5m, is anchored in Freshwater Bay. The echo sounder indicates a depth of 2.0m. You need to know whether there will be sufficient water beneath the boat at low water for safe anchorage or whether you will need to prepare to take the ground.

The transducer is positioned 0.4m below the surface so the actual depth of water is 2.4m. You calculate that the height of the tide in the bay is 1.9m. The seabed at the anchorage therefore has a depth of 0.5m below chart datum (2.4 −1.9). You need to work out the height of the tide at low water to determine if there will be sufficient water.

	Time differences				Height differences			
Portsmouth	HW		LW		MHWS	MHWN	MLWN	MLWS
	0000 & 1200	0600 & 1800	0500 & 1700	1100 & 2300	4.7	3.8	1.8	0.6
Freshwater	−0210	+ 0025	−0040	−0020	−2.1	−1.5	−.4	−.0

Tide table extract for that day:

8	0259	4.1
Tu	0816	1.3
	1528	4.1
	2037	1.5

For high water the height difference (X) to be applied clearly lies between 2.1 and 1.5.

Range on the required day $= 2.6$

Portsmouth MHWS $= 4.7$
Portsmouth MHWN $= 3.8$

Difference $= 0.9$

HW on day in question $= 4.1$
MHWN $= 3.8$

0.3

Freshwater spring
difference $\quad = 2.1$
Freshwater neap $\quad\quad\quad$ } X must be between these figures
difference $\quad = 1.5$

0.6

therefore $X = \dfrac{0.3}{0.9} = \dfrac{X}{0.6}$

or, $X = \dfrac{0.3}{0.9} \times 0.6$

$= 0.19, \quad (\text{say } 0.2)$

From NP 204 it will be seen that the height correction is:

$$1.5 + 0.2 = 1.7$$

For low water the height difference (X) to be applied clearly lies between 0.4 and 0.0

Range on the required day $= 2.6$

Portsmouth MLWN $= 1.8$
Portsmouth MLWS $= 0.6$

Difference $= 1.2$

LW on day in question $= 1.5$
MLWN $= 1.8$

0.3

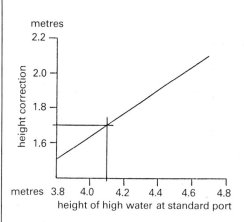

TIDAL PREDICTION FORM

NP 204

STANDARD PORT PORTSMOUTH TIME/HEIGHT REQUIRED......
SECONDARY PORT FRESHWATER DATE Tues 8th TIME ZONE GMT

	TIME		HEIGHT		
STANDARD PORT	HW	LW	HW	LW	RANGE
	¹1528	²2037	³4·1	⁴1·5	⁵2·6
Seasonal change DIFFERENCES		Standard Port	6	6	
	7	8	⁹1·7	10	
Seasonal change SECONDARY PORT		Secondary port	11	11	
	12	13	¹⁴2·4	15	
Duration	16				

metres

2.2 —
height correction
2.0 —
1.8 —
1.6 —

metres 3.8 4.0 4.2 4.4 4.6 4.8
height of high water at standard port

High water height correction for Freshwater.

Freshwater spring
difference $\quad = 0.0$
Freshwater neap $\quad\quad\quad$ } X must be between these figures
difference $\quad = 0.4$

0.4

therefore X $= \dfrac{0.3}{1.2} = \dfrac{X}{0.4}$

or, X $= \dfrac{0.3}{1.2} \times 0.4$

$= 0.1$

From NP 204 it will be seen that the height correction is:

$$0.4 - 0.1 = 0.3$$

The time difference to apply for high water clearly lies between −0210 and +0025, while

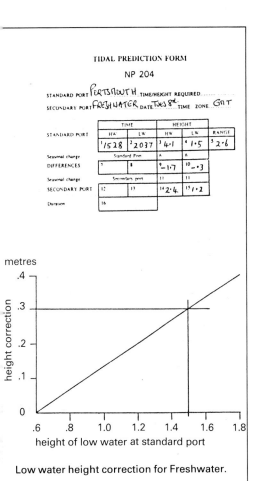

Left form

TIDAL PREDICTION FORM

NP 204

STANDARD PORT PORTSMOUTH TIME/HEIGHT REQUIRED..........
SECONDARY PORT FRESHWATER DATE TUES 8th. TIME ZONE GMT

STANDARD PORT	TIME		HEIGHT		
	HW	LW	HW	LW	RANGE
	¹1528	²2037	³4·1	⁴1·5	⁵2·6
Seasonal change	Standard Port		⁶	⁷	
DIFFERENCES	⁷	⁸	⁹−1·7	¹⁰−·3	
Seasonal change	Secondary port		¹¹	¹¹	
SECONDARY PORT	¹²	¹³	¹⁴2·4	¹⁵1·2	
Duration	¹⁶				

metres

Low water height correction for Freshwater.

Right form

TIDAL PREDICTION FORM

NP 204

STANDARD PORT PORTSMOUTH TIME/HEIGHT REQUIRED..........
SECONDARY PORT FRESHWATER DATE TUES 8th. TIME ZONE GMT

STANDARD PORT	TIME		HEIGHT		
	HW	LW	HW	LW	RANGE
	¹1528	²2037	³4·1	⁴1·5	⁵2·6
Seasonal change	Standard Port		⁶	⁷	
DIFFERENCES	−0040	⁸	⁹−1·7	¹⁰−·3	
Seasonal change	Secondary port		¹¹	¹¹	
SECONDARY PORT	¹²1448	¹³	¹⁴2·4	¹⁵1·2	
Duration	¹⁶				

time of high water
at standard port

High water time correction for Freshwater.

---

that for low water must be between 0040 and 0020.

Standard port times	1200
	1800
Difference	6

Standard port HW on day	1528
	1200
	0328 = 3.47 hours

Secondary port
correction   − 0210 } X must be between
             + 0025 } these figures
             ─────
             0235   (ie 2.58 hours)

therefore X $= \dfrac{3.47}{6} = \dfrac{X}{2.58}$

or, X $= \dfrac{3.47}{6} \times 2.58$

= 1.49 hours (ie 0130)

− 0210
+ 0130
─────
HW correction = − 0040

Standard port times	1700
	2300
Difference	6

Standard port LW on day	2037
	1700
	0337 = 3.62 hours

Secondary port
correction

$\left.\begin{matrix} 0040 \\ 0020 \end{matrix}\right\}$ X must be between these figures

$$\begin{array}{r} 0020 \end{array}$$

therefore $X = \dfrac{3.62}{6} = \dfrac{X}{20}$

or, $X = \dfrac{3.62}{6} \times 20$

$= 12.06$

$$\begin{array}{r} 0040 \\ 0012 \\ \hline \end{array}$$

LW correction $= 0028$

	HW time	Height	LW time	Height
Portsmouth	1528	4.1	2037	1.5
Freshwater difference	−0040	−1.7	−0028	−0.3
	1448	2.4	2009	1.2
	+ 0100 BST		+ 0100 BST	
	= 1548		= 2109	

At low water the depth of water above the seabed would therefore be:

1.2 (the height of LW above chart datum)
+0.5 (the depth of the sea floor beneath chart datum)

1.7m

As the boat draws 1.5m that will give a clearance of only 0.2m at low water, which will be too small for comfort because, in only a slight sea, grounding and possibly serious damage will occur. At least the navigator now knows the situation and may act on that basis.

In the same bay on the same day a boat with a draught of 2.35m has anchored and subsequently taken the ground. The crew wish to know at what time they should prepare to refloat. The depth of water has been calculated to be 1.85m at low water. Clearly the tide needs to rise at least 0.5m to 1.7m before the boat will begin to refloat.

To tell them the answer find 1.7m on the range line you have drawn on the tidal curve. From that draw a horizontal line to intersect the rising limb of the curve. From there go vertically to the time scale. That gives a time of 2 hours 25 minutes after low water. They should therefore expect to begin to refloat at about 2334.

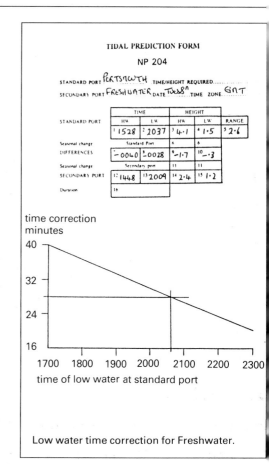

Low water time correction for Freshwater.

The rule of twelfths

The rule of twelfths is a simple, rough method of working out the depth of water at times between high and low water. It is not applicable to harbours and estuaries at which the tidal curve is asymmetrical or at which the duration of the rise and fall varies greatly from 6 hours: it would be of no use in an area such as the Solent. The duration and range are obtained from the tide tables and the rule is applied. It states that the tide may be expected to rise and fall at the following rate:

$\frac{1}{12}$ of the range in the 1st $\frac{1}{6}$ of duration = roughly 1st hr
$\frac{2}{12}$ of the range in the 2nd $\frac{1}{6}$ of duration = roughly 2nd hr
$\frac{3}{12}$ of the range in the 3rd $\frac{1}{6}$ of duration = roughly 3rd hr
$\frac{3}{12}$ of the range in the 4th $\frac{1}{6}$ of duration = roughly 4th hr
$\frac{2}{12}$ of the range in the 5th $\frac{1}{6}$ of duration = roughly 5th hr
$\frac{1}{12}$ of the range in the 6th $\frac{1}{6}$ of duration = roughly 6th hr

The time at which you would expect to begin to refloat at Freshwater.

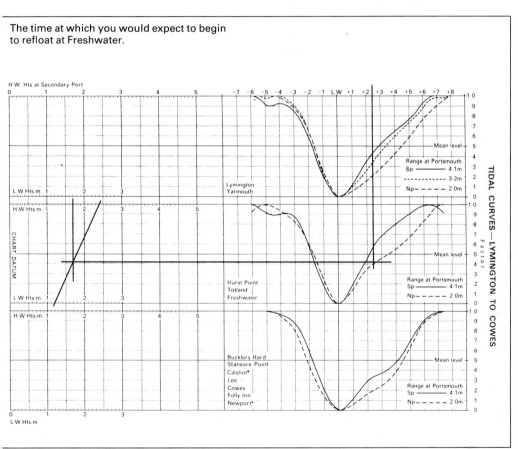

Tidal definitions

Amplitude   Vertical displacement of the level of the sea from a mean level.

Chart datum   The plane from which all soundings or drying heights are measured. All heights of tide shown in tide tables are measured upwards from this line. Chart datum on a chart is at the approximate level of the LAT (see below). Mean high water spring is the datum level for the heights of all land features.

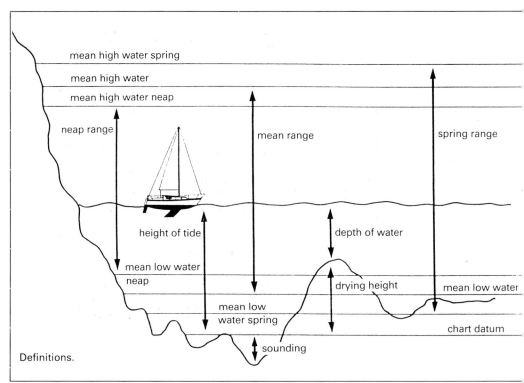

Definitions.

Current	Horizontal flow of water, but not periodic. Produced by meteorological phenomena.
Drying height	The height of a feature which is periodically covered or uncovered by the sea.
Duration	The time between successive high and low waters.
Range	The vertical distance between successive low and high waters.
Sounding	The depth of a feature which is permanently covered by the sea.
Tide	Periodical movement of the level of the sea surface through a vertical plane. This movement is produced by lunar/solar gravitational pull.
Tidal stream	A horizontal flow of water produced by gravitational pull.
Mean high water spring (MHWS)	The average height throughout the year of two successive high waters when the range is at its greatest.
Mean low water spring (MLWS)	The average height of two successive low waters during the same period as MHWS.
Mean high/ low water neaps (MHWN/MLWN)	As for springs, but this is the average of two successive high and two successive low waters respectively during the period when the range is at its lowest.
Highest/lowest astronomical tides (HAT/LAT)	The highest and lowest levels of tide that are predicted to occur under a particular combination of astronomical conditions and average meteorological conditions. It is possible for storms to produce levels in excess of these.

IALA Maritime Buoyage Systems.

LATERAL MARKS

PORT HAND

Colour:	Red
Shape (Buoys):	Cylindrical (can), pillar or spar
Topmark (if any):	Single red cylinder (can)

STARBOARD HAND

Colour:	Green
Shape (Buoys):	Conical, pillar or spar
Topmark (if any):	Single green cone point upward

DIRECTION OF BUOYAGE

LIGHTS, when fitted, may have any rhythm other than composite group-flashing (2+1) used on modified Lateral marks indicating a preferred channel. Examples are:

Red light		Green light
Q.R	Continuous quick light	Q.G
Fl.R	Single-flashing light	Fl.G
L Fl.R	Long-flashing light	L Fl.G
Fl(2)R	Group-flashing light	Fl(2)G

The lateral colours of red or green are frequently used for minor shore lights, such as those marking pierheads and the extremities of jetties.

PREFERRED CHANNELS

At the point where a channel divides, when proceeding in the conventional direction of buoyage, a preferred channel is indicated by a modified port or starboard Lateral mark as follows.

Preferred channel to starboard

Colour:	Red with one broad green horizontal band
Shape (Buoys):	Cylindrical (can), pillar or spar
Topmark (if any):	Single red cylinder (can)

Preferred channel to port

Colour:	Green with one broad red horizontal band
Shape (Buoys):	Conical, pillar or spar
Topmark (if any):	Single green cone point upward

DIRECTION OF BUOYAGE

Red light		Green light
Fl(2+1)R	Group-flashing (2+1) light	Fl(2+1)G

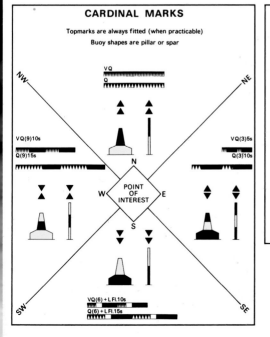

CARDINAL MARKS

Topmarks are always fitted (when practicable)

Buoy shapes are pillar or spar

VQ
Q

VQ(9)10s
Q(9)15s

VQ(3)5s
Q(3)10s

NW   NE

N

W — POINT OF INTEREST — E

S

SW   SE

VQ(6) + L Fl.10s
Q(6) + L Fl.15s

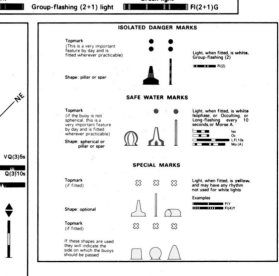

ISOLATED DANGER MARKS

Topmark
(This is a very important feature by day and is fitted wherever practicable)

Shape: pillar or spar

Light, when fitted, is white. Group-flashing (2)

Fl(2)

SAFE WATER MARKS

Topmark
(if the buoy is not spherical, this is a very important feature by day and is fitted wherever practicable)

Shape: spherical or pillar or spar

Light, when fitted, is white. Isophase, or Occulting, or Long-flashing every 10 seconds or Morse A.

Iso
Oc
L.Fl.10s
Mo (A)

SPECIAL MARKS

Topmark
(if fitted)

Shape: optional

Topmark
(if fitted)

If these shapes are used they will indicate the side on which the buoys should be passed

Light, when fitted, is yellow, and may have any rhythm not used for white lights

Examples

Fl.Y
Fl(4)Y

165

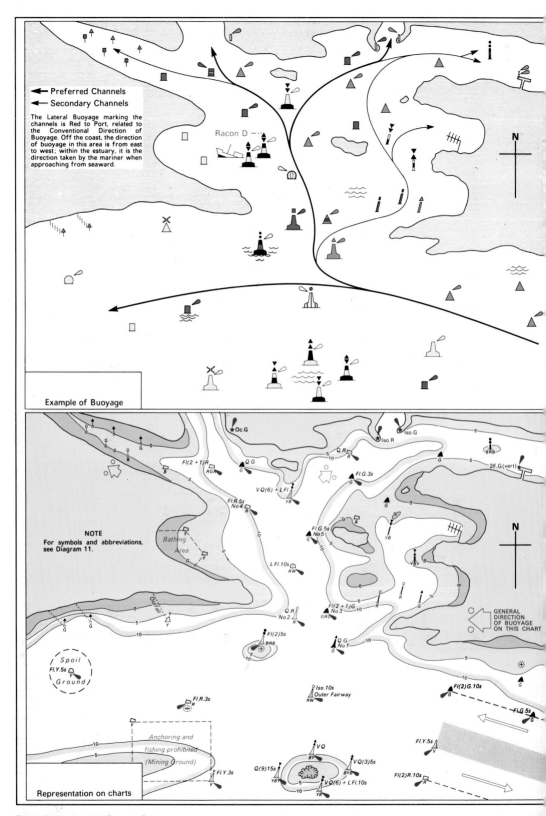

Buoyage representation on charts.

Questions

Answers are on page 225.

All times are given as BST where appropriate. All answers should be given in BST.

RIVER TYNE NORTH SHIELDS

Lat. 55°00′N. Long. 1°27′W. **HIGH & LOW WATER 1989**

GMT ADD 1 HOUR MARCH 26 — OCTOBER 29 FOR B.S.T.

MAY

Day	Time	m	Time	m		Day	Time	m	Time	m
1 M	0537	1.7	1130	4.2		16 Tu	0039	4.0	0646	1.7
	1812	1.0					1239	4.1	1907	1.2
2 Tu	0031	4.3	0639	1.4		17 W	0121	4.1	0728	1.6
	1229	4.6	1910	0.7			1321	4.2	1947	1.2
3 W	0121	4.6	0731	1.1		18 Th	0157	4.3	0808	1.4
	1321	4.9	2002	0.5			1359	4.3	2023	1.1
4 Th	0206	4.9	0819	0.9		19 F	0229	4.5	0843	1.2
	1409	5.2	2050	0.5			1436	4.4	2056	1.1
5 F	0249	5.0	0905	0.7		20 Sa	0258	4.6	0917	1.1
	1457	5.3	● 2135	0.6			1512	4.5	2129	1.1
6 Sa	0331	5.1	0950	0.6		21 Su	0328	4.7	0950	1.1
	1546	5.3	2219	0.7			1549	4.6	2203	1.2
7 Su	0413	5.1	1035	0.6		22 M	0400	4.7	1024	1.0
	1637	5.0	2259	0.9			1626	4.6	2237	1.2
8 M	0457	4.9	1120	0.7		23 Tu	0433	4.7	1101	1.0
	1727	5.0	2342	1.2			1706	4.6	2313	1.3
9 Tu	0542	4.8	1207	0.9		24 W	0509	4.6	1140	1.1
	1819	4.7					1750	4.5	2353	1.4
10 W	0024	1.5	0628	4.6		25 Th	0551	4.5	1224	1.1
	1257	1.1	1914	4.4			1836	4.3		
11 Th	0112	1.8	0720	4.1		26 F	0038	1.5	0639	4.4
	1357	1.3	2013	4.1			1314	1.2	1931	4.2
12 F	0209	2.0	0819	4.1		27 Sa	0130	1.6	0734	4.3
	1507	1.4	2122	3.8			1413	1.2	2032	4.1
13 Sa	0328	2.1	0929	3.9		28 Su	0232	1.7	0836	4.3
	1623	1.5	2240	3.8			1519	1.2	2141	4.1
14 Su	0449	2.1	1044	3.9		29 M	0343	1.7	0945	4.3
	1727	1.4	2347	3.8			1627	1.1	2249	4.2
15 M	0554	1.9	1147	3.9		30 Tu	0455	1.6	1054	4.4
	1822	1.3					1733	1.0	2353	4.3
						31 W	0600	1.5	1156	4.6
							1835	0.9		

JUNE

Day	Time	m	Time	m		Day	Time	m	Time	m
1 Th	0048	4.5	0700	1.3		16 F	0112	4.2	0728	1.6
	1253	4.8	1931	0.9			1326	4.1	1942	1.5
2 F	0138	4.7	0755	1.1		17 Sa	0151	4.3	0812	1.5
	1349	4.9	2025	0.9			1411	4.3	2025	1.4
3 Sa	0225	4.8	0847	1.0		18 Su	0227	4.5	0853	1.3
	1443	5.0	● 2114	1.0			1453	4.4	2104	1.4
4 Su	0311	4.9	0936	0.9		19 M	0304	4.6	0932	1.2
	1535	5.0	2200	1.1			1534	4.5	2143	1.3
5 M	0356	4.9	1024	0.8		20 Tu	0341	4.7	1012	1.0
	1627	4.9	2244	1.2			1614	4.6	2223	1.2
6 Tu	0440	4.9	1111	0.8		21 W	0417	4.8	1052	0.9
	1716	4.8	2325	1.3			1655	4.6	2302	1.2
7 W	0523	4.8	1157	0.9		22 Th	0457	4.8	1134	0.9
	1804	4.6					1739	4.6	2343	1.2
8 Th	0005	1.5	0608	4.6		23 F	0540	4.8	1219	0.8
	1243	1.0	1852	4.4			1825	4.5		
9 F	0048	1.8	0655	4.5		24 Sa	0027	1.2	0625	4.8
	1333	1.1	1942	4.1			1306	0.8	1916	4.4
10 Sa	0133	1.8	0744	4.3		25 Su	0113	1.3	0717	4.7
	1425	1.2	2036	3.9			1358	0.9	2011	4.3
11 Su	0226	1.9	0837	4.1		26 M	0206	1.5	0813	4.6
	1519	1.4	2135	3.8			1453	1.0	2108	4.2
12 M	0329	2.0	0938	3.9		27 Tu	0307	1.6	0915	4.4
	1617	1.4	2238	3.8			1553	1.1	2212	4.2
13 Tu	0440	1.9	1041	3.9		28 W	0414	1.7	1020	4.3
	1715	1.5	2336	3.8			1658	1.2	2316	4.3
14 W	0544	1.9	1142	3.9		29 Th	0527	1.6	1129	4.5
	1810	1.5					1807	1.3		
15 Th	0028	4.0	0641	1.8		30 F	0019	4.4	0638	1.5
	1236	4.0	1857	1.5			1238	4.5	1913	1.4

JULY

Day	Time	m	Time	m		Day	Time	m	Time	m
1 Sa	0119	4.5	0742	1.4		16 Su	0117	4.2	0745	1.6
	1342	4.6	2012	1.4			1351	4.2	2001	1.6
2 Su	0213	4.6	0840	1.2		17 M	0202	4.4	0833	1.4
	1440	4.7	2104	1.3			1437	4.4	2046	1.4
3 M	0301	4.7	0932	1.0		18 Tu	0244	4.6	0917	1.1
	1531	4.8	2150	1.3			1519	4.6	2129	1.2
4 Tu	0346	4.6	1019	0.9		19 W	0324	4.8	1000	0.9
	1619	4.8	2231	1.3			1600	4.7	2210	1.1
5 W	0427	4.6	1102	0.8		20 Th	0402	4.9	1042	0.7
	1701	4.7	2308	1.3			1641	4.8	2249	1.0
6 Th	0506	4.8	1143	0.9		21 F	0441	5.1	1123	0.6
	1743	4.6	2343	1.3			1723	4.8	2329	0.9
7 F	0546	4.6	1222	0.8		22 Sa	0523	5.1	1207	0.5
	1824	4.5					1807	4.7		
8 Sa	0018	1.4	0624	4.6		23 Su	0010	1.0	0607	5.1
	1300	0.9	1904	4.3			1249	0.5	1853	4.6
9 Su	0055	1.6	0704	4.6		24 M	0052	1.1	0651	5.0
	1338	1.1	1948	4.1			1334	0.7	1942	4.5
10 M	0134	1.7	0748	4.5		25 Tu	0140	1.3	0749	4.8
	1419	1.3	2033	3.9			1423	1.0	2036	4.4
11 Tu	0220	1.9	0837	4.3		26 W	0236	1.5	0837	4.6
	1505	1.6	2124	3.8			1519	1.3	2136	4.2
12 W	0318	2.0	0935	3.9		27 Th	0345	1.8	0956	4.4
	1559	1.8	2220	3.8			1631	1.6	2245	4.1
13 Th	0431	2.1	1041	3.9		28 F	0511	1.8	1116	4.2
	1704	1.9	2322	3.8			1753	1.8		
14 F	0547	2.0	1151	3.9		29 Sa	0004	4.2	0633	1.7
	1811	1.9					1239	4.3	1910	1.8
15 Sa	0024	4.0	0653	2.0		30 Su	0114	4.3	0745	1.6
	1257	4.0	1910	1.8			1348	4.4	2011	1.6
						31 M	0211	4.5	0842	1.5
							1442	4.6	2100	1.4

AUGUST

Day	Time	m	Time	m		Day	Time	m	Time	m
1 Tu	0256	4.7	0929	1.0		16 W	0223	4.7	0901	1.0
	1527	4.7	● 2141	1.3			1503	4.7	2111	1.1
2 W	0335	4.8	1012	0.8		17 Th	0303	4.9	0943	0.6
	1606	4.7	2216	1.2			1542	4.9	2152	0.9
3 Th	0412	4.9	1048	0.7		18 F	0341	5.2	1026	0.4
	1642	4.7	2248	1.1			1623	5.0	2231	0.8
4 F	0444	4.9	1122	0.6		19 Sa	0420	5.4	1105	0.3
	1718	4.7	2318	1.1			1702	5.0	2309	0.7
5 Sa	0518	4.9	1153	0.7		20 Su	0501	5.3	1146	0.3
	1751	4.5	2347	1.2			1743	5.0	2349	0.8
6 Su	0550	4.8	1224	0.9		21 M	0546	5.4	1225	0.5
	1825	4.4					1827	4.9		
7 M	0018	1.3	0625	4.6		22 Tu	0029	1.0	0634	5.2
	1253	1.1	1900	4.3			1307	0.8	1914	4.7
8 Tu	0052	1.5	0704	4.4		23 W	0116	1.3	0728	4.9
	1326	1.4	1938	4.1			1354	1.3	2006	4.4
9 W	0130	1.7	0748	4.2		24 Th	0212	1.6	0829	4.5
	1404	1.7	2020	4.0			1451	1.7	2107	4.2
10 Th	0218	2.0	0840	3.9		25 F	0328	1.9	0945	4.2
	1453	2.0	2111	3.8			1614	2.1	2227	4.0
11 F	0324	2.1	0946	3.8		26 Sa	0511	1.9	1122	4.0
	1602	2.2	2217	3.8			1756	2.1		
12 Sa	0454	2.2	1111	3.7		27 Su	0001	4.1	0641	1.7
	1730	2.2	2337	3.8			1230	4.2	1910	1.9
13 Su	0621	2.0	1235	3.8		28 M	0112	4.3	0745	1.4
	1845	2.0					1351	4.4	2005	1.7
14 M	0049	4.1	0724	1.9		29 Tu	0202	4.6	0836	1.1
	1334	4.2	1942	1.7			1436	4.5	2047	1.5
15 Tu	0141	4.3	0815	1.3		30 W	0243	4.8	0917	0.9
	1422	4.5	2029	1.4			1512	4.7	2124	1.2
						31 Th	0317	4.9	0953	0.7
							1546	4.8	● 2155	1.1

TIDAL DIFFERENCES ON RIVER TYNE (NORTH SHIELDS)

PLACE	TIME DIFFERENCES				HEIGHT DIFFERENCES (Metres)			
	High Water		Low Water		MHWS	MHWN	MLWN	MLWS
RIVER TYNE .... (NORTH SHIELDS)	0200 and 1400	0800 and 2000	0100 and 1300	0800 and 2000	5.0	3.9	1.8	0.7
River Tyne								
Entrance	+0005	+0005	−0005	−0005	+0.1	0.0	0.0	+0.1
Newcastle-upon-Tyne	+0003	+0003	+0008	+0008	+0.3	+0.2	+0.1	+0.1
Blyth	+0005	−0007	−0001	+0009	0.0	0.0	−0.1	+0.1
Coquet Road	−0010	−0010	−0020	−0020	+0.1	+0.1	0.0	+0.1
Amble	−0023	−0015	−0023	−0014	0.0	+0.2	+0.2	+0.1
Alnmouth	−0030	−0022	−0032	−0026	0.0	+0.1	+0.1	+0.1
Craster	−0035	−0030	−0040	−0038	−0.1	0.0	0.0	0.0
North Sunderland (Northumberland)	−0048	−0044	−0058	−0102	−0.2	−0.2	−0.2	0.0
Holy Island	−0043	−0039	−0105	−0110	−0.2	−0.2	−0.3	−0.1
Berwick	−0053	−0053	−0109	−0109	−0.3	−0.1	−0.5	−0.1

1. a) What is the time of LW at North Shields before 1200 on 16 May?
   b) What is the time of HW at North Shields during the evening of 23 June?
   c) What is the range of the tide at North Shields on the morning of 18 June?
2. a) On 1 August, what will be the height of LW at Berwick before 1200?
   b) On 24 May, what will be the height of HW at Berwick after 1200?
3. a) What is the depth of water in position 51°24′.50N 01°24′.85E (chart 5061) at MLWS?
   b) What will be the depth of water in the same position at MHWN?
   c) Would the extreme north of the drying part of the Goodwin Knoll (chart 5061) be visible at MHWN?
4. What height of tide will be required for a boat drawing 1.3m to pass over the shallowest part of South Calliper (chart 5061) with a clearance of 0.5m?
5. What is the least height of tide required to allow a boat with a draught of 2.1m to enter a harbour protected by a bar with a charted depth of 1.3m if a clearance of 0.5m is required?
6. Using tidal diamond A on chart 5061, what will be the direction and rate of the stream at:
   a) 1 hour after Dover HW with a neap tide?
   b) 4 hours before Dover HW with a spring tide?
   c) 2 hours after Dover HW midway between springs and neaps?
7. Using tidal diamond E on chart 5055 and PNT work out the direction and rate of the stream at:
   a) 1740 on 7 June
   b) 0240 on 27 May
8. a) What will be the height of the tide at North Shields at 1850 on 15 August?
   b) At what time after the morning HW of 13 May will the tide at North Shields have fallen to 2.5m?
9. What will be the height of the tide at Berwick at 1600 on 28 August?
10. Using the tidal stream chartlet of the English Channel (in PNT) work out:
    a) When the tidal stream becomes east-going off Folkestone on the morning of 18 July.
    b) What the rate of the tidal stream is off Shoreham at 0500 on 10 August.

CHAPTER 13

Position Finding and Course to Steer

Position finding

It is important at all times to know either where you are or to be able to work it out quickly. Without this ability you will not be able to plan a safe passage or check the progress of that passage. You may simply wish to arrange a rendezvous with another boat at a given point, or may, in an emergency, need to inform the coastguard of your precise position. When conditions such as wind direction change you will wish to react as quickly as possible. The navigator who is unsure of the present position will not be able to react when a wind shift takes the boat downtide and downwind of the destination. Position must be given either as latitude and longitude or as a compass bearing combined with distance off.

While close to clearly identifiable marks, whether they be lights at sea or conspicuous land features, you may accurately plot your position on a chart. Once you are no longer 'buoy-hopping' you must be able to find your position by dead reckoning and ultimately be able to check that position with a fix.

Direction and distance are the two parameters from which you will resolve your position. Time is a key point in this because it provides a constantly changing navigational reference point.

You probably know that navigators use the term 'knot' for speed, but what does it mean? It is the distance travelled in a given period of time. This is not quite as straightforward as it initially seems. At sea distance is measured in sea miles, which are not the same as terrestrial miles. The sea mile is equal to 1' of latitude (about 2,000yd, compared with the terrestrial mile of 1,760yd). Therefore 1kn means 1 sea mile per hour.

Knowing the heading of your boat and the distance run over a period of time you may work out the dead reckoning position (DR)

on a chart.

From the chart you can determine the angle between true north and the direction in which you wish to travel, your 'course'. The course to steer will be the course from the chart corrected for variation and deviation.

The diagram shows a true course of 165°.

True bearings are measured from true north.

165° T

The track of the boat over the seabed *should* be the same as the course on the chart, but is unlikely to be so because of the effect of the wind and the tidal stream. To clarify this point we will first follow a track, on Admiralty chart 156 of the Northumberland coast, where neither effect was considered. On this extract the initial position at 1030 had been fixed as 4.1 miles from the Coquet Island lighthouse on a bearing of 295°T. The log at that moment read 247.8. The position was plotted on the chart with the time and log reading. The navigator then plotted a course of 305°T towards the port lateral to the north-north-east of Coquet Island. The boat followed that heading for 1 hour at a constant speed of 4kn. At 1130, with a log reading of 251.8, the navigator decided to update the position. Using a parallel rule the heading of 305°T was laid off from the initial position.

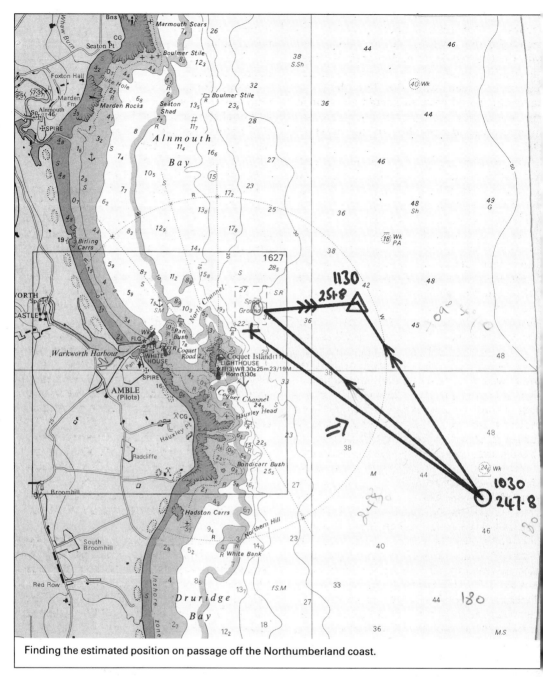

Finding the estimated position on passage off the Northumberland coast.

A pair of dividers was then placed on the adjacent latitude scale and opened out to 4′ (ie 4 miles, the distance travelled in 1 hour). One point of the dividers was placed at the initial position while the other marked a point 4 miles along the previously drawn course. This last point was therefore the DR of the boat at 1130. This was marked on the chart with the correct symbol, +, and the time and log reading (for clarity not shown on the diagram).

The navigator then searched the shoreline for a conspicuous charted object which would help to verify the position. A hand-bearing compass was used to find the bearing of the spire of Alnmouth church. This was found to be 314°T. The reciprocal was plotted and passed close enough to the DR to satisfy the navigator that the position was reasonably accurate. The echo sounder reading corrected for the height of tide was compared with the charted depth in that area. If either the bearing of the spire or the echo sounder had not agreed with the DR then the navigator would have suspected an error in the plotting of the DR. In this particular situation the danger lies to the west of DR.

The position the navigator plotted at 1130 was useful but not 100% accurate because it did not take into consideration the effects of leeway and tidal stream.

Leeway is the effect of the wind pushing the boat downwind of its destination. It is the amount by which the course over the seabed differs from the apparent heading according to the steering compass. You should work out the amount of leeway by looking astern and using a hand-bearing compass to measure the angle between the boat's fore–aft line and its wake. The figure is usually about 5° but may reach 10° for a small cruiser in a force 4–5 wind. The figure varies according to wind strength, point of sailing and boat design. It is at its greatest when you are close-hauled but progressively reduces as you move off the wind until it is zero on a dead run. A boat with a high superstructure and shallow draught will experience much more leeway than one with a low superstructure and deep keel. You must get to know how your boat drifts downwind in different conditions. It is clear that pronounced drift may lead to disaster if not taken into consideration when plotting position or a course to follow. A simple but often made error is to plot the leeway in the wrong direction. If the leeway is 5° and you apply it in the wrong direction your course will be 10° in error. To avoid this mistake you should place a wind arrow next to your plot. The boat's heading corrected for leeway is known as the water track and is drawn as a straight line with one arrow in the relevant direction.

Tidal drift is the direction and amount by which the water track is affected by the tidal stream. The rate and set of the stream will be obtained either from tidal diamonds or a tidal stream atlas, as described in chapter 12. It helps to plot positions at the change of the tidal hour. That way your working is not further complicated by having to work out the rate for a fraction of an hour. It is also

sensible to do as much as possible of the required interpolation between springs and neaps before you set out on a passage. The stream is plotted as a line with three arrows in the relevant direction.

Taking the example of the boat off Northumberland we will now look at how leeway and tidal stream affected its course between 1030 and 1130 and its position at 1130. On the day in question the leeway was 5°, due to a south-west wind. The stream set 085° at 1.3kn between 1030 and 1130.

From the 1030 fix, plotted as before, the boat's water track was plotted to give the DR at 1130. Note that the navigator drew an arrow against the plot to emphasise the direction in which the boat was pushed by the wind. Compare this water track with the previous course. From the DR position the tidal stream was laid off using a parallel rule to give the correct set of 085°T, and dividers were used to mark off the correct distance of 1.3 miles. The point at the end of the tidal vector was the position at 1130 which, because the course had been corrected for leeway and tidal stream, was the EP (estimated position). This was marked with the correct symbol, △, and the time and log reading recorded alongside.

The navigator also drew a line connecting the 1030 fix with the 1130 EP. This was the course that the boat made good over the seabed, described as the CMG (course made good) and ground track. The distance of this line was the DMG (distance made good) between the two positions.

To obtain SMG (speed made good) you divide the DMG by the time elapsed between the two points. In the case of a one hour passage, such as in our example, the SMG is clearly the same as the DMG. You will see from the chart extract that between 1030 and 1130:

CMG = 327°T   COURSE
DMG = 3.20 miles   DISTANCE
SMG = 3.20 kn   SPEED

Do not make the mistake of putting too much faith in your EP. You have produced it from a collection of parameters that have an unknown degree of accuracy. The information given in tide tables, tidal atlas and diamonds is predicted and is liable to vary from the actual figures because of variations in the weather. The steering compass and the log may not be totally accurate and the helm may well have wandered from the given course. You are also unlikely to have calculated the leeway perfectly. Such errors do tend to cancel each other out and with practice you will find that you achieve phenomenal levels of accuracy. You must, however, always bear in mind the possibility of error for the reasons stated and be able to check your plotting. As with DR, the EP should be checked with reference to conspicuous charted features and the echo sounder.

To go beyond the accuracy of the EP you need to combine two or more position lines. If you can cross the first position line with a second then the position of the boat will be at the intersection of the two. A position line is obtained by using a hand-bearing compass to take a bearing on an object. The reciprocal of that bearing is then plotted from the object with a single arrow at the end of the line pointing away from the object.

On the following chart extracts the navigator of *Red Devil*, on passage from Fowey to Falmouth, was attempting to find the boat's position. A bearing of 220°T was obtained on the Yaw Rock buoy at 0530 and converted to the reciprocal so that on the chart a line was drawn 040°T from the buoy. An arrow was placed on the end of the line to emphasise that it was a position line. Although the navigator knew that the boat was somewhere on that line where there was no indication of exactly where.

At 0630 the navigator managed to take, within 30 seconds of each other, the following bearings:

| Yaw Rock buoy | 315°T |
| Church at Gorran Haven | 285°T |

The reciprocals of these were then plotted from the two points. Where the two lines intersected the navigator drew the symbol ⊙ to indicate that that was the observed position

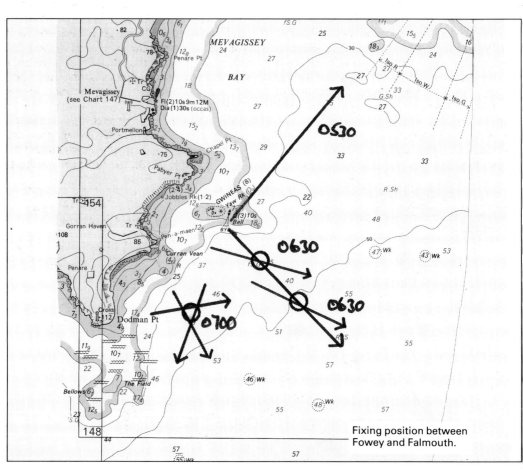

Fixing position between Fowey and Falmouth.

(fix). The time and log reading would be marked next to the fix.

Three position lines would have produced a more reliable fix because of the difficulty of taking accurate bearings from a small boat. A slight error in one bearing, and therefore position line, leads to a significant error in the fix. The position of *Red Devil* at 0630 would have changed significantly had the bearing of the church been taken as 295°T.

At 0700 the navigator managed to take, within a minute of each other, the following bearings:

Yaw Rock buoy	020°T
Church at Gorran Haven	330°T
Cross on Dodman Point	260°T

The three position lines produced from these bearings did not intersect at one point but formed a small triangular 'cocked hat'.

This is what you should expect from your position lines too, because however efficient you are you cannot hope to be perfectly accurate with each line. The third line effectively provides a check on the other two. The boat will be inside the triangle and if there is danger in or close to that triangle the boat will be presumed to be in that part of the triangle closest to the danger. In the case of *Red Devil* the position was taken to be in the shore side of the triangle.

You will note that the position lines are only drawn long enough to show the point of intersection.

The planning of a fix is an art in itself. The greatest accuracy will be achieved by taking bearings on identified conspicuous shore objects such as chimneys or fixed navigational marks such as lighthouses. Bearings taken on buoys may be a little less accurate because of their tendency to drift on their moorings. You must ensure that you have correctly identified the buoy and be confident that it is where it should be and has not broken away from its mooring. The most accurate position will be derived from a transit on two shore features.

Less reliable, but still useful, are bearings taken on prominent topographic features such as headlands. These may be highly accurate, but all too often it is not easy to determine where the headland cuts the water. This will be particularly true where there are offlying rocks immediately beyond the headland. For example, the precise point where Manacle Point (south of the Helford River) bisects the sea is not always easy to discern. You must also remember that the constantly changing level of the sea will affect the headland's profile. The best position line obtained from a bearing on a headland will be achieved when the headland descends steeply into the sea with no offlying rocks. The edge of an island may be used in the same way.

You should take the bearings as quickly as possible, noting the log reading before you start. Bearings on the beam should be taken last because they change the quickest.

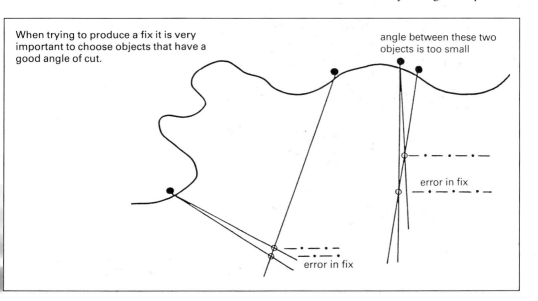

When trying to produce a fix it is very important to choose objects that have a good angle of cut.

angle between these two objects is too small

error in fix

error in fix

Always choose the closest of two objects that are in the same general area because while an error of 3° may be of little significance over a ¼ mile it may be very serious if the distance is 10 miles. You should try to achieve a good angle of cut between the objects. Ideally the angle should be between 60° and 90°. If the angle is too small it only requires a small error in one bearing to make a large error in the fix. Where the angle is too large it becomes difficult to determine precisely where the lines intersect.

With the increased use of hyperbolic systems some navigators are becoming complacent and are not updating their chart plot as often as they should. The EP should be plotted every hour, and preferably be backed up by a fix. During a difficult passage in heavy weather or fog, or when you are approaching harbour, you should plot more frequently.

Course to steer

The techniques that we used in order to find our position will be much in evidence when plotting a course to steer.

The navigator of *Red Devil*, on passage from Sunderland to Scarborough, fixed the boat's position at 2100 as 1 mile due east of the Tees Fairway buoy. For the next leg of the passage a course to steer, to the special mark north-north-west of Cowbar Nab, needed to be worked out.

The navigator first drew a line between the 2100 fix and the special mark. That was the course that the boat had to make good over

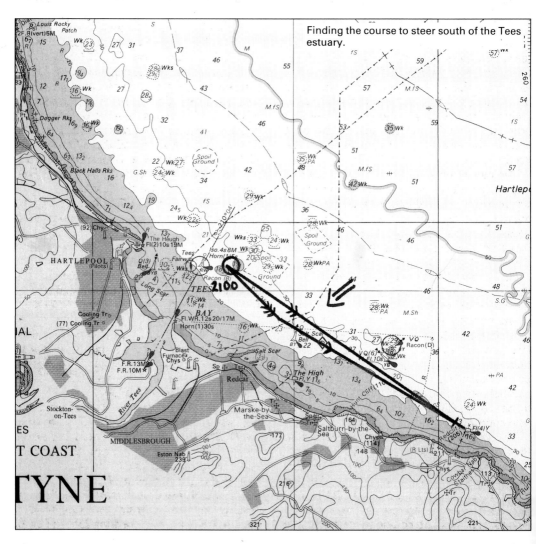

Finding the course to steer south of the Tees estuary.

the seabed. From the chart we can see that the required CMG was in fact 124°T. The boat would not have reached the special mark if the helm had been given that course to steer. The effects of the tide, wind, variation and deviation all had to be considered.

The relevant information was as follows:

Tidal stream   135°T   1.5kn
Leeway   4° due to a north-east wind
Variation   5°W
Deviation   1°E
Expected boat speed 4kn

You will immediately see that the tendency will have been for the stream to take the boat to the south and east of the required course while the wind will have pushed it to the south and west.

When working out a course to steer the stream effect is applied first. As in this case, the stream rarely runs in line with the course. It is usual for the tide to be flowing at an angle to the required course. A course therefore has to be produced so that the boat slides crabwise to the destination. You need to point up towards the tide so that the boat apparently effects a straight line to the destination.

The navigator of *Red Devil* used a parallel rule to lay off a line in the direction of the stream from the 2100 fix. As the navigator estimated that the passage should take about 2 hours, dividers were used to mark off from that point the distance that the stream would have travelled in 2 hours: 3 miles (1.5 x 2).

Using the latitude scale the dividers were then set to 8 miles (the boat's speed through the water multiplied by 2 hours). One point of the dividers was placed at the end of the tidal vector while the other was placed on the line between the two points. The navigator then drew a straight line between the two points described by the dividers. Using the parallel rule the bearing of this line was found to be 120°T. This was almost the required true course.

The navigator then took into consideration the fact that the wind would push the boat 4° downwind of the required course. The leeway was therefore subtracted from 120°T to give the required true course of 116°T. This figure was then corrected for variation and deviation to give the course to steer to make

good a course of 116°T between the two buoys. The helm therefore had to follow a course of 120°C.

A frequent mistake made by beginners is to join the end of the tidal stream with the destination. This gives an inaccurate course-to-steer vector because it represents the wrong speed for the boat. To the inexperienced the completed vector diagram appears misleading. Although the diagram is constructed to enable you to work out the course to steer, the boat in fact stays on the CMG line throughout. You will find that the vector diagram is rarely the precise size that you require. More often than not the track of the boat's speed laid off from the end of the tidal vector intersects the CMG either before or beyond the destination. This does not matter because the boat simply slides down the track until it reaches the destination.

From the vector diagram constructed it was possible to work out the probable DMG and SMG. From these the ETA was calculated. The DMG is the distance from the initial point to the point at which the water track intersects the CMG. In this passage the DMG in 2 hours was found to be 10.9 miles. As this diagram was drawn for 2 hours the SMG was 5.45kn. To find the ETA the total distance of the passage (measured between the two buoys) was divided by the SMG to give the total time for the passage:

$$11.5 \div 5.45 = 2.11 \text{ hours}$$

Fractions of an hour are easy to calculate if you remember that:

0.1 hour =   6 minutes
0.2 hour = 12 minutes

To be really accurate remember that:

0.01 hour = 0.6 minute = 36 seconds
0.02 hour = 1.2 minutes = 1 minute 12 secs

Red Devil's navigator calculated the total time for the passage to be 2 hours 7 minutes. This was added to the time when the position was fixed off the Tees Fairway buoy (2100). The ETA was therefore 2307.

The calculation is just as straightforward if the water track intersects the CMG beyond the destination. Where this occurs after the construction of a 1 hour vector diagram then the passage is going to take less than 1 hour.

The navigator of *Red Devil*, this time on passage to Lowestoft, fixed the boat's position as 0.4 miles from the Corton east cardinal with the buoy bearing 235°T at 1700.

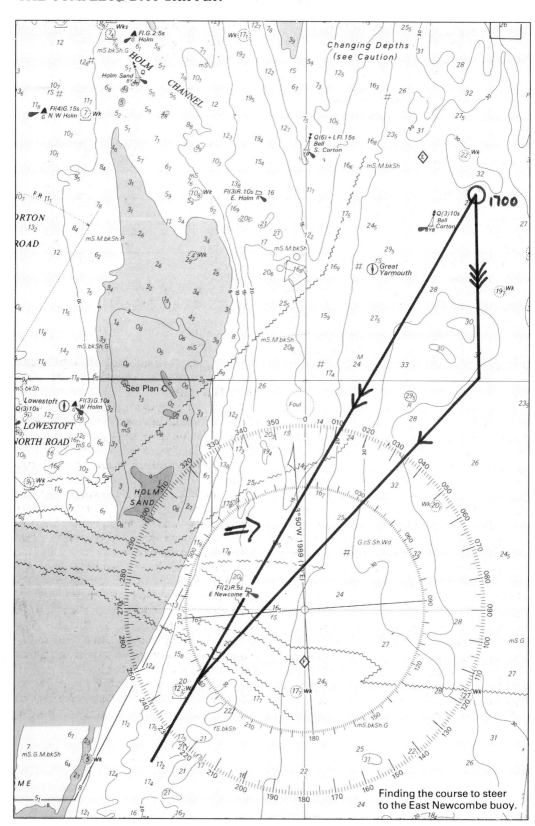

Finding the course to steer to the East Newcombe buoy.

In a light breeze with falling visibility it was decided to lay off a course for the East Newcombe buoy.

The relevant information was as follows:

Tidal stream	179°T 1.3kn
Leeway	2° due to a west wind
Variation	5°W
Deviation	1°W
Expected boat speed	3kn

The vector diagram was plotted as in the previous example. In this case the water track cut the CMG beyond the destination so the passage was clearly going to take less than 1 hour.

From the plot the water track was found to be 224°T. When leeway, variation and deviation were applied this gave a course to steer of 232°C. The DMG and SMG were calculated to be 4 miles and 4kn respectively. As the distance between the two positions was 3.3 miles this gave an estimated time for the passage of 3.3 miles divided by 4 knots, which was 0.825 hours. Added to 1700 this gave an ETA of 1750.

If a passage looks as though it might last 2 hours then you must plot two tidal vectors of 1 hour's duration each. From the end of the second vector you then plot a track equal to twice the boat's expected speed. Should the two tidal vectors be significantly different the boat might wander from the track during the passage. The boat might in fact not be on the ground track until the end of the passage.

When a passage is clearly going to last several hours then your method of drawing the tidal vector will depend on the nature of that stream. Where the tides are rectilinear (flowing first in one direction and then reversing to flow in the opposite direction) you may average the tidal effect for the expected length of the passage and then proceed as above. Where the stream is rotary, so that it changes its angle every hour, you will have to plot tidal vectors for each hour in order to find the resultant for the entire passage.

With a rectilinear tidal stream you need first to calculate your estimated passage time and then to aggregate the east and west streams for that period:

Hours	Set	Rate
1	110°	0.4
2	110°	0.8
3	110°	1.2
4	110°	0.7
5	110°	0.3
6	slack	
7	290°	1.6
8	290°	1.9
9	290°	1.4
10	290°	1.1
11	290°	0.8
12	slack	

Total drift 110° = 3.4
Total drift 290° = 6.8
———
Balance 290° = 3.4

You then plot the balance of the tidal stream from the initial position and lay off the course as explained above.

Where the stream is rotary you must plot all the individual tidal vectors from the initial point. The course is then plotted from the end of the resulting tidal vector chain.

In both these situations the boat will trace a wide sweep, first one side of the ground track and then the other. You must therefore make quite sure that such a sweep does not take you towards potential danger. If it does you will have to modify the course to take these into consideration.

Whatever the situation you must plot regular DR and EP and work out a new course to steer each time you halve the distance to your destination. On an 80 mile passage you will therefore do this after 40, 20, 10 and 5 miles, bearing in mind that you will need to aim either upstream or upwind of your destination so that you are not fighting an adverse stream or strong headwind. Whether you decide to be upstream or upwind depends upon which is going to cause you the least trouble.

Questions

Answers are on page 225.

All questions are based on chart 5061. Variation for the whole exercise is 3°W and deviation is zero. All times are BST.

1. At 1000 a navigator obtains a fix at 51°20′N 01°30′E. The boat then heads 220°T making 4kn. If the leeway due to an east wind is 4° and the tidal stream sets 150°T at 1.5kn:
   a) What is the EP at 1100?
   b) What is the true course, distance and SMG?
2. The position of a boat is fixed by a navigator at 1200 as 51°10′N 01°35′E. The boat heads for 2 miles on a course of 315°T before tacking onto 050°T for a further 3 miles until the time is 1300. If leeway is 5° due to an east wind and the tidal stream sets 135°T at 1kn:
   a) What is the EP at 1300?
   b) What is the true course, distance and SMG?
3. The navigator of a boat heading south towards Deal has taken the following bearings:

North Foreland light	355°M
North Goodwin buoy	087°M
East Brake buoy	024°M

   Plot the fix and find the latitude and longitude.
4. With the flagstaff at Walmer Castle in transit with the church immediately to the west a boat has just crossed the 20m contour. Plot the position at that moment and find the latitude and longitude.
5. The navigator of a boat has fixed the position as precisely 1.5 miles due north of the North East Goodwin buoy. What is the true course to the Quern buoy (Ramsgate Road) if:
   - leeway is 5° due to north-west wind,
   - tidal stream sets 289°T at 2kn,
   - and expected boat speed is 4kn?

For questions 6–11 use the tide table at the end of question 10.

6. At 0930 on 5 June a navigator obtains a fix at 51°08′.5N 01°25′E. For the next hour the boat heads 060°T making 3kn. Leeway due to a south-east wind is 5°. At 1030 the boat's heading is changed to 020°T while speed and leeway remain constant. Using tidal diamond N work out:
   a) The EP at 1030.
   b) The true course, distance and SMG.
7. At 1930 on 27 July a navigator obtains a fix at 51°24′·10 N 01°36′·90 E. For 1 hour the boat heads 169°T making 3 kn. Leeway due to a west wind is 4°. At 2030 the boat's heading is changed to 210°T while the speed and leeway remain constant. Use tidal diamond B to work out:
   a) The EP at 2130.
   b) The true course, distance and SMG.
8. At 1810 on 4 August a fix is obtained by Decca at 51°06′·1 N 01°19′·40 E. The boat's speed is 4kn and the leeway is 4° due to a south-easterly wind. Use tidal diamond P to work out:
   a) The magnetic course to the South Goodwin light vessel.

    b) The SMG.

    c) The ETA at the light vessel.

9. At 0455 on 12 June a fix is obtained by Decca at 51°17'·10 N 01°36'·60 E. The boat's speed is 4kn and the leeway is 3° due to a south-westerly wind. Use tidal diamond E to work out:

    a) The magnetic course to the Goodwin knoll buoy.

    b) The SMG.

    c) The ETA at the buoy.

10. At 1855 on 15 August a boat is at the entrance to Ramsgate harbour. The boat's speed is 4kn and the leeway is 3° due to a north-easterly wind. Use tidal diamond H to work out:

    a) The magnetic course to the Goodwin Fork buoy.

    b) The SMG.

    c) The ETA at the buoy.

TIDE TABLE EXTRACT (DOVER) FOR QUESTIONS 6 TO 10

Date	Time (GMT)	Height (m)
5 June	0031	6.7
	0811	0.6
	1300	6.6
	2027	0.7
27 July	0137	1.6
	0703	5.7
	1411	1.7
	1930	5.8
	0256	1.5 (28 July)
4 August	0123	6.4
	0710	1.1
	1340	6.6
	2124	1.0
12 June	0206	1.8
	0724	5.4
	1436	2.0
	1940	5.7
15 August	0554	1.1
	1042	6.4
	1818	1.0
	2254	6.4

CLASS OF LIGHT		International abbreviations	Older form (where different)	Illustration Period shown ⊢──────⊣
Fixed *(steady light)*		F		
Occulting *(total duration of light more than dark)*				
Single-occulting		Oc	Occ	
Group-occulting	*e.g.*	Cc(2)	GpOcc(2)	
Composite group-occulting	*e.g.*	Oc(2+3)	GpOcc(2+3)	
Isophase *(light and dark equal)*		Iso		
Flashing *(total duration of light less than dark)*				
Single-flashing		Fl		
Long-flashing (flash 2s or longer)		L Fl		
Group-flashing	*e.g.*	Fl(3)	GpFl(3)	
Composite group-flashing	*e.g.*	Fl(2+1)	GpFl(2+1)	
Quick *(50 to 79–usually either 50 or 60–flashes per minute)*				
Continuous quick		Q	Qk Fl	
Group quick	*e.g.*	Q(3)	Qk Fl(3)	
Interrupted quick		IQ	Int Qk Fl	
Very Quick *(80 to 159–usually either 100 or 120 –flashes per minute)*				
Continuous very quick		VQ	V Qk Fl	
Group very quick	*e.g.*	VQ(3)	V Qk Fl(3)	
Interrupted very quick		IVQ	Int V Qk Fl	
Ultra Quick *(160 or more—usually 240 to 300 – flashes per minute)*				
Continuous ultra quick		UQ		
Interrupted ultra quick		IUQ		
Morse Code	*e.g.*	Mo(K)		
Fixed and Flashing		F Fl		
Alternating	*e.g.*	Al.WR	Alt.WR	

COLOUR	International abbreviations	Older form (where different)	RANGE in sea miles	International abbreviations	Older form
White	W (may be omitted)		*Single range* *e.g.*	15M	
Red	R				
Green	G		*2 ranges* *e.g.*	14/12M	14,12M
Yellow	Y				
Orange	Y	Or	*3 or more ranges* *e.g.*	22-18M	22,20,18M
Blue	Bu	Bl			
Violet	Vi				

ELEVATION is given in metres (m) or feet (ft)		**PERIOD** in seconds *e.g.*	5s	5sec

Light characteristics   Reproduced by kind permission of H.M. Stationery Office and the Hydrographer of the Navy

CHAPTER 14

Pilotage and Passage Planning

Trinity House

The Trinity House Corporation, which is controlled by a board of elder brethren, is the culmination of the growth of pilotage since Elizabethan times. The brethren consist of master mariners from all walks of maritime life. There is a separate board controlling lighthouses. Both of these boards are supported by technical and administrative staff.

It was during the first quarter of the sixteenth century that 'marks' first began to appear, especially in the Thames estuary. Although in 1514 Henry VIII proclaimed by royal charter that Trinity House had the power to regulate pilotage it was not until the Seamarks Act of 1565 that Elizabeth I gave the corporation the authority to erect seamarks. This was followed in 1604 by James I giving Trinity House the right to compulsory pilotage.

Although the first Trinity House lighthouse was built at Lowestoft in 1609 the following two hundred years saw much coastal pilotage remain in the hands of private individuals. This is illustrated by the histories of the Nore light vessel and the Eddystone lighthouse. The former was in fact the first manned light vessel. Previously Trinity House had considered light vessels to be impractical but in 1732 two private individuals were given permission by the government to station a light vessel at the Nore in the Thames estuary and to charge tolls on passing ships. The first lighthouse on the Eddystone was built by Henry Winstanley in 1698. He died in his lighthouse when the largest storm ever to hit the British Isles destroyed the structure in November 1703. In 1709 the government granted Captain Lovett a 99 year lease to the rock with permission to build a lighthouse and charge dues on passing ships. His wooden structure, designed by John Rudyerd, was burnt down in 1755. The significance of that light was recognised by

Trinity House, which immediately placed a light vessel off the rock. John Smeaton completed a new structure in 1759 from local granite. This building stood until 1882 when it was replaced by the present structure. The remains of Smeaton's lighthouse are still to be seen on the rock.

It was George III who established the Trinity House pilot districts in 1808. However, it was not until 1836 that the government gave the corporation the power to buy out private lights compulsorily. At a time of rapidly increasing seaborne trade the importance of this to the authorities was evidenced by the purchase of the Skerries lighthouse off Anglesey for £444,000 in 1841. The government provided loans for such purchases.

Over the centuries the power of the light used in lighthouses and vessels has obviously increased. The Smeaton light on the Eddystone, with its two-tiered chandelier of twenty-four candles, was visible for 5 miles. Coal burning was impractical for all but the most sheltered shore locations. It was Argand who invented the first oil burner suitable for lighthouse use. When this was combined with the parabolic reflector, invented by William Hutchinson in 1763, a very much more powerful and reliable light was produced. This was further improved when Augustin Fresnell successfully utilised the refractive qualities of glass for lighthouse requirements. Present-day lights are powered by electricity with bulbs ranging from 150W to 3,000kW.

The numerous roles Trinity House played during the early part of the nineteenth century have now been rationalised to a certain extent. The district pilotage, for instance, passed to the control of harbour authorities as a result of the Pilotage Act of 1987. Trinity House retains responsibility for deep-sea pilotage and currently employs some 650 pilots.

The corporation is one of three lighthouse

authorities responsible for the coastline of the United Kingdom and Eire. Trinity House coverage stretches as far north as the Solway Firth on the west coast and Berwick-upon-Tweed on the east coast and includes the Channel Islands. The lighthouse service is responsible for all visual, audible, fixed and floating seamarks as well as for managing the Decca chain, radio beacons and racon. In total there are some 82 lighthouses, 11 light vessels, 6 lanbys and 550 buoys. Of the latter some 400 are lit. The operational control centre is at Harwich, and the engineer's department and depot are at East Cowes. Under the trusteeship of the Department of Transport the lighthouse service levies dues on vessels arriving at UK and Irish ports. These dues are based on tonnage. As the reliance of large commercial vessels on these lights has declined there has been pressure for owners of leisure boats to pay towards the system. So far such pressure has been successfully resisted.

Trinity House allows local harbour and port authorities to lay their own marks under its guidance. Any changes to such local buoyage must be approved by Trinity House. The corporation played a leading role in the establishment of the world-wide IALA (International Association of Lighthouse Authorities) buoyage system which replaced some thirty different systems with one common one. Its responsibility for marking special areas such as traffic separation schemes gives it a vital role to play in areas such as the Dover Straits.

Since the 1980s Trinity House has been involved in the comprehensive automation of its lights: the last light vessel was automated in 1989. It now has a fleet of eleven light vessels, including the Sevenstones and St Gowans. These vessels have to be towed to their stations because they do not have functional engines. Less than one-third of the lighthouses are now manned: the aim being complete automation by 1997. This has been made possible by the use of more reliable machinery, lighthouse tenders and a helicopter. The service has one helicopter on permanent charter and two tenders. The latter are used for surveying and marking wrecks and shoals, as well as for maintenance work on buoys.

There are three types of lighthouse. Bishop Rock, at 53.4m, is the highest of the six remaining tower lights built on isolated rocks surrounded by sea. Island lighthouses such as Coquet Island off the Northumberland coast are a short distance from the shore. The third category, shore lights, is illustrated by lights such as Dungeness and Start Point.

Although the number of floating aids is decreasing because of the improved navigation systems of commercial shipping the increasing size of such vessels has required some deep shoals to be marked. Many light vessels have been replaced by lanbys (large automatic navigation buoys). These massive steel buoys weigh about 40 tonnes, are ballasted by a further 40 tonnes of sea water and are about 12m in diameter. Other buoys are classified according to whether they are deep-water (C1) buoys or inshore (C2) buoys. The former are 15m high, weigh about 10 tonnes and are 3m in diameter. Made of 10mm welded steel they are attached by heavy chain to a 3–5 tonne cast-iron sinker. Many buoys have fog signals and some have racon. The latter gives a radar image of the buoy over a distance of 25 miles. Recent additions to the buoyage have included fast-water buoys designed to keep their positions in fast tidal streams and air-portable buoys. The latter are placed from a helicopter to mark the positions of new hazards such as wrecks.

Pilotage

Pilotage is the art of moving safely from one part of the coastline to another, using the various navigational aids and any conspicuous shore features.

Although you may carefully work out a course to steer between two points it will not necessarily take you clear of danger. This may be because of variations in the tidal stream or because of helming errors. Once within sight of the coast, chart-plotting methods alone will not suffice and you will have to supplement them with visual techniques. The various aids you might use include buoys, lights, lighthouses and beacons as well as prominent land features such as church towers, chimneys and radio masts. It is essential that you are able to recognise instantly and interpret correctly the characteristics of the navigational aids. You must familiarise yourself with the marks, hazards and safe-water channels of your home port and usual sailing area. Before you set off on a passage to a harbour you do not know well you must study thoroughly the hazards, channels and navigational aids to build up a clear mental picture of the approach. With a particularly difficult entrance a list of the equivalent buoys and beacons should be ready in the cockpit.

These marks are the navigational equivalent of the signpost. The buoyage system, which is very much the core of pilotage, is constructed in such a way as to lead the navigator from one mark to the next, away from danger.

BUOYAGE SYSTEM

Around the coastlines of northern and western Europe, including the British Isles, the system in operation is the IALA System A. This consists of lateral, cardinal and special marks which are standardised in shape, colour and relative position.

In busy commercial harbours and estuaries there are numerous closely spaced buoys and beacons because of the density of traffic. Where there is less traffic, such as in the upper reaches of an estuary or in a quiet harbour, there are far fewer marks. In the upper reaches of a river the channel may be marked not by buoys and beacons but by withies or perches (tree branches).

Most of the marks within each of the following categories have distinctive light characteristics which operate on a regular cyclical period. Familiarise yourself with these.

On a chart each mark is shown by a mini version of the relevant symbol. A tiny circle at the base of the symbol gives the true position of the mark while if it is named this is printed alongside the symbol (on larger scale charts). If the light is lit then this is shown by a magenta flash radiating from the symbol. The light characteristics are printed alongside the flash. Beacons are shown by an * if lit, and their characteristics are shown as for any other mark. If unlit they are shown by an o with the top mark indicated.

Lateral marks Primarily, these indicate the margins of a navigable channel. They delimit the channel by their position, while their colour (red for port and green for starboard) informs the navigator which side of the buoy the vessel should pass to remain within the channel. In general the direction of buoyage

is west to east along the English Channel and south to north through both the Irish and North Seas. Within coastal waters the direction is always inward from the sea. When navigating in the opposite direction to the buoyage, out of harbour for instance, you must treat the buoys in the opposite sense. Where the marks are numbered it will be upwards from the seaward end of the channel. Port marks are always given the even numbers. This is clearly illustrated by the channel east of the Dunkerque lanby shown to the north-east of Calais on chart 5055.

Port marks tend to be cylindrical and starboard conical, but this does vary. Lateral marks do not necessarily have top marks or lights. Where they do the top mark will be either a can or a cone and the light will be red or green depending on whether the mark is port or starboard. The shape of the larger steel lattice marks is difficult to make out from a distance and they can be confused with another type of mark until their top mark or light is identified. Where the channel is of less importance the buoys will probably be replaced by red and green posts driven into the seabed. Invariably referred to as beacons, these usually have a small top mark but are rarely lit.

Where the channel splits into two or more distinct sections the lateral marks are modified to indicate the preferred or main channel. A port buoy with a green horizontal band indicates that the starboard channel is the preferred route, while a red horizontal band on a starboard buoy indicates that the port channel is the preferred route.

If the channel is frequently used by commercial traffic then it may be best to keep just outside it, but *do* keep a check on the depth.

Cardinal marks These are positioned north, east, south and west of a danger such as rock, shoal or wreck. There may be more than one cardinal marking a particular danger. Each cardinal effectively guards one quadrant: so the north cardinal, for instance, guards the area between 315° (north-west) and 045° (north-east). They are black and yellow pillars or spars and have two black top marks. The specific cardinal at a given location is defined by the direction that its top marks point in, the position of its black band, and the characteristics of its light. The top marks point up for the north cardinal and down for

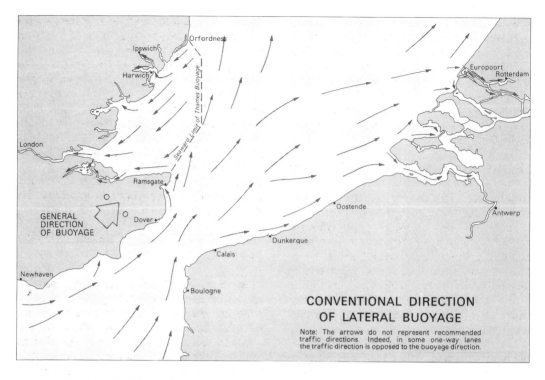

London

GENERAL
DIRECTION
OF BUOYAGE

**CONVENTIONAL DIRECTION
OF LATERAL BUOYAGE**

Note: The arrows do not represent recommended
traffic directions. Indeed, in some one-way lanes
the traffic direction is opposed to the buoyage direction.

the south cardinal. Above the west cardinal they point in towards each other while above the east cardinal they point away from each other. The colour arrangement of the four marks is equally distinctive. The north and south cardinals each have just two bands, with the black being at the top on the north cardinal and at the base on the south cardinal. The west cardinal has yellow bands at the top and bottom with black in the centre while this pattern is reversed for the east cardinal (yellow in the centre and black at the top and base). The number of light flashes for each cardinal corresponds to the clockface position of the mark. So while the north cardinal flashes continuously, the east exhibits three flashes, the south six and the west nine. All of these may be 'very quick' or 'quick' as indicated on the chart. The south cardinal also exhibits a long flash after the short.

A cardinal mark stands on its own side of the danger. In other words, if it is a north cardinal the danger lies to the south of it, so you must pass well to the north. The Long-rose Spit buoy to the east of Margate on chart 5061 illustrates this point.

Isolated danger marks As their name suggests, these are placed over an isolated danger such as a wreck, with safe water all round. They should be given a wide passage on either side. They are very distinctive, having two black balls as top mark and a white group-flashing light. By day black and red horizontal bands make them easily distinguishable once you are close to them. Like cardinals they occur either as pillars or spars.

Safe water marks These indicate an area free of hazard to navigation. They are used as landfall buoys to mark the seaward end of a buoyed channel or to mark the middle of a wide channel. Their colour is an unmistakable pattern of vertical red and white stripes on a structure that may be either a sphere, a pillar or a spar. The top mark, if fitted, will be a red sphere. If a light is fitted it will be white and either isophase, occulting, a long flash every 10 seconds or Morse A. On chart 5055 a safe water mark is shown in the centre of Rye Bay.

Special marks These are used in conjunction with the lateral and cardinal marks. They indicate the position of anything which needs marking but does not fall into one of the above categories. This includes specific dangers or safe water. They are used to indicate areas of water set aside for a specific use, such as water skiing or submarine exercises. A new, as yet uncharted danger, would also be indicated by a special mark. Special marks are always yellow and may be any shape. The top mark, if fitted, will be a yellow cross. The light, if any, will also be yellow and may exhibit any rhythm. On chart 5055 they are shown marking sewer outfalls off the English coast and the separation zones on both sides of the Channel.

Lighthouses, light vessels and beacons

Lighthouses and beacons are placed to give warning of specific dangers such as headlands or rocks. Where lighthouse construction has not been possible, for example in areas such as shifting sands, light vessels are used instead, as with the Goodwins. Both houses and vessels are progressively being automated, with some vessels being permanently replaced by lanbys and some lighthouses being switched off.

Like marks, these warnings have distinctive light, and often sound, characteristics. A light is marked on a chart by a magenta flash, alongside which are printed its characteristics. As with buoys, the precise position of lights is given by a small circle at the base of the symbol, while the position of a vessel is given by a small circle at the base of the hull.

The major characteristics common to lights around the British Isles coastline are:
– class or character of light;
– colour(s);
– period;
– elevation;
– luminous range.
Anvil Point lighthouse, for example, is shown on a chart as:
  Fl 10s 45m 24M Horn (3) 30s
This translates as follows:

Fl	Single flash.
10s	Period of light in seconds: in this case 10 seconds from the beginning of one flash to the beginning of the next flash.
45m	Elevation of the light in metres above mean high water spring.
24M	Luminous range in sea miles.
Horn (3)	3 blasts of horn.
30s	Period of horn in seconds: in this case 30 seconds from the beginning of one 3 blast sequence to the beginning of the next.

If a light colour is not indicated then you should assume it to be white. It is very useful to have either a wrist-watch with a second hand or a digital stop-watch to check the timing characteristics of a light that you have sighted. More detail will be found in the *Admiralty List of Lights* or a nautical almanac. The local pilot will also have additional data, plus detailed drawings to aid day recognition. The structure of a lighthouse is painted distinctively to help identification.

The height of a lighthouse means that in ideal visibility its loom (beam reflected back down from the sky) will be seen before the actual light becomes visible.

Leading marks, transits and clearing lines

These are either lights or significant objects and are positioned in a straight line so that a continuation of the line (transit) indicates the safe channel. A transit exists when you are trying to keep two clearly identifiable objects in line. If the objects 'open out' then you are no longer on the transit and are heading into danger. If you do drift off the line then head towards the lower of the two marks.

Leading marks are positioned at the entrance to a harbour to give a leading line along which you should approach. Some charts show these lines. The marks are usually so positioned that the projection of the line seaward indicates the safe line to take into the harbour or estuary. While you remain on that line you are safe. Once inside the harbour or estuary you follow the buoyed channel. It would be sensible to make a note of the bearing of the leading line as part of your pilotage plan so that you know the general direction in which you should be looking.

A transit is far better than a compass bearing because it lacks the ambiguity of the latter. In fact in a pilotage situation a compass bearing alone is not just useless but positively dangerous. The steering compass is often difficult to read accurately at sea and there may be local disturbances in the magnetic field because of structures in the rock of the seabed. Transits, on the other hand, are instant, visual, do not move around and are not affected by the earth's magnetic field. The moment the objects appear even the slightest distance apart the helm knows that the boat is off track and must then act instantaneously to correct the course.

Where no official transits are available you should form your own. Any readily identifiable and conspicuous shore features will suffice. You could use two towers, a church and a water tower, the end of a pier and a tower or a buoy and a tower. On chart 5061 several church towers close to Broadstairs could be used to form transits. The list of possibilities is endless. Should you use a buoy for one of your transit marks then you must appreciate that your transit will be a little less accurate because of the buoy's tendency to range slightly on its chain. You might also use two headlands, although this is not quite so easy or accurate because of the difficulty in precisely pinpointing the edge of the land.

The approach to Beaulieu river across the spit is along a leading line. The spit should be approached from the south along the transit of the two beacons that will be observed just to the west of the conspicuous boathouse.

You maintain that transit, with the entrance piles on your port side, until you have rounded the north-eastern tip of the spit. The channel westward is clearly marked by withies (posts sunk into the river bed).

The approach to the buoyed channel into the marina at Etaples (chart 5055) is well marked by lights (including a sectored light). There are also several transits available to help pilotage. A boat approaching from the west may use a transit on the high house and the church next to the railway line which will lead to the north end of the marked channel.

A clearing line allows you to keep on the safe side of a danger such as rocks just below the surface. A bearing is taken on a prominent object near the danger and then drawn, using the reciprocal, from the object on the chart. As long as you remain on the correct side of this clearing line you will keep out of danger. A second clearing line in the same

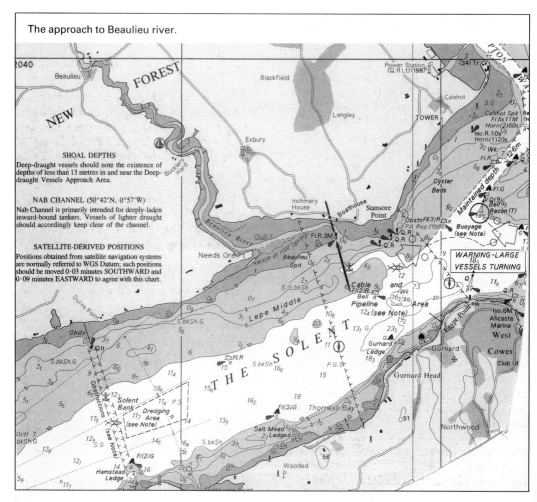

The approach to Beaulieu river.

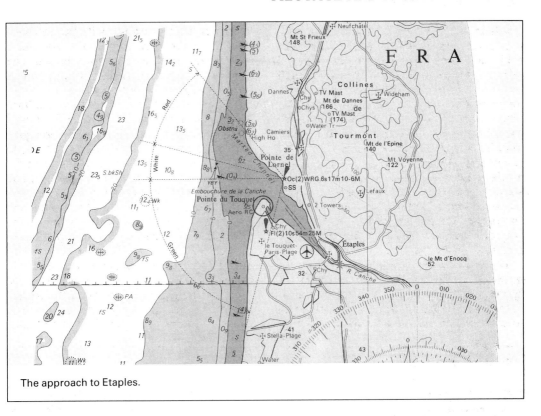

The approach to Etaples.

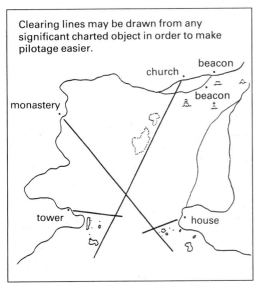

Clearing lines may be drawn from any significant charted object in order to make pilotage easier.

oided. The navigator is fortunate that there are four conspicuous objects on which to take bearings. Approaching from the south-east the navigator uses three clearing bearings to ensure that the boat does not run onto the rocks. To avoid the rocks to the east the bearing of the monastery must not be less than 320° and that of the house must not be less than 278°. Once the tower bears 072° the navigator makes towards the beacon while using a clearing bearing on the church to

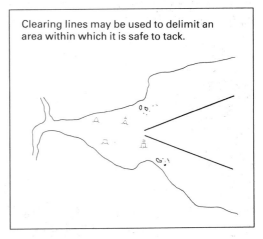

Clearing lines may be used to delimit an area within which it is safe to tack.

area will allow you to determine when you have safely passed the danger area. Transits and clearing lines may be used together.

In the diagram the two beacons provide a leading line to the beginning of the buoyed river channel. Before that line is reached there are offlying rocks and shallows to be av-

keep away from the shallows. Once the two beacons are in transit they are followed as a leading line until the buoyed channel is reached.

In much the same way two clearing lines

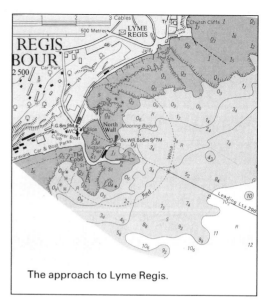

The approach to Lyme Regis.

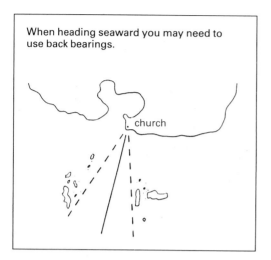

may be used to delimit the area within which a boat may safely tack. If the buoy at the river mouth bears more than 285° or less than 245° the boat will be in trouble.

If you are heading seaward out of an estuary with limited safe water and no marks to either port or starboard you will have to use a mark astern to keep you on track. This is termed a back bearing. In this instance the boat is navigated between the offlying rocks by taking a bearing on the church. As long as that bears 015° from the boat the heading is safe. If it increases to 036° or decreases to 357° the boat is heading into danger.

Leading lights help the entry into many harbours. When the lights are in transit and appear as one you know that you are in the channel. If they are not in line then you are out of the channel and must head for the lower light. Entry to Lymington at night is helped by leading lights bearing 318°T. Entry to Ramsgate (chart 5061) is assisted by leading lights bearing 270°T.

Many lights are sectored to help the navigator in the same way as transits and clearing lines. The sector visible to the navigator gives an idea as to the position of the boat: a change from one sector to another may be used to indicate the point at which to turn into a harbour or estuary. It is a convention that the bearings of the different sectors

are always given as true directions as observed from the sea.

The entrance to Lyme Regis has both leading lights and a sectored light. The transit of the lights along 296°T will take you to the seaward end of the south harbour wall (The Cobb). When approaching the harbour you should be within the red sector at all times. If you are in the white sector or cannot see either colour you are in grave danger of running aground.

The Needles light, guarding the western approaches to the Solent, is an excellent example of a sectored light. To the north the red sector covers the Shingles Bank while the green shines over the Five Fingers Rocks and the white indicates safe water. The North Foreland light (chart 5061) is similar.

Passage planning

Passage planning begins with deciding upon your destination. Even if at this stage your 'passage' is simply a round trip of the immediate coastal area you must have a plan.

You need to take into consideration the weather, the tidal streams and the experience of the crew. In the first instance do not be too ambitious by aiming for a destination too far away. An inexperienced crew are likely to become tired and frustrated if you do not arrive when expected, or do not arrive at all. The passage must be the right pace for the crew. Bear in mind that once the wind in-

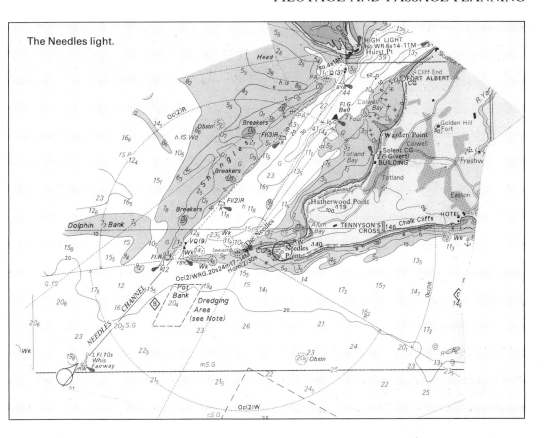

The Needles light.

creases beyond moderate a downwind course is much less tiring than sailing into the wind. When the wind exceeds force 4 the boat will heel if close-hauled or reaching and sail-changing will become progressively more difficult. Your first passages should keep well clear of any situation that could cause a problem, whether it be shoal waters or deteriorating weather. As you become more experienced so your passages may become more demanding. A 6 hour passage in shoal waters or poor visibility is too demanding for the inexperienced and may lead some to lose their interest in sailing.

It is far better to begin with short day passages to get the crew acclimatised to the boat and the rigours of sailing. Be conservative in how far you expect to get in a given period of time. The inexperienced skipper frequently underestimates how long a passage will take. You must take into consideration the suitability of the boat and its equipment for your intended passage. Once you become more adventurous you will have to ensure that there is someone on board who can act competently as skipper if you are injured or taken ill.

The time of departure is very important. Night-time departures are enjoyable but not for the inexperienced. Departure should be timed so that you gain the most from the tide. Should you be heading for another port then tides at the destination are of equal importance. You need to make sure that there is enough water to enter the harbour and that any locks or marina gates will be open. There is no point in arriving only to have to wait for 2 hours to access the mooring.

When planning a short coastal passage there are various publications to study. These include *Reed's Nautical Almanac* (or similar), the local pilot, the tidal stream atlas and the various relevant charts.

You should obtain a small-scale chart on which to plan the whole passage, and various large-scale charts for the approach to harbour and anchorage. In case of a change of plan once on passage you need charts covering those areas that are immediately adjacent to that passage. All charts must be up-to-date, with all relevant corrections in the latest *Notices to Mariners* clearly marked.

Having decided upon the general direction you must work out bearings between the major landmarks, lighthouses and buoys. Plan your course to avoid obvious hazards such as rocks, overfalls and separation zones. Work out tidal streams, especially at headlands, so that you will be going with and not against them. If you intend navigating across a tidal stream you will have to plan a course that takes this into consideration. In case of bad weather you need to note escape routes to sanctuaries such as harbours and sheltered bays. Make lists of all these features and the bearings between them. It is important to have large-scale harbour plans and any relevant port signals to make port entry easy. Lay off your course on the chart, with the compass course and distance noted on each leg. You should have a waterproof copy of all this pre-planned data available in the cockpit.

Shortly before departure you must carry out a rigorous check of the engine. The important checks are:

- *oil level in the engine and gear box;*
- *fuel level;*
- *existence of oil and fuel leaks;*
- *existence of water in the fuel;*
- *water tank full (if fresh water cooled);*
- *if sea water cooled, open the cooling water seacock if the engine is to be used immediately and check water circulation.*

It is equally important that you check the outboard if this is the auxiliary.
- *Check the spark plugs are clean and their gaps are set correctly.*
- *Check that the fuel tank and spare tank are both full.*
- *Check the oil-petrol mixture.*
- *When running observe the water outlet to ensure water is circulating properly.*

It is just because little weaknesses will gradually grow into a major fault that leads to disaster that you must make a final check on all boat and personal equipment. This includes running and standing rigging, anchor line, warps, battery, navigation lights, bilge pumps, safety equipment (flares, lifejackets, lifelines), clothes, fuel, gas, food and water.

You must carry the necessary flags to ensure that your boat is correctly 'dressed' at all times, so that you always observe flag etiquette. Flags nations use at sea are described as ensigns and may not be the same as their national flags. You will not, for instance, see the Union Jack flown from a British-registered vessel. At sea UK vessels fly the Red Ensign unless the ship's master has a special warrant to display another ensign. The Blue Ensign of HM Customs is one special ensign that you will frequently see. An ensign is flown from the stern of a vessel.

All too often the skipper of a cruising boat fails to brief the crew clearly. When the crew are inexperienced a briefing must be in plain language that avoids the use of nautical terms. Allocate a job to each crew member and explain the importance of each job to the whole crew so that you will all act as a team. Make clear the reason for and the need to follow all instructions, and that there can only be one skipper on the boat. Explain the thinking behind the different legs of the course and the significance of the different marks you are likely to encounter. It is very important that you make quite clear the function of all safety equipment on the boat and go through all the relevant safety procedures.

The right food is important for even the shortest passage. You need to stock up with more food than you expect to use and to plan your menus carefully. Fresh perishables should be put into the coolest lockers, although as purpose-made cool boxes are available for boats you should really have one of these. Cool plates are available, allowing you to convert empty lockers into refrigerated space. You should concentrate on energy-giving, nourishing food. Meals should be organised so that they are easy to prepare once you are underway. Always start the day with a good breakfast followed by frequent snacks during the passage. High energy foods such as chocolate and biscuits are vital.

Immediately before departure advise someone of your plans and make sure that they have the tear-off slip of the coastguard safety scheme card. Should you change your plans while on passage then use the radio-telephone to inform either the coastguard or your shore contact.

Finally, before you slip your mooring obtain the most up-to-date weather forecast that is available.

In the first instance you will probably head for a familiar mark just outside the harbour. Despite the apparent familiarity of this mark and the immediate area you should make no assumptions and must treat this as a pilotage situation. This means using a heading on the buoy, and clearing bearings if necessary. As soon as you are clear of the harbour set your log to zero and get onto the required heading for your first leg. When you have a steady heading and speed fix your position if possible, if not you must at least plot your EP.

When you are starting to windward you need to decide upon the best tack. Your tacks have to be planned so as to avoid hazards and to make the best of wind shifts and tidal streams. One method is to draw a 20° cone from the destination point and keep within that. Remember that a plotting or helming error of 1° will take you 1 mile off course in a 60 mile passage. The best skippers rarely manage better than a 3° error while the inexperienced will be in excess of 5°. Every time you plot your position you therefore need to put a circle of error around that position and keep well clear of any hazards within it.

For a passage of more than 3–4 hours you need a watch-keeping system. For the crew to be alert and fresh at all times they need adequate rest because passage making is mentally and physically tiring. In rough conditions, or when visibility is poor, fatigue comes on even more quickly. The more inexperienced the crew the more rapidly they will tire. The watch pattern varies from boat to boat. It is very important that experience is evenly distributed between the watches. The traditional cruising watch is one of 4 hours on and 4 hours off, with two short 'dog-watches' when the whole crew is awake. Especially on a long passage, it is important that conditions below are such that the off-duty watch can sleep without being disturbed. This means keeping noise and light to an absolute minimum. If at all possible sail changes requiring the whole crew should be carried out when they are all awake, so that no one's sleep is interrupted. The off-duty watch should be roused some 15 minutes before the beginning of their watch so that the changeover is punctual.

During the passage, however short, you must keep a log. This can either be one that you have bought from a chandler or simply an exercise book divided into the relevant columns. Most boats make do with just one log, but some have separate logs for navigation, weather and interest. The navigator's log (or the log) must start with the departure time and log reading. At hourly intervals you should record the course steered, EP and/or fix, distance run, log, wind direction and strength and barometer reading. Between these hourly records you must note any changes in heading and any navigation marks passed. As soon as a new object comes into view you should make a note of the time and its bearing from the boat. All of this information will allow you to back track more easily if you should get lost. You will find that it will add to your general enjoyment if you keep a record of interesting sights such as dolphins or rare birds. You may also like to record the names of the crew on different passages.

Remember that the log is the official record of your passage and as such can be used in a court of law if witnessed and signed.

Your first passages should not involve you in a night landfall. These are particularly difficult where the destination is unfamiliar and when the crew are tired. Your passage planning should dictate daytime landfall only, until you are more experienced. Should gear failure or deteriorating weather create a situation in which a night landfall is unavoidable then you will need to be aware of the problems. It is usually best to approach land close to dawn because you will have the benefit of the shore lights to help fix your position followed immediately by a visual view of the coast as the sun comes over the horizon. A night arrival is never easy because of the difficulty of picking out navigation lights from the background urban lights. The harbour entrance is quite likely to be marked by red and green lights, which you would expect to make the situation quite clear. However the green harbour entrance light you aim for may turn out to be the starboard light of a slow-moving boat and the red light may be the neon light of a hotel behind the harbour. In these circumstances fix your position before beginning the final approach to the harbour. This approach must be slow and deliberate with constant use of the echo sounder to check the depth. You must identify navigation lights positively. Two red lights close to the harbour may have identical or very similar characteristics and be positioned against a similar background. The danger in mistaking one for the other is quite obvious.

A daytime landfall is obviously less hazardous but not necessarily simple. Even moderate visibility may affect the profile of the coastline. Where a coastline is dominated by headlands and bays, with buildings such as coastguard lookouts and churches on some of the promontories, it will be all too easy to attempt to enter the wrong bay thinking that it is the harbour you are seeking. Take care not to jump to conclusions, especially in the identification of buoys.

Before entering the harbour you must make sure that you are aware of all the entry signals and keep a lookout for traffic, particularly if it is a commercial port. It is both courteous and sensible to contact either the harbourmaster (if a commercial port) or the marina on the VHF to seek permission to enter (if necessary) and advice on mooring. The rubric on chart 5061 makes clear the need to report your movement to Ramsgate harbour authority.

In harbour the ensign is flown from 0800 (summer) or 0900 (winter) until 2100 or sunset, whichever is the earliest. At sea it is courteous to dip the ensign, by lowering it, as a warship of any nationality passes. Keep your ensign dipped until the warship has

dipped and rehoisted her ensign. To save wear the ensign need not be displayed continuously while at sea, but it must be displayed when close to other vessels and when entering or leaving harbour.

The small triangular flag flown at the head of the mainmast is the burgee. It indicates membership of a sailing club or similar organisation. If the owner belongs to more than one club other burgees may be flown from beneath the spreaders. You will probably find that on a modern cruiser it is not possible to fly a flag from the top of the mast so all flags will be flown from the spreaders.

A cruising boat is correctly dressed when displaying the national ensign and her club burgee. When racing the ensign is not worn.

When visiting a foreign port it is courteous to fly the ensign of that country from the starboard yardarm. If an important national event is being celebrated in the country that you are visiting you should fly the ensign of that country from the masthead, or from the spreaders if that is not possible.

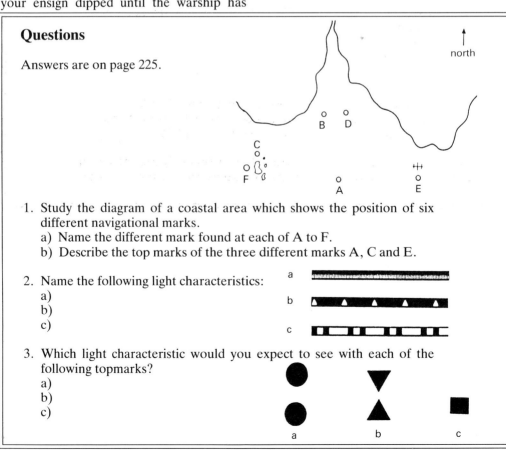

Questions

Answers are on page 225.

north

1. Study the diagram of a coastal area which shows the position of six different navigational marks.
   a) Name the different mark found at each of A to F.
   b) Describe the top marks of the three different marks A, C and E.

2. Name the following light characteristics:
   a)
   b)
   c)

3. Which light characteristic would you expect to see with each of the following topmarks?
   a)
   b)
   c)

4. Which light characteristic would you expect to see with each of the following buoys?
   a)
   b)

5. While entering a harbour you come across the following three light sequences. In each case say what type of buoy you are approaching and what action you should take.
   a)
   b)
   c)

6. How would you recognise the East Goodwin light vessel (chart 5061) in poor visibility?

7. What is the direction of buoyage to the east of Calais beyond the Dunkerque lanby? (Chart 5055.)

8. Approaching Hastings (chart 5055) you see two fixed red lights in the following positions:
   a) What do you deduce from this?
   b) What action should you take?

9. While heading due north for Ramsgate (chart 5061) in poor visibility you suddenly see a starboard lateral buoy about 100m to starboard. What quick check would confirm whether it is B1 or B2?

10. On passage due south in poor visibility you suddenly see the North Goodwin buoy (chart 5061) immediately to the north-north-west. What action should you take?

CHAPTER 15

Sail Trim and Aerodynamics

The flow of air around a sail is described as a flow field and is illustrated by streamlines. The lines give the direction of the flow, while the spacing of the lines indicates the speed. The closer the spacing the faster the flow. The velocity of the air determines the local air pressure, according to Bernouilli's law. This considers air to act as a fluid, and states that the pressure in a fluid is constant while the speed is constant. The pressure will fall as the speed increases and will increase as the speed falls. The streamlines behave in a different manner according to the number of sails set. The following discussion considers the dynamic flow around the typical headsail and mainsail rig.

The two sails must be considered to act as a single airfoil and not as two separate shapes. The streamlines approaching the boat have a uniformity in their spacing which suggests a constancy in flow velocity. Some distance in front of the rig the flow begins to divide, with some flowing to leeward of the headsail and some to windward of the mainsail. The air between these two flows moves through the slot between the sails. The streamline that separates the flows above and below the airfoil is the stagnation streamline. You will observe that while the spacing of any two streamlines alters as they pass over the airfoil they return to their original spacing on leaving the airfoil.

The deflection of the air from its path is described as upwash or downwash according to the direction in which it has been deflected. The upwash is greater in front of the headsail than in front of the mainsail. It is the upwash in front of a sail that produces lift.

Close-hauled with genoa lead well aft. Air from the leech of the genoa is causing backwind in the luff of the mainsail.

Running with the spinnaker boom well aft and a headsail set to reduce the power of the spinnaker.

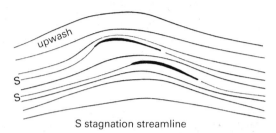

S stagnation streamline

Streamlines showing the flow of air over main and headsail. Upwash is prominent in front of the headsail.

What happens next is not perfectly understood. There is general agreement that flow velocity is at its greatest on the leeward side so that pressure there is therefore lower than on the low velocity windward side. There is not total agreement as to the precise reason for the velocity difference and consequent pressure difference across the sail surface.

Air is essentially lazy in its movement and will resist any change in direction to the extent of taking the line of least resistance. The air forced to leeward of the headsail will therefore change direction as little as possible in order to pass around the leading edge of the airfoil. The streamlines therefore converge as they pass the headsail luff. This leads to high velocity and, as governed by Bernouilli, lower pressure along the leeside leading edge. Meanwhile the air passing to windward behaves in a very different manner. The streamlines spread out, showing the reluctance of the air to flow directly into the draft. The flow therefore slows and produces high pressure. It is this pressure difference acting against the surface of the sail from the high pressure (windward) side to the low pressure (leeward) side that provides the aerodynamic force which drives and heels the boat.

The mast and mainsail act to deflect some air over the leeside of the headsail which would otherwise have passed over the mainsail. This creates higher speeds and therefore lower leeside pressures and so increases the pressure difference.

Aerodynamic research shows quite clearly that in order to maintain balanced flow around the airfoil the air must leave the leech with equal speed and pressure either side of the stagnation line. This might seem unlikely because the faster moving air on the leeward side must decelerate once it has passed the luff while the slower air on the windward side would accelerate. By the time the leech was reached the speed/pressure differentials at the luff would have been reversed and they would not be equal either side of the stagnation line.

Empirical and theoretical research shows that the required balance is created by air circulating around the airfoil in a clockwise direction. This flow is known as circulation flow. On the windward side it flows in the opposite direction to the non-circulation flow and so leads to lower speeds. On the leeward side the circulation flow reinforces the non-circulation flow so that the speed is increased. There is therefore equal speed and pressure either side of the stagnation streamline.

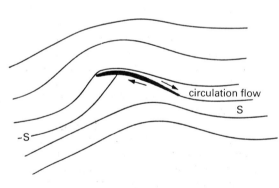

Circulation flow around a single sail. On the windward side this is in opposition to the streamlines.

Awareness of the balanced nature of the flow around correctly set sails will help you to realise the potential of your rig.

Recent research has forced a fresh consideration of the slot effect. The simple argument that it allows a proportion of air passing to windward of the headsail to be channelled to the leeward surface of the mainsail so that it reinforces the flow on that surface and delays possible stall no longer holds true. Neither is it correct to argue that the slot produces a Venturi effect such that the flow accelerates through the slot so further lowering pressure on the leeside of the mainsail and thereby increasing lift.

The flow through the slot is slowed by friction, with separated air peeling off the mast and the two sail surfaces. On entering the slot this friction slows the air, the opposite of the alleged Venturi effect. It is only as the air reaches the aft part of the slot that it accelerates back to the velocity of the free air.

The acceleration or deceleration along a sail surface produces a pressure gradient in a lateral direction along the surface. The greater this gradient the more turbulent the airflow and the more it separates from the airfoil surface so as to produce a stall. While the stagnation streamline for the mainsail goes straight into the mast there is no need for significant upwash ahead of the mainsail. This means that the air does not have to deflect so far in order to pass onto the leeward side, and the acceleration is not as great as that over the leading edge of the headsail. The pressure along the luff is therefore not as low as might otherwise be expected. The lateral pressure gradient along the leeside towards the leech is therefore also less than expected. This is because the air does not have to slow down as much in order to reach the velocity of the free air by the time that it exits the leech. This relatively small pressure gradient is significant because it creates a smoother airflow, making separation and stall less likely.

The point at which the streamlines are closest together on the leeward surface is the point of lowest pressure. The centre of lift will therefore be in that area. Should the draft in that area be increased then the air will find it very difficult to cling to the surface and will therefore separate from the leeward surface as it is drawn on by its own momentum. A turbulent flow is therefore created on that side with a consequent fall in pressure and an increase in frictional drag. It is this decrease in the pressure difference between the two sides that leads to decreased lift and consequent stalling.

Of probably even greater significance is the fact that the sails are very sensitive to the

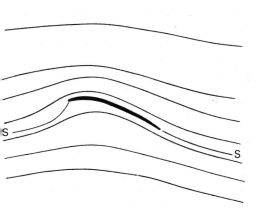

It is important to maintain an angle of attack to the wind that gives a smooth flow over the sail so that a stall is avoided.

angle of attack to the wind. If the helm bears off the wind the angle of attack will increase so that the stagnation streamline hits the windward surface of the sail instead of hitting the airfoil straight on. The apparent wind will therefore accelerate rapidly in order to pass onto the leeside but then has to decelerate rapidly in order to leave the leech at a velocity close to that of the free airflow. The air will therefore separate from the leeside and cause the sail to stall. If the helm heads up into the wind the angle of attack will decrease so that the stagnation streamline will go into the leading edge of the leeside. This will probably cause the pressure on that side to be greater than on the windward side and so the sail will luff. The disadvantage of not maintaining a steady angle of attack is that the pressure on both sides of the leading edge of the airfoil will constantly change so the sail will not maintain a stable shape. The result is turbulence and reduced drive.

The width of the slot must always be taken into consideration when adjusting the various sail controls. If the slot is too wide the sails will effectively become two separate air-foils and have an increased tendency to stall. If the slot becomes too narrow not enough air will pass through to the leeward side and there will be pronounced turbulence and drag on that side.

It is because modern cruisers typically have overlapping headsails that the relation-ship between the two sails and the slot be-comes even more important. If the genoa is allowed to hook to windward it will reduce the width of the slot and so reduce the amount of air passing along the leeside of the mainsail. The leech will then drive air into the leeside of the mainsail luff and create tur-bulence and drag as it interferes with the airfoil shape of the mainsail. When the over-lap is small the slot will be too wide. When the overlap is large the slot will be too narrow.

Apparent wind

Sitting in the cockpit of a moored boat you will sense the true wind on your body. This is the movement of air produced by the atmos-pheric pressure gradient. You will also see it in the motion of flags, trees and smoke.

Once you begin to move through the air you create your own wind. Ride a motor cycle at speed and you will feel this apparent wind quite clearly. The apparent wind is a combination of the true wind and the force that you create as you move through the air. The electronic wind indicator in your cockpit and the tell-tales on the sails show the direction of the apparent wind.

If you motor due north, say, on a calm day you will feel the apparent wind head-on. The velocity of this wind will increase as your speed increases so that when you are moving at 5kn the apparent wind will be 5kn. If the true wind were then to develop from, say, due west, you would still sense only one wind but it would then be a combination of the true wind and that produced by your movement. The apparent wind so formed is a resultant of the two winds; it comes from a point forward of the true wind.

The velocity and direction of the apparent wind may be established by drawing a paral-lelogram using the speed and direction of the boat and the true wind, drawn to scale. The direction of the apparent wind will be given by the angle that the diagonal makes with the boat's heading, while the length of the diagonal gives the velocity of the apparent wind.

While it is not essential to know the direc-tion of the true wind the helm should have a definite awareness of the apparent wind di-rection and strength, and must have an un-derstanding of how that will change as the heading of the boat changes.

The apparent wind will be forward of the true wind except when the latter is either dead ahead or dead astern. When the true wind direction is greater than 100° to the bow

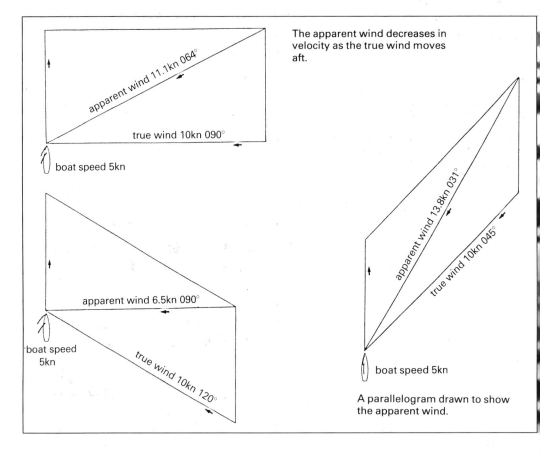

The apparent wind decreases in velocity as the true wind moves aft.

apparent wind 11.1kn 064°

true wind 10kn 090°

boat speed 5kn

apparent wind 6.5kn 090°

boat speed 5kn

true wind 10kn 120°

apparent wind 13.8kn 031°

true wind 10kn 045°

boat speed 5kn

A parallelogram drawn to show the apparent wind.

then the apparent wind speed will be less than that of the true wind. When the true wind speed is increasing in strength the boat speed will also increase, although at a slower rate. The effect of this will be to increase the apparent wind velocity and to bring it further aft.

As the true wind moves aft the apparent wind will decrease in velocity. This means that on a run you will not have a clear idea of what the wind strength would be were you to be going upwind in the same conditions. While you are heading downwind the apparent wind will be equal to the true wind minus the boat speed. If the true wind is 18kn and the boat speed 7kn then the apparent wind would be 11kn – a moderate breeze. Should your passage require you at that moment to turn upwind then you would be faced with very different conditions. The boat speed would probably fall to about 5kn, so that in the same true wind the apparent wind would increase to over 20kn. With more than double the downwind apparent wind that you just experienced you will then be in a strong breeze and

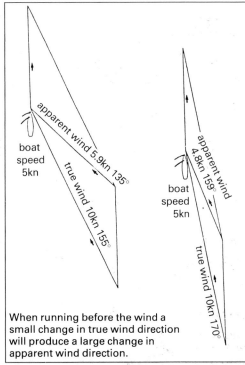

boat speed 5kn

apparent wind 5.9kn 135°

true wind 10kn 155°

apparent wind 4.8kn 159°

boat speed 5kn

true wind 10kn 170°

When running before the wind a small change in true wind direction will produce a large change in apparent wind direction.

Navigation lights and sound signals.

1 Sound signals are shown coming from vessels.
2 All signals are repeated at intervals of not more than two minutes.
3 All vessels are shown underway except those at anchor.
4 Consult the RYA booklet G2 'International regulations for preventing collisions at sea' for detailed variations to the above.

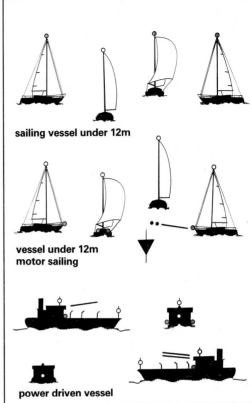

sailing vessel under 12m

vessel under 12m motor sailing

power driven vessel

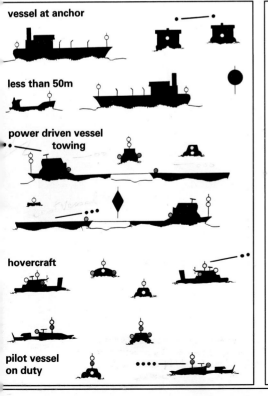

vessel at anchor

less than 50m

power driven vessel towing

hovercraft

pilot vessel on duty

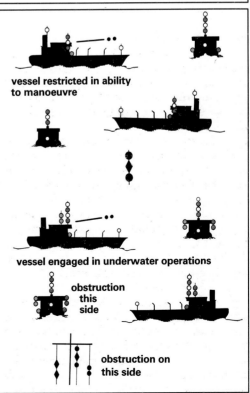

vessel restricted in ability to manoeuvre

vessel engaged in underwater operations

obstruction this side

obstruction on this side

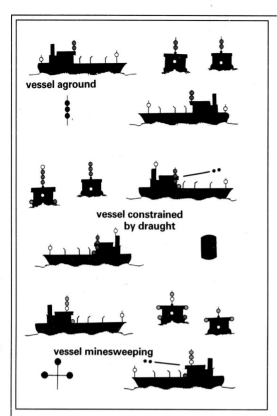

vessel aground

vessel constrained by draught

vessel minesweeping

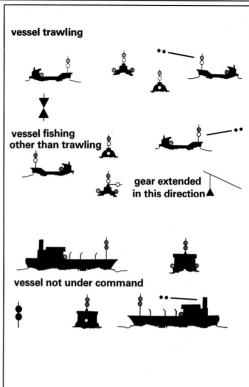

vessel trawling

vessel fishing other than trawling

gear extended in this direction

vessel not under command

Cowes, during Cowes Week.

may well need to reduce sail. The change in apparent wind may well take the inexperienced crew by surprise. You would be well advised to consider shortening sail before turning from a run to a beat.

When the velocity of the wind doubles, the force of that wind on the sails increases fourfold. The pressure on the sails is therefore increased fourfold, so the heeling moment is considerably increased as you go from run to beat. This helps to explain the sensation of suddenly feeling overpowered as you change heading.

When the true wind is well aft only a small change in true wind will produce a large change in apparent wind direction. The change in the apparent wind direction may be twice that of the true wind. This is one of the reasons why sailing downwind can be difficult. The helm only has to wander slightly from side to side of the course to cause the apparent wind to swing wildly back and forth. It is such movement that leads to the rolling motion that is both typical of a run and so dangerous.

On a beam reach, or when close-hauled, the apparent wind velocity is always greater than that of the true wind. This means that you are effectively making your own wind. This helps to explain why reaching is in fact the fastest point of sailing.

Sail draft and shape

Draft is the key to correct sail setting. The problem is that the often quoted rule of deep draft in light airs and a flat sail in strong winds does not hold true for every situation. If it were only the wind strength and direction relative to the boat that were significant then the rule would apply in all conditions. The state of the sea and the shape of the boat also have an important role to play.

The effect of driving into a wave is to slow the boat. If this happens at regular intervals, as is likely, then it follows that the boat will be constantly decelerating as it hits waves and accelerating between them. When the waves are coming thick and fast the overall boat speed will be drastically reduced. In this situation you need to sacrifice a certain amount of pointing ability by using a deeper draft to provide sufficient propulsion to drive through the waves without being slowed too much. If the boat is relatively beamy or has a

shallow keel the need for the powerful sail shape is even greater.

A boat with a more streamlined hull, sailing upwind through smooth water, will get close to its hull speed in a wind no stronger than force 3. The reason for this is simply that the smooth water offers minimum resistance to the hull. Setting a full sail in such conditions would generate more energy but little of that would be converted to forward speed because the boat would already be close to its hull speed. The excess energy would therefore be converted to heeling power which, because it creates increased drag, would lead to a reduction in speed. In light to moderate winds with smooth water you would therefore be advised to set a flat sail.

Sail trim

Sails provide the primary propulsion of the auxiliary cruiser. To get the most enjoyment from your sailing and to maximise passage speed you need to set the sails so that, as near as possible, they are the perfect shape for the given wind and sea conditions. Although there are many detailed texts on the subject it is the feel of the boat at any one moment that will tell you if you are getting the most from it. In the same way that a car driver will feel the lack of performance from a car which is misfiring, the experienced crew will feel hesitancy or stiffness in a boat when the performance is not maximised.

There are relatively clear theories as to how the sails should be set for different conditions and on different points of sailing. The more experienced you become the more you will realise that no two boats or sets of conditions are identical: what makes one boat perform to the limit of its ability on one point of sailing may not suit another boat. You will also realise that the experts do not always agree.

Although there are obviously a limited number of physical controls on sail trim these are all interdependent, to the extent that altering one will require an alteration of at least one other. There are so many possible combinations that all you can hope to achieve is an understanding of the basic theories so that you can progressively adapt these to your boat and the various sea and wind conditions that you may be faced with.

There is perhaps more jargon used by

crew, sailmakers and designers in this field than in any other aspect of sailing. You need to be able to work confidently with these terms in order to develop fully the performance of your boat.

CAMBER OR DRAFT
This is curvature of the sail.

CHORD
This is the straight-line distance between luff and leech.

CAMBER OR CHORD RATIO
This is the ratio between the sail's maximum depth and the chord. It is described as the camber or draft of the sail or simply the amount of fullness. If the chord is 150″ and the draft 15″ then the ratio is 10%. A full sail, achieved by shortening the chord, has a higher ratio than a flat one.

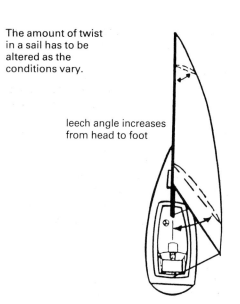

The amount of twist in a sail has to be altered as the conditions vary.

leech angle increases from head to foot

may be up to 300%, while the wind at the mast top may be veered by as much as 20°.

SLOT
This refers to the gap between the headsail and the main, and the flow of air between the two.

WEATHER HELM
This describes the situation in which the boat rounds up into the wind as you free the helm. The amount of weather (or lee) helm is measured as the angle between the rudder and the centreline. It develops when the centre of effort of the sails is aft of the centre of lateral pressure of the underwater shape. A small amount of weather helm, up to about 5°, is desirable because it will help you to point. You should not have more than this figure because the rudder will then have such a steep angle of entry into the water that it will create excessive drag. The usual cause of excessive weather helm is a leech that is too closed or a mainsheet that is too tight. Excessive heel will also produce weather helm.

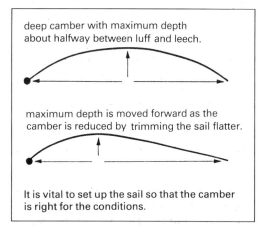

deep camber with maximum depth about halfway between luff and leech.

maximum depth is moved forward as the camber is reduced by trimming the sail flatter.

It is vital to set up the sail so that the camber is right for the conditions.

TWIST
This describes the situation in which the leech does not present a constant angle from foot to head. The changing angle or twist is observed from beneath the boom, by looking along the leech from clew to head. The amount of twist is determined by mainsheet trim and the position of the traveller.

SHEAR
This describes the situation in which friction with the surface of the earth causes the wind to be backed and reduced in velocity compared to the wind at a higher altitude. This difference is noticeable even between deck level and mast top. Differences in wind speed

LEE HELM
This is the tendency for the boat to head off the wind when you free the helm. It results in a loss of lift from the rudder surface and is not desirable in any situation.

The controls

It is important that every sail produces its

maximum efficiency on each and every point of sailing. It is just because windward performance is the most sensitive to sail shape and set that the mainsail, the key driving force in most small boats, is designed to maximise its close-hauled characteristics. You will use the various controls to maximise the effectiveness of the sail when not beating. Adjusting the controls will allow you to change through a variety of sail shapes.

Although the various sail controls are interdependent it is useful to learn how they work in isolation. Only then will you begin to appreciate the intricate interrelationships that exist.

BACKSTAY

This is usually adjustable by means of a small wheel fitted towards the base of the stay. Slackening the backstay will slacken the headstay, which therefore sags to leeward while the mast bends forward. This helps to produce a full shape in the sail with a round entry and maximum draft in the centre. This gives increased power but decreased pointing ability. The resulting closure of the leech will also lead to an increase in weather helm when you have an overlapping genoa set. You will tend to slacken the backstay when heading downwind because power is then more important than pointing ability. Tensioning the backstay will have the opposite effect: decreased power but improved pointing. This is because you have brought the maximum draft forward to a distance about one-third behind the luff. You have also lengthened the chord and therefore reduced the ratio and flattened the sail. This moves the flow further aft in the sail and opens the leech.

LOWER SHROUDS

These hold the mast in place by supporting it against potential lateral movement. Downwind these are particularly important because they act against the thrust of the spinnaker pole when reaching. The mast will lean to leeward if they are set up too slack. On the other hand if they are too tight the top of the mast will lean over them.

MAINSAIL CONTROLS

Mainsail halyard This controls creases in the sail and the draft position. The airflow over the sail will be disturbed and therefore less efficient if there are creases in the sail. Insufficient tension will cause diagonal creases radiating from clew to luff. Too much tension will lead to creases in the luff parallel to the mast.

As the wind strengthens you need a flatter sail with the drive further forward. We have seen that tensioning the backstay flattens the sail but it also takes the draft further aft. You need to increase the halyard tension at the same time so that you keep the drive as far forward as required.

Kicking strap This control is particularly important when sailing off the wind. When either running or reaching both the mainsheet and traveller are eased out. With the traveller at its leeward limit any further easing of the mainsheet will cause the boom to lift and the leech to open and twist. Tensioning the kicking strap restricts the lifting motion of the boom and so reduces these tendencies. You should not overtension the kicking strap because that will create turbulence at the leech by closing it too far. When the kicking strap is too slack the drive will be lost because the air will leave the upper part of the leech too early.

When heading upwind a tensioned kicking strap will flatten the lower half of the mainsail and so open the slot. In light to medium winds the kicking strap should be slackened to increase drive.

Mainsheet and traveller In combination these are used to form the shape of the sail. The mainsheet controls the twist in the leech while the traveller controls both the angle of attack of the sail to the wind and the width of the slot. The prime task of the leech is to ensure that the airflow leaving the sail is smooth. Any turbulence will increase drag and therefore reduce speed.

When conditions allow the boat's balance to be of only secondary importance the sheet may be kept very tight so that the leech is closed. The tension should be fine-tuned so that the top leech tell-tale is just flowing. When it collapses you have too much tension.

A closed leech in a strengthening wind will increase heel because the air cannot easily escape from the sail. If you allow this to continue unchecked your speed will fall because of decreased forward drive and increased hull drag. At the same time weather helm will increase and the boat will become increasingly difficult to steer. To reduce heel you need to reduce the effectiveness of the upper part of the leech. You will achieve this by either easing the sheet or moving the traveller to leeward. We have already seen that tensioning the backstay will have the same effect. Opening the leech will allow the air to escape from the sail and so reduces heel.

In light airs the weight of the boom will tend to close the leech even when the sheet is relatively slack. Set like this the sail will not respond properly to a puff because the straight set of the sail will cause turbulence and therefore drag. The traveller needs to be moved to windward to open the leech and produce a more laminar flow. This causes the sheet to be angled away from the traveller, thus allowing the boom to lift more easily and therefore twist the leech during a puff. As the wind strength increases you will have to ease the traveller to leeward, as suggested previously.

As you go further off the wind the kicking strap will increasingly be used to control twist rather than the sheet.

Leech line You should tighten this just enough to prevent the edge of the leech fluttering. Do not overtighten it because that will hook the leech to windward and increase drag. Whilst running you can tighten the leech line significantly because that will deepen the draft.

Cunningham This is a more practical control for bringing the draft forward in stronger winds than is the halyard. Easing the cunningham moves the draft aft and so gives the powerful shape that you require in light airs.

Clew outhaul The correct adjustment of this allows the foot of the mainsail to be set to the required shape. Increased tension flattens the foot, while easing increases the depth.

Leech tell-tales These give you more information about the efficiency of sail trim than a cockpit full of instruments. Four strips of light spinnaker cloth, each about 20cm long, are placed along the length of the leech (normally, one close beneath each batten pocket). If these stream aft then there is a smooth laminar flow over the sail with little

turbulence. When the angle of attack to the wind is too large the airflow across the leech begins to separate from the sail. If you do not correct this by easing the sheet or by heading up to the wind the set of the sail will progressively deteriorate, with separation spreading across the sail. The turbulence created by this separation will lead to the formation of vortices around the leech, indicated by the leeward tell-tales flying forward and lying close to the sail. When air completely separates from the leeside it is stalled and forward drive is drastically reduced.

Topping lift This has little to do with the set of the sail: its primary function is to prevent the boom falling onto the deck. In very light airs it is used to take the weight of the boom off the sail. In all conditions you must avoid setting it too tight because that will create a permanently open leech.

HEADSAIL CONTROLS

Halyard This is eased to keep the draft aft in light airs, and tensioned to bring it forward in stronger winds. If the tension is too high a fold will appear parallel to the headstay, running from head to tack. If the tension is eased too much the leech will close and folds will run from luff to clew.

Sheet lead Probably the most important part of the set of the sail is the positioning of the sheet lead. The correct position is determined by a combination of wind strength, angle of attack to the wind and sea state. The lead is moved forward when you require greater depth in light airs. The immediate effect of this will be to close the leech so much that the tell-tales no longer break together. You should attempt to alter the lead so that they lift in unison. When the lower ones break first the lead should go aft, and when the upper ones break first it should go forward. Easing the sheet will also help to unify the lift of the tell-tales. This does have the negative effect of widening the slot, so if you have an inner track you should transfer to that in order to maintain slot width. Most medium-sized cruisers only have one track so you will have to accept the reduction in slot width. As the wind strengthens you will have to move the lead aft to help flatten the sail. You will also have to tension the sheet to ensure that all the tell-tales break together.

When sailing off the wind the lead needs to go forward because the leech will open as you ease the sheet and the head of the sail will then spill air. Moving the lead outboard (if possible) will close the leech sufficiently for the luff to have a uniform angle of attack. If the sea should become heavier you will need to position the lead further forward to produce greater drive from a deeper sail. On a boat which does not have an outboard track the slot will be reduced because you have eased the mainsheet. This leads to backwinding of the mainsail which is why, if possible, you should move to an outboard track to keep the slot open. Inevitably, if you cannot control the backwind the performance of the main will suffer.

Many cruisers have roller-reefing headsails, which make sail handling that much easier. The leech will open as you roller-reef so you will have to move the lead forward to close it again. Failure to do so will lead to increased weather helm.

Leech line This is used to control flutter along the leech.

Tell-tales These should be positioned about 20cm from the luff at roughly one-third, one-half and two-thirds height above the foot, measured along the luff. The leeward tell-tales are the most important because the flow over the leeward side determines the amount of power developed by the sail. Even dark threads are not easy to see through the sail so you should have at least one small window in the sail at a point where you have a tell-tale.

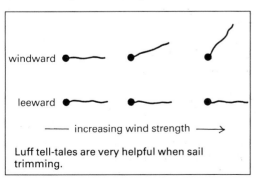

windward

leeward

⟵ increasing wind strength ⟶

Luff tell-tales are very helpful when sail trimming.

With smooth laminar flow all six tell-tales will flow smoothly aft. When heading upwind you must consider the windward and leeward tell-tales separately. The latter must fly

smoothly aft, but those on the windward side will be affected more by the wind strength and sea state. In light airs they should parallel those on the leeward side, but as the wind increases they will progressively turn upwards. In moderate wind and sea they will fly at an angle of 30°–40° to the horizontal. In an increasing sea the effect of the waves stopping the boat, and its subsequent acceleration, will increase the airflow across the headsail so those on the windward side will turn up less than they do in light conditions. If the windward tell-tales turn upwards more than you would expect for the conditions then it will be because the boat is being sailed too close to the wind. The solution is to bear away. If you bear away too much the leeward tell-tales will turn upwards or even flow forward. This is because the sail has stalled in the turbulent flow of the leeward surface. You will then have to ease the sheets or head up again. The leeward tell-tales should always fly horizontally, irrespective of wind strength, when beating and reaching.

The tell-tales also help to determine the accuracy of the lead position. If only the lower windward tell-tale flutters when luffing then the lead is too far forward. When it is too far aft it will be the upper windward tell-tale which breaks first. When all three on the leeward side respond in an identical manner then the lead position is correct.

Beating

LIGHT AIRS

Sailing in these conditions is very difficult and requires a great amount of patience. You have to concentrate thoroughly on every aspect of the weather and tidal stream to utilise them to your advantage.

The wind strength will be so low that the sails hang slack and have virtually no drive. If left like this they will provide little acceleration when a puff does come. To resolve this you need to heel the boat to leeward so that the weight of the cloth will force the sail into a more powerful camber. This will allow acceleration to occur when a puff arrives. A further benefit from such artificial heel is a reduction in the drag produced by the motion of the hull through the water. Such a drag is greater at low speeds, so it is essential that you lift as much of the hull out of the water as possible. To lift more of the windward hull

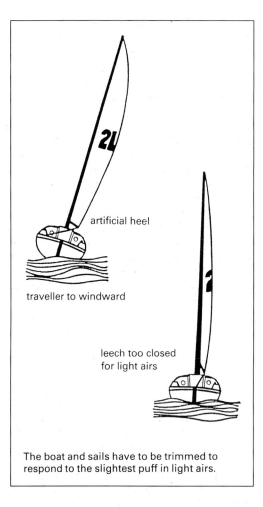

artificial heel

traveller to windward

leech too closed
for light airs

The boat and sails have to be trimmed to
respond to the slightest puff in light airs.

they will increase both rudder and hull drag. For similar reasons you should adjust sheets carefully and slowly. Just one jerk of the sheet will cause the airflow on the leeward side to separate. During the two or three seconds that it will take for it to reattach itself you will lose all momentum. You cannot alter the sheets fast enough to match the wind shifts so you will need to play constantly with them. In such conditions where constant slight alterations are required, winches are more efficient than hands.

In light airs the sail must be kept working as a lifting surface because an aerodynamic surface is more likely to stall at low speed. Stalling massively decreases forward drive and does little for balance. A boat will accelerate only slowly in light winds so you must do all you can to keep it moving. This means that you must obtain every ounce of power from the sails.

Mainsail In light airs, between 5 and 10kn, the mainsail should be set to its maximum depth, with the deepest part of the camber about half-way between luff and leech. The cunningham should be eased off to the point of putting wrinkles in the luff. If you were to tension the cunningham the draft would go right the way forward and form a depression along the mast. A puff would be unable to follow such a deep curve and would therefore fail to produce lift. The outhaul should be similarly slack, perhaps pulled about half-way out. The leech should be open, because if it is too tight it will cause excessive drag as the air attempts to flow off the sail. The aft third of the sail should hook slightly to windward to induce a little weather helm. The mainsail traveller should be slightly to windward so that the boom is positioned close to the centreline without having to oversheet, which would cause the battens to hook to windward and the leech to tighten. The purpose of centring the boom is to increase pointing ability in conditions which tend to reduce pointing by as much as 10° when compared with a moderate wind. If you find that a puff tends to generate leeway rather than forward drive you will need to position the traveller a little to leeward. Circumstances may dictate that you position it all the way to windward so that you have the sheet running at an angle. In a faint puff, this would encourage the boom to lift far more easily than if the

out of the water than you submerge the leeward side the crew sits on the leeward side of the boat. Shifting the weight of the crew forward will be even more effective in reducing the wetted surface because while you are lifting the relatively wide transom out of the water it is the narrower bow section that is being submerged. All of this gives a nett reduction in wetted surface, reduced friction and therefore reduced drag. A further benefit from heeling like this is that it will create slight weather helm and give more lift to the rudder so that it is easier to steer than might otherwise be the case at such slow speed. You need a little weather helm to allow some progress to windward. Lee helm in light airs must be avoided because it will produce excessive drag.

Never try to point too high in light airs because that will reduce your speed. You must also avoid rapid tiller movements because

sheet was perpendicular to the boom. The action of the boom rising causes the leech to open. Releasing the kicking strap will also help this action.

In light airs it is vital that you keep the sails at the correct angle to the wind. A slight increase in wind speed is much more significant at low speed than high. There is a 25% increase in velocity when the wind strengthens from 4 to 5kn, compared with a 5% increase when it moves from 20 to 21kn. With a 25% increase the increase in apparent wind may be as much as 35%.

When you have the correct set in the sails the top batten will either parallel the boom or be up to 5° from it. The lower battens may be well to weather without causing the sail to stall. When you are too close to the wind the luff will tend to bulge. If you stray too far off the wind the leeside tell-tales will start twirling. Both situations lead to a significant drop in the drive produced by the sails. Wandering between the two will also reduce the boat's speed.

Headsail This must be set to a full shape with maximum draft in the centre of the sail so that the weak air will pass across the sail without stalling. This will allow you to obtain the maximum drive possible from the genoa. To allow the air to flow easily between the genoa and mainsail you need more twist than would be desirable in a stronger wind. This will open the slot and ease the airflow. To achieve this shape ease the halyard until diagonal folds begin to appear just behind the luff. To increase the draft you need to move the fairlead further forward. This may cause the leech to close, in which case you should ease

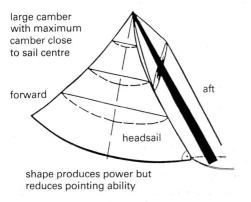

large camber with maximum camber close to sail centre

forward

aft

headsail

shape produces power but reduces pointing ability

A powerful sail shape is more important than pointing ability in light airs.

the sheet slightly. You may find the weight of the sheet alone is enough to collapse the leech. If you do not have lightweight sheets then try holding the sheet close to the clew.

The flow over the mainsail is dependent on the flow over the genoa. As you ease the latter its head will twist out and therefore widen the upper slot. This causes the apparent wind for the upper part of the mainsail to swing aft rapidly. You must therefore twist out the upper part of the mainsail at the same time if the mainsail is not to stall. During a puff, regardless of strength, the apparent wind will move aft so that heel increases and drive decreases. This movement is more significant in light airs because of the proportionately greater increase of wind speed for a given velocity. The angle of attack alters as the apparent wind moves aft, so the sail will no longer be correctly trimmed. To rectify this you must either head into the wind or ease the sheet or traveller. Which action you take depends on whether your priority is to maintain heading or to maintain speed.

When the true wind drops the apparent wind comes forward so that the sail begins to luff. The inexperienced helm may believe that the problem is one of pointing too high. Assuming that a constant heading has been maintained the boat will either be going through a hole in the wind or is being headed by the wind. If it is a hole then heading off will kill the boat's speed, so the best action will be to use the boat's momentum to get through the hole and to pick up the breeze on the other side. When it is a wind shift you should head off so as to fill the sails. If you are not sure whether it is a hole or a header you should try bearing away about 25° from the wind. If the sails still luff then it is probably a hole. Your movement through 25° must be gentle because if it is too rapid you will force air against the leeside of the sail so that the luff effect becomes even more pronounced and backwind may develop. At that stage you will probably become very confused as to the wind direction.

In a puff the apparent wind will go aft so the sail will tend to stall unless you head up. When the wind goes aft this is described as 'lifting' and you are being 'lifted'. You should recognise a puff because of the cat's-paws on the surface of the water.

When a header makes you tack, remember

that the turning movement will bring the apparent wind aft so that the genoa will fill again before you are properly into the tack. That may give you the false impression that the wind has shifted back again. Should you think that you have been lifted, and so decide to stop the tack, you will find yourself back on the original course facing the same header.

When the boat feels underpowered increase the draft and the drive-to-heel ratio by easing both sails and falling off the wind by 10°–15°. This will increase the angle of attack and therefore the power developed by the genoa. On a long passage in light airs this will significantly increase your speed made good.

In the section on draft and shape it was made clear that the boat will retain its speed more easily in smooth water. In such conditions you may therefore adjust the controls so that you have a significantly flatter headsail and mainsail. The advantage of the flatter shape is that the air will not have to deviate far from its path in order to attach to the sail, whereas with the fuller shape a puff has to make a larger turn in order to attach itself to the leeward side. The result is that with the fuller shape it does not attach so easily. To obtain the flatter shape the lead needs to be further aft.

MODERATE BREEZE

A moderate breeze gives the best sailing conditions, in which the mainsail is very stall resistant. As the wind strengthens from a light breeze you should sail a little off the wind with the sails slightly fuller. When you get to the point at which you do not need to create artificial heel and the crew have to be on the weather side then you should begin to flatten the sail. A streamlined hull will require a flatter sail earlier than will a beamy hull. With the latter you should briefly delay any significant change of trim. A heavy sea would also require such delay.

Mainsail The luff tension should be increased to reduce the draft and to bring it further forward. The tension should be just enough to hold the draft near the middle of the mainsail. You do not want it too far forward because that will increase backwind and over-flatten the sail so that less power is produced. You shoud also increase tension on the outhaul to flatten the lower third of the mainsail.

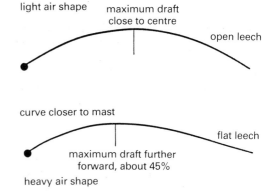

The maximum draft position must be varied according to the wind strength.

While the stability and balance of the boat permit, this point of sailing should have the least twist in the sails. Twist is eliminated by trimming the sheet hard in. You will probably find that you need to ease the traveller to leeward to prevent the leech hooking to windward and so creating drag.

Unless weather helm becomes a problem the curvature of the mainsail should extend well back into the batten panels, to add power and to help pointing. Should weather helm become a problem you will have to ease the traveller further to leeward. You must take care to avoid over-trimming, which is easily done in a moderate breeze, as it will take much of the power out of the sail and will create a tight leech. Once you have gone so far off the wind that the boom extends beyond the end of the traveller you will have to use the kicking strap to provide the downward tension necessary to control twist.

Headsail In a moderate breeze most of the boat's drive comes from the genoa. It is therefore vital that this sail is set correctly. This requires a flatter sail with limited twist. When the sea is heavier the amount of twist should be increased. By tightening the headstay you will be able to point higher. Increased halyard tension produces a flatter shape and you should also move the fairlead further aft. When you have the three taletales lifting together you have a uniform angle of attack. If the mainsail is significantly backwinded you should move the lead further aft to flatten the headsail further and decrease the amount of air being deflected into the mainsail. By adjusting the lead position you will eventually achieve the optimum amount of backwind.

In a heavy sea you will require more power from the genoa if you are to punch through the waves. If you try to point too high the waves will drastically reduce boat speed. You should therefore bear off, ease the sheets and move the lead forward.

STRONG BREEZE

Mainsail The helm balance is the most important consideration in these conditions. If the sea is relatively smooth then this means that the mainsail should be flat but opening towards the head. To achieve this shape bend the mast back to its limit. This will considerably reduce drive from the mainsail and therefore reduce heeling. The draft should be in the middle third of the sail. A straight entry with a smooth arc will minimise backwind and put the power-producing centre of the sail far enough aft of the mast to be away from the turbulent flow associated with the mast and rigging. The luff should be tensioned to flatten the leech and move the draft

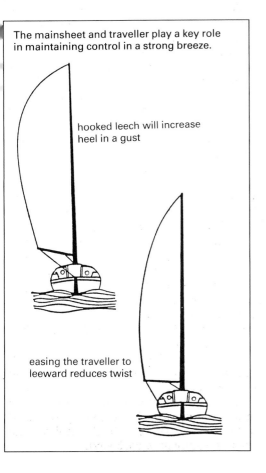

The mainsheet and traveller play a key role in maintaining control in a strong breeze.

hooked leech will increase heel in a gust

easing the traveller to leeward reduces twist

forward. The tension on the outhaul should be increased to draw the clew aft. This will help to reduce the overall depth of the sail and to flatten the lower part of it.

The head of the sail is particularly important in these conditions. Although you do not want excessive twist in the sail you must bear in mind the effect that the upper part of the sail has on heeling. The increased heel of the boat, as the wind strengthens, leads to a decrease in thrust and an increase in hull drag, giving a marked reduction in boat speed. The weight of the air on the top of the mast and sail causes them to act as a massive lever. To reduce heel and weather helm you should make the upper part of the sail less effective by inducing some twist. You can do this by easing either the kicking strap or the mainsheet.

If you can keep the boat flat, position the traveller on the centreline. Otherwise ease the traveller to leeward to prevent a tightened or hooked leech, as these create increased heel. The leech is aft of the boat's centre of rotation, so the weight of the air, unable to escape easily from this part of the sail, will push the stern to leeward and the bow to windward. If a traveller is not fitted you will have to ease the mainsheet. Should the wind ease then you can always bring the traveller back again. You will find that it is best to use the traveller to respond to changes in wind velocity. Easing the traveller maintains the angle of attack of the luff to the apparent wind as the latter comes aft in gusts. On a boat that does not have a traveller you will have to ease the mainsheet, which has the disadvantage of allowing the boom to rise, which will probably induce too much twist.

In gusts you must ease the traveller, or the mainsheet if a traveller is not fitted. Poor trim and excessive heel may lead to substantial weather helm which will cause a significant reduction in boat speed as the bow comes up into the wind. Such weather helm may be the result of an overtightened leech, in which case you will have to ease the mainsheet and accept any backwind that develops. As the boat comes back level after a gust you should haul in the traveller (or sheet).

In a strong wind with a heavy sea running the lower part of the sail needs more depth in order to provide the power that is required to punch through the waves. If this causes excessive heel you should reef rather than flatten the sail.

Headsail Once conditions have become heavy it will be better to set a full jib rather than a flattened genoa. The latter should be trimmed flat with the head more open than the foot, as with the mainsail. Increasing the halyard tension will bring the flow forward and therefore open up the head of the sail. If the mast has been bent aft for the mainsail set then this will also open the headsail leech and so help to reduce heel. It will also tighten the forestay, which is vital. Opening the leech will reduce backwind on the mainsail by making it easier for the air to escape aft from the headsail. Moving the fairlead aft will help to keep the slot open and to increase twist by opening the leech. By significantly reducing the effectiveness of the upper part of the sail the centre of effort will be lowered and so the heel will be reduced.

When the sea is dominated by a short chop you may have to put the bow into the waves to prevent the boat being stopped. The sails will probably luff as boat speed falls. You should then head off to pick up speed. Watch the tell-tales to make sure that you do not go too far off the wind and stall. Try to avoid being hit by the next wave as you head off.

Reaching

The initial effect of changing from a beat to a reach is to bring the apparent wind aft. You therefore need to ease the sails, otherwise the wind will hit them at too large an angle. The result of this would be an increase in heel and a decrease in forward drive because of the lack of drive-producing flow over the lee of the mainsail. Moving off the wind you can maximise forward drive because pointing is no longer a factor. To achieve this both sails should be set a little fuller. Heel is less significant than when on a beat because drive from the sails is more in the direction of the boat's heading. The lift produced by the rudder blade is not very important on this point of sailing so you may set your sails so that you have neutral helm.

MAINSAIL
The maximum draft is achieved with the mast bent forward about 10° from upright. This is done by easing the backstay. Luff tension must be eased until diagonal creases just

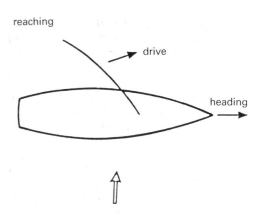
reaching

Well trimmed sails will reduce heel and produce more power when reaching.

begin to form, while the outhaul must be eased until vertical creases just begin to form in the foot.

The sail should be set with no twist and an angle of attack to the apparent wind of about 20°. If the angle is increased to 30° then the drive produced by the sail will decrease by

Close-reaching in squally conditions. The poor set of the mainsail and the angle of heel suggests that the boat is overpowered and that both sails should be reefed.

only about 5% but the heel will increase by perhaps 50%. Easing the traveller will keep the boom from lifting and producing twist. As you bear further off the wind, and the traveller is eased further, the mainsheet will become angled over the water so that it no longer exerts a vertical force on the boom. To prevent twist developing in this situation the kicking strap must be tensioned.

As the wind strengthens you will have to compromise between boat safety and optimum boat speed. Should you decide that conditions dictate that safety is the prime concern then some of the drive should be taken out of the sails and the leech should be opened to reduce the sails' effectiveness. The kicking strap then becomes the key control; if you begin to lose control, ease it further.

The settings are essentially the same for light and moderate winds when reaching. In very light air the kicking strap should be slackened and the mast bent further. The only variation with the genoa is that the halyard may require extra tension as the wind strengthens, to prevent severe creasing in the luff. As with the mainsail you will have to open the leech progressively. This also helps to reduce backwind on the mainsail. You need to play the sheets constantly when reaching because if you over-trim the boat's speed will fall markedly.

HEADSAIL
As the genoa is eased out the head will twist open. You must therefore move the lead further forward to keep a uniform angle of attack. If the upper tell-tail breaks after the others then the lead is too far forward. The halyard should be eased until horizontal creases begin to appear in the luff. This will move the flow aft and give the sail greater depth.

As the wind goes beyond 50° to your heading the efficiency of the genoa falls. Once the angle reaches 80°–85° you should set a spinnaker.

Broad reach

The fastest point of sailing occurs when the true wind is aft of the beam. Depending on the boat, wind and sea conditions this will be when the true wind is between 120°–150° relative to the heading. Although the apparent wind will then be slightly less than

the true wind in velocity, the increase in drive-to-heel ratio and consequent decrease in heel and leeway will permit increasing hull speed until equilibrium is reached between propulsion and drag forces.

The greatly increased drive potential is associated with an increase in draft. The maximum absolute thrust occurs with a draft of about 23%. To achieve this a small amount of twist is desirable, but excessive twist must be avoided because that will lead to a loss of thrust. Twist will become a problem, because of the tendency of the boom to lift and therefore produce a smaller projected sail area. The rise and fall of the boom with the gusts and waves will produce disturbed airflow, which will also diminish thrust. These effects should be minimised by tensioning the kicking strap and hauling the traveller well to leeward.

When heeling increases to an unacceptable degree the sail needs to be flattened to a limited extent. You will achieve this by bending the mast aft to its original upright position.

Run

LIGHT TO MODERATE BREEZE

Mainsail The following points refer to the mainsail irrespective of whether you set a spinnaker. The sail needs to be set up full so that it drags the boat downwind in the manner of a spinnaker. To achieve this in light airs the kicking strap is eased slightly and the leech line tensioned. As the wind increases from light to moderate, ease the leech line and tension the kicking strap to prevent the leech opening too far. (In strong winds the kicking strap must be as tight as possible to prevent even the slightest opening of the leech. If it were to open the upper part of the sail would fly forward and might start the boat rolling.)

Headsail The trim is the same in light and moderate winds. Large headsails such as a genoa do not set very easily on a run. Better results are achieved with a smaller headsail pushed out to windward with a pole. The sail should be set to produce the largest possible projected area by pulling the pole aft as far as possible and ensuring that it is horizontal. Avoid having a tight leech or one that is set

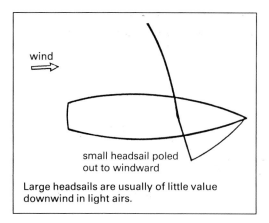

wind

small headsail poled
out to windward

Large headsails are usually of little value
downwind in light airs.

too hard; both will allow air to escape from the foot of the sail. (In strong winds the headsail must be trimmed flat to prevent it oscillating with the wave motion and exacerbating any tendency to roll. Pulling the pole as far as possible to windward will flatten the sail.)

HEAVY SEAS
An increase in wind strength usually means an increase in wave size. It is therefore vital for safety, comfort and boat speed that you effectively handle the growing sea. It is helpful if you understand the mechanics of wave motion. What you see when looking at a wave is not an ever onward movement of water but the movement of a form, ie a wave. In relation to the seabed the water is effectively stationary, whatever the size of the wave. Any one molecule of water will describe a near circle as the wind-driven form passes through. Ignoring the effect of tidal stream or current, the molecule therefore maintains its position relative to the seabed. There is, however, some surface flow on the wave, which is very relevant. The water on the crest slides forward towards the trough, while the water in the trough slides back towards the next crest. This means that any object in the water will be pushed forward by the crest before sliding back into the next trough.

The effect of this surface flow on a boat is twofold. The effectiveness of the rudder is reduced because as the crest passes under the stern the surface flow is moving in the same direction as the boat and therefore reduces the amount of water flowing past the boat. With a 3.0m wave the surface velocity is about 3kn. If the boat speed is 7kn the steer-

ing force exerted by the rudder is equivalent to a boat speed of only 4kn (7 −3kn). This problem is exacerbated by the second effect of the surface flow, which is to exert a twisting motion on a boat as its bow goes into the trough while its stern is lifted on the crest. The tendency of the bow to dig into the trough and plough under increases the torque effect produced by the trough pushing the bow back while the stern is pushed forward by the crest. This torque attempts to push the boat around, thus increasing the difficulty of steering. Such a problem will be increased when the wind and waves are in opposition to a tidal stream or current.

It is best to steer the boat in a line parallel to that along which the torque operates. This means that it is better to run rather than to beam or broad reach in such conditions. Attempting the latter you will allow the crest to hit the quarter and so increase the torque, but if you run off in front of the crest the tendency to twist will fall significantly. Modern cruisers are very buoyant aft, and lift well, so that in normal conditions there is no danger of the wave pouring over the stern. The danger comes in a severe storm, when the crests break over the stern. The inexperienced skipper should not be out in such conditions.

A major problem downwind is the tendency to roll. Once initiated this will become self-perpetuating because the buoyancy inherent in the boat will cause it to roll first to one side and then back again. The momentum back to the upright position, coupled with the forces initiating the roll, will cause the boat to roll to the other side and then come back upright. The severity of the roll will increase with each successive roll.

When the mast rolls to windward the apparent wind moves forward on the sail. As the rolling motion gathers momentum the apparent wind again moves further forward. This therefore rapidly increases the proportion of the mainsail that develops airflow and lift on its leeside. This lift rolls the mast to windward, so as the lift increases the speed of roll increases until the motion of the boat is totally out of control.

Prevention being better than cure you should trim your sails so that this is unlikely to occur. The kicking strap should be tensioned so that the boom will not lift. If the boat begins to roll try to increase the tension

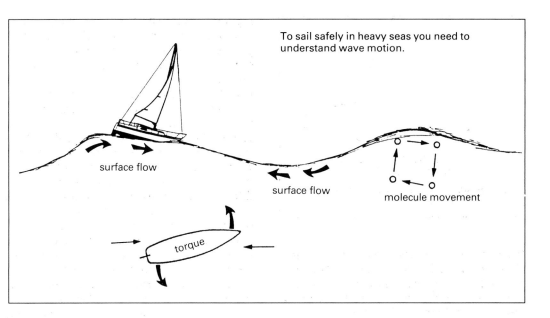

To sail safely in heavy seas you need to understand wave motion.

surface flow

surface flow

molecule movement

torque

on the kicking strap. Should that fail then tighten the mainsheet slightly to reduce its effectiveness by stalling the top part of the sail.

Spinnaker handling

Spinnaker handling is one of those areas of sailing that worries the inexperienced crew. The first decision to be made is whether or not you are going to fly the spinnaker. Your decision will depend on the strength of the wind (it could be too strong or too light), whether the wind is too far forward or aft, the sea state and the experience of the crew.

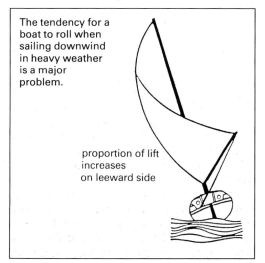

The tendency for a boat to roll when sailing downwind in heavy weather is a major problem.

proportion of lift increases on leeward side

There are a wide variety of spinnakers you may set, depending on whether you are close reaching, beam reaching or running, and depending on the wind strength. Most family auxiliary cruisers will have just one spinnaker, which may in fact be a cruising chute. The latter are favoured on many smaller boats because they do not require a spinnaker pole. These poles are difficult to stow on a smaller boat and tend to be in the way on deck. The cruising chute may be used on any point of sailing between close reaching and running. You may fly it in an apparent wind of 0–18kn when reaching and up to 30kn when running.

In very light airs you need to set a lightweight spinnaker. The apparent wind needs to be kept well forward because if it is aft in such conditions the sail is likely to flap back and forth and could possibly wrap itself around the headstay. When there is a left-over sea running such problems will be exacerbated. If you have to head with the wind well aft in these conditions you would be best advised to take the spinnaker down and set a headsail.

Some spinnakers may be set when the apparent wind is as far forward as 55°–65° relative to the bow. This will be possible in light to moderate winds but in a stronger wind would lead to significant weather helm and the likelihood of broaching. A spinnaker should not be set when the wind is forward of the beam and more than 25kn: if you have a large headsail then you would make more progress with that than with a spinnaker.

You may look at your boat speed and decide that you are so close to maximum hull speed that there is nothing to be gained by setting a spinnaker. That would be the wrong decision because in the trough of a wave, and going up the other side, the boat is unlikely to achieve hull speed and therefore needs the extra thrust of a spinnaker. Any boat can surpass hull speed in surfing conditions. The spinnaker will give sufficient extra power to surf earlier and for longer.

The spinnaker is a triangular nylon sail. When not set the two vertical edges are called luffs because the sail is symmetrical. When set the edge leading up from the pole is the luff and the other is the leech.

The frequently exaggerated problems of using a spinnaker will lessen if you pack it so that it does not twist as it is hoisted. The common name 'turtle' is given to the various objects into which a spinnaker may be packed. These include sail bags and buckets. When you pack a spinnaker you are said to 'turtle' it.

Having decided upon a suitable turtle you need to find the head of the sail. Hold one luff near that point and run your other hand along that luff, flaking the edge from side to side. Then repeat this with the other luff. While holding the three corners of the sail to one side stuff the remainder into the turtle, then lay the corners on top of the sail. This usually prevents problems whilst hoisting, although the three corners may twist through 180°. If that happens lower and start again.

The various 'snuffer' designs now on the market have largely made the turtle redundant. With a snuffer the spinnaker is permanently fitted inside a lightweight sock. It is sensible either to buy the snuffer already fitted or send your spinnaker to a sailmaker to have one fitted. Instead of hoisting the sail you hoist the snuffer (with the spinnaker inside) using the spinnaker halyard. When the top of the snuffer is at the masthead you pull on a continuous line so that the snuffer tube is pulled to the masthead thus allowing the sail to open. The tube remains at the top of the mast while the sail is in use. To snuff the sail you let the wind out of the spinnaker and then pull on the line to bring the tube down over the sail. The snuffer (containing the spinnaker) is then lowered and stowed.

The sheets need to be attached before you hoist the spinnaker. One sheet or the other is referred to as the guy on one tack and then reverts to being the sheet when you gybe. This does cause some confusion at first. The spinnaker pole is always set to windward opposite the main boom, with the guy running through its outboard end. The sheet is attached to the free corner of the sail. When

The spinnaker controls.

1 spinnaker pole
2 uphaul
3 downhaul
4 sheet
5 guy

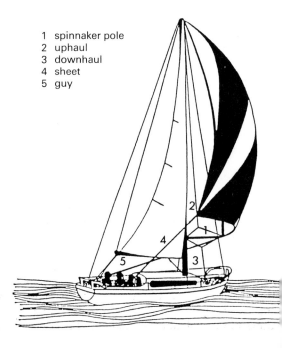

A snuffer considerably eases the handling of a spinnaker.

you gybe the pole is moved across the boat to the new windward side. The old guy then becomes the new sheet and the old sheet becomes the new guy.

The spinnaker pole is attached to a downhaul and an uphaul. The former prevents the pole from angling upwards when the sail is full; the latter prevents it from angling downwards when it is not full. Much of the

The spinnaker pole close up.

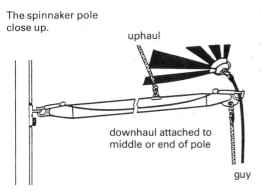

uphaul

downhaul attached to middle or end of pole

guy

set of the spinnaker relates to the pole. When using a cruising chute you are unlikely to be using a pole, but trim theory is very similar.

Most problems occur when setting, even if you are using a snuffer. To minimise such problems get the sail up as quickly as possible. Before hoisting ensure that the sheets and halyards run outside all shrouds, rigging, stanchions and lifelines and that they do not foul other sheets. It is particularly easy for the sail to twist and become wrapped around the forestay or jammed between halyard and forestay. Once the sail is half up and filling (snuffer not used) it will be too late to prevent such problems. Make sure that the three corners are well separated before hoisting. If the sail begins to rotate with the tack and clew close together then a wrap may develop and produce a tangle with an hour-glass shape. The middle section will be wrapped around itself or the forestay while the upper and lower parts may be drawing. This is a very difficult problem to resolve. The immediate worry is that the sail will shred itself. To avoid the complete destruction of the sail you must act fast.

Where the spinnaker is twisted around itself but free of the forestay you should stretch out the foot by hauling on the sheets. This may allow it to unwrap. Alternatively, head downwind to blanket the sail with the main-

sail. The crew should then pull down on the leech and shake it. Should that not work then lower the halyard a few feet in case the problem has been caused by a swivel jammed in the halyard block. If all else fails lower the sail until the crew can reach the wrap and attempt to twist it back.

Most of these problems will be avoided if you indulge in the modest expenditure of a snuffer.

With a spinnaker set you should rig a rubber boom-preventer to cushion the effect of an unexpected gybe. This line should be led to the cockpit from the main boom so that it may be released quickly if necessary. Rubber should be used so that the preventer will stretch should the boom drag into the water during a roll. Any other material would probably cause you to lose the mast because of the pressures on the rig as the boom is dragged through the water.

The opening of the spinnaker will lead to a sudden and massive increase in sail area. To reduce the impact it is sensible to ease the mainsheet kicking strap initially to reduce weather helm and therefore the danger of a broach. In the first instance you should not oversheet the spinnaker because that will drive the boat into the wind and possibly begin a roll.

When running the spinnaker is more or less stalled and therefore drags the boat along. This explains why one of the guiding principles of sail trim is to achieve the greatest possible projected sail area. The effectiveness of the sail is proportional to the area of the sail exposed to the wind. You will achieve this by keeping the pole well aft and the sheet well trimmed. This action does, however, have a negative effect. In setting the pole and sheet as described you bring the spinnaker closer to the mainsail so that it is drawn progressively into the disturbed air in front of that sail. This naturally leads to a decrease in efficiency. Easing the pole forward and easing the sheet will move the spinnaker away from the disturbed air. You will have to vary between these two extremes (of the spinnaker being further forward or further aft) in order to try and find a happy medium. Easing the halyard will help to draw the spinnaker away from the mainsail, but you cannot do this in light or strong winds.

The pole should be perpendicular to the mast, not to the water, so that you produce the maximum projected sail area by keeping the spinnaker as far away from the mainsail as possible. When you move one end of the pole you will therefore have to move the other an equal amount in the same direction. You should note, however, that even when 20° out of true the loss of pole length will only be an insignificant 5%. There is therefore nothing to be gained by endlessly moving the pole to try and get it perfectly perpendicular.

The height of the pole is even more important. It should be set so that the tack and clew are level with the plane of the deck and each other. Although the clew may be slightly higher than the tack you must never have the tack higher than the clew. If the pole is too high too much air will escape from the sail and you will lose drive. If it is too low the air will be unable to escape and may cause the sail to start oscillating. When the wind is gusty or the waves are long you will be constantly playing with the pole to try and keep it at an optimum height.

When close reaching the pole should be almost touching the forestay in order to move

the spinnaker as far from the boat as possible and therefore maximise its sail area. If the conditions suggest the possibility of a broach then bring it aft about 30–40cm.

When you are happy with the position of the pole ease the sheet until you see a slight curl along the luff. You should constantly trim so that this curl just disappears. Ease the sheet when decelerating and then sheet in as you begin to accelerate. As you ease the sheet the clew will lift and therefore you will have to raise the pole to keep it perpendicular. When you tighten the sheet the reverse will occur and you will have to lower the pole. On a smaller boat, or on any boat where the sea is causing a rolling motion, you will have

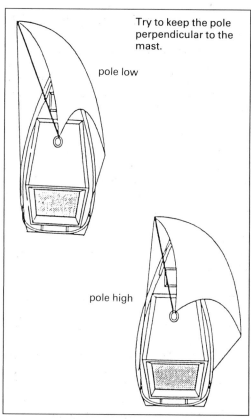

sheet eased with pole well forward

The angle of the spinnaker pole to the mast is a significant factor.

sheet trimmed tight with pole well aft

Try to keep the pole perpendicular to the mast.

pole low

pole high

to play the guy constantly. As the boat rolls to windward ease the pole aft and ease the sheet. Try to keep the leech open so that the air can escape easily.

Remember that whenever the true wind velocity changes or the boat begins to surf or falls off a plane the apparent wind will change and the spinnaker will have to be trimmed by altering the pole position and the sheet trim.

The alert crew will anticipate such changes.

Do not begin to trim the mainsail until you are satisfied with the performance of the spinnaker.

LIGHT AIRS

For perhaps 90% of the time the spinnaker will be ineffective in light airs. The sail must be set correctly to maximise its effectiveness when a puff does occur. To achieve this the pole should be very low, with the outboard end a little higher than clew. Do not have the pole so low that the luff is stretched and folded over. Set like this the spinnaker would be unable to fill in a puff because of the shape of the luff and the amount of unsupported cloth in the foot that needs to be filled. It is equally incorrect to have the pole too high, because the sail would then sag to leeward and therefore require a strong puff to fill it.

You cannot get the spinnaker far forward of the mainsail by easing the halyard because the lack of air in the sail will simply cause it to drop straight down.

MODERATE BREEZE

When running downwind in a moderate breeze you should ease the halyard 15–25cm to take the sail away from the disturbed air in front of the mainsail. This will also allow the spinnaker to set closer to the vertical.

HEAVY WIND

The spinnaker will overpower the boat if it is allowed to develop full power. You must therefore either reduce its effectiveness or change to a headsail. The clew must be higher than the tack to allow air to escape. Constantly play both the mainsail and spinnaker to keep the luffs breaking.

The oscillation of the spinnaker from side to side that may develop will increase the natural tendency of the boat to roll when the wind is well aft. As the oscillating spinnaker rolls from side to side it will inevitably cause a broach. Although you cannot completely dampen this motion you can at least reduce it and so lessen the risk of a broach. The major cause of spinnaker oscillation is an eased halyard, so try to tension that. If this is the case, and the oscillation continues unchecked, you will have to lower the spinnaker.

If the oscillation is not being caused by an eased halyard it is likely to be the result of the sail being too far in front of the boat and

therefore in undisturbed air. In an attempt to prevent oscillation occurring you should try to reduce the effectiveness of the sail by easing the pole down and forward to a point where it is at an angle of less than 90° to the apparent wind. At the same time you should

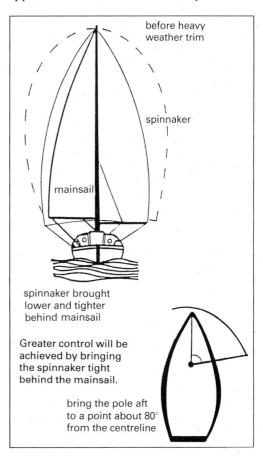

before heavy weather trim

spinnaker

mainsail

spinnaker brought lower and tighter behind mainsail

Greater control will be achieved by bringing the spinnaker tight behind the mainsail.

bring the pole aft to a point about 80° from the centreline

harden the sheet and bring the guy and sheet leads forward. The idea behind these actions is to pull the sail down and to keep it tight behind the mainsail. This will reduce its effectiveness and in particular will prevent airflow reaching its leeside. If you do not prevent such leeside flow it will pull the sail to weather and cause the mast to roll in that direction. The centre of effort in the sail will then move to weather of the hull so that lee helm develops. The natural response of the helm to round the boat up will then exacerbate the problem because the rudder will push down on the water and lift the stern rather than turn the boat. The boat may then broach as the spinnaker rolls to leeward of it.

The helm can help to prevent such a roll

continuing by luffing immediately the boat begins to heel to windward, or by immediately bearing away if it heels to leeward. Keeping crew weight aft will also help because the broader stern will create more drag than the bow.

If you should be unfortunate enough to broach then simultaneously ease the sheet to spill wind and ease the boom-preventer. As the boat rights itself you will need to tighten both again if you are to prevent the development of an oscillating tendency.

Should the pole be too low the spinnaker will tend to collapse frequently because the luff will be too full. The jolt of the sail refilling again will exert so much pressure that gear may fail. To avoid this you will need to raise the pole. You must also ensure that the pole is secured effectively so that it does not swing as the boat rolls.

You will realise that because it is important in these conditions to get the spinnaker behind the mainsail you must not reef the latter. Doing so would only let more air get to the spinnaker and worsen any problems; you would also lose the blanketing effect when dousing. Tensioning the mainsail cunningham and the backstay will flatten the mainsail and reduce its drive. This will help to ease the situation.

To obtain maximum speed you should ease the sheet as you go into the back of a wave and then tighten it as you surf down the next wave.

REACHING

When the wind is close to the beam you must avoid a tight leech because that will create drag both backwards and to leeward. As long as the sheet lead is not too far aft the leech should not tighten as you trim the sheet to stop the luff curling.

GYBE

Turn the boat downwind and simultaneously bring the pole aft and ease the sheet. You must keep the spinnaker downwind throughout the manoeuvre. Take the pole off the mast but do not disconnect the old guy. Hold the pole out and reach for the sheet (new guy). This will help to keep the spinnaker full during the gybe.

When gybing from reach to reach you will have to take the pole completely off. First disconnect it from the mast and then re-move it from the old guy. Freewheel the sail through the gybe and connect the pole to the guy on the new windward side. Should reattaching the pole to the mast prove difficult, momentarily ease the sheet to collapse the spinnaker.

TAKE DOWN

The skipper must judge when conditions and crew experience make it necessary to lower the spinnaker. When you decide to lower it come further off the wind and adjust the mainsail accordingly (as you use it to blanket the spinnaker). To bring the spinnaker under the lee of the mainsail slacken the sheet and guy. Tighten the guy again afterwards. When the crew have hold of the foot you can ease the halyard. Try then to gather in the sail as a slim column so that it is easier to handle. The helm should give the commands because the best overall view of the operation is from the cockpit. Should the sail go into the water you must act fast. Release all but one line to the spinnaker so that it will stream behind the boat as a slender column. Two lines attached to the sail would cause it to act as a sea anchor and it would be shredded by the force of the water.

Obviously a cruising chute with a snuffer is much easier to douse than a spinnaker without one. You will still need to control the sails as you would if you did not have a snuffer.

Roller-furling headsails

It would be inappropriate to refer to these as roller-reefing systems because that would suggest the ability to reef the sail in a way that any portion of it would be set correctly for any given conditions. The furling genoa, as the name suggests, is just a mechanism to get sufficient area of the sail out of the way so as to maintain control over the boat. The advantages of such a system are that it makes handling heavy sails much easier and that you do not have to go onto a violently pitching foredeck in order to reduce sail area. You also avoid the struggle of getting a heavy, wet sail down below from the foredeck.

Using such a system it is difficult to keep an ideal sail shape. As you roll-in the sail there will be an increase in the thickness of the cloth at the leech and foot. At a time when you want a flatter sail you will find that the draft is actually increasing. Such a mis-shapen sail with significant draft will push the boat off the wind, reduce pointing ability and make tacking difficult. In difficult conditions you may need to tack and to point high.

The clear advantage of the roller-furling genoa is that you should never be over-powered. You can and should get around the problem of the poor set of the furled sail by rigging a secondary forestay to which you may attach a storm jib. This will allow you to cope with the most extreme conditions. You should also bear in mind that furling systems can jam. If this happens in heavy conditions and you do not manage to free the problem you will have to find some way of securing the sail so that you are not overpowered.

Care and maintenance of sails

Modern sails are strong, hard and dimension-ally stable so that stretch is no longer a major problem. The common material in use today is polyethylene terephthalate, known as Terylene or Dacron. Sails are designed to work within the limits of the forces that are operating on them, both in term of the mag-nitude and direction of those forces. This is why they have high dimensional stability. If you use the sails incorrectly, by setting them up so that the forces are applied in the wrong direction, you will rapidly stretch and ruin them. You will find that Terylene sails handled properly maintain their designed shape and give many years of high quality performance.

Although Terylene is very tough you should break the sail in for some 3–4 hours in a light to moderate breeze. You should not reef the sail until it has been used for some 5–6 hours.

When you hoist the mainsail you must not leave the boom unsupported or the leech will be stretched because it will be carrying the weight of the boom. To avoid this problem uses the topping lift to support the boom. On a smaller boat without a topping lift you must support the boom with your hand while hoisting.

The headsail must be treated equally care-fully. Before hoisting make sure that all the hanks are on the forestay and that the halyard is not twisted around the stay or jammed aloft. The sail must not be sheeted in until it is fully hoisted. While sailing try to keep it clear of any rigging which will cause

chafe or a possible tear. Any sharp surfaces on the boat, such as split pins, should be taped to avoid the risk of a tear.

When lowering a sail, simply release the halyard and it should come down under its own weight. Resist the temptation to pull the sail down by the leech because that will stretch the cloth. If you are leaving the sail wrapped around the boom, take out the battens and cover the sail with a boom cover to protect it from the sun and dirt.

There are a variety of dangers to synthetic sails. Although the sail material itself is durable the stitching on the outside surface is prone to chafe. The most likely places for this to occur are where the mainsail is in contact with the shrouds when off the wind, and along the leech where it brushes against the topping lift. The stitching around batten pockets frequently suffers from chafe. The problem may occur at either end of the pocket. At the forward end the batten may chafe through the end of the pocket and therefore the sail, while the stitching along the leech may be damaged by the effect of pushing the batten into the pocket. You will avoid such problems by using battens of the correct size that are tapered towards the inner end. You must always remove battens before wrapping the sail around the boom or putting it into a bag.

The leech and clew of a headsail are prone to chafe if they are allowed to flog and hit rigging. The foot is very likely to be chafed against the lifelines and stanchions, especially when the boat is tacked. Taping the outer ends of the shrouds will reduce chafe on the headsail leech. It is a good idea to put tape wherever chafe is likely to occur.

The spinnaker will particularly suffer where the foot tape and the clew rings are in contact with the forestay.

Areas prone to chafe must be inspected frequently. One or two loose stitches will soon lead to a whole seam or panel coming undone if they are not attended to. When you find a loose stitch you should either restitch it or cover it with adhesive sail tape. You should keep a roll of such tape on the boat so that you can deal with the problem immediately.

If you do not look after the sails you will find that they rapidly develop creases. This will be because they have been folded, bagged or stowed incorrectly. Creases distort the flow of air across the sail and lead to a significant fall in performance. Should a sail develop a bad crease then wash it and hang it loosely along the luff to dry. (You must never hang it by the leech because that would cause the sail to stretch.) If this does not succeed then take the sail to a sailmaker. Do not iron it!

A sail should be folded carefully, with either vertical or horizontal folds. Alternate the direction of such folds each time you stow the sail otherwise they will become creases. If you are not leaving the sail for long then you can roll it round the boom without creasing it. To stow it for a longer period bunch the sail down on top of the boom. Pull the foot out and wrap it around the mass of the sail.

Damp will cause unsightly stains on a sail, although it will not actually harm the fabric. Sails are full of minor surface irregularities that harbour dirt, salt and moisture. These act as nuclei for the growth of mould. The mould grows on the nuclei and the the sail material itself. Although it does not affect the strength of the fibres mould leads to discolouration which is very difficult to remove. To prevent this problem you should thoroughly wash and dry the sails. Moisture is likely to remain longest in the batten pockets, so these are a good guide as to when a sail is dry and ready to be stowed.

To help keep sails in good condition you must clean all the surfaces with which they are likely to come into contact. If possible wash the decks before handling the sails. You should run a cloth soaked in heavy detergents along the length of all stays and spars.

When salt water evaporates from the surface of a sail it leaves layers of salt crystals which keep the sail damp by absorbing moisture. The result is stiff cloth and increased weight aloft, both of which have a negative effect on performance. The easiest way to avoid this problem is to hose down the sails with fresh water and leave them to dry. Rather than hanging them you should spread them on the decks to dry.

Cleaning stained sails is not very easy, which is why sailmakers offer a cleaning service. A small sail you could soak in a bath of detergent and hand-warm water. A larger sail you would have to lay out on a flat surface such as concrete, having first cleaned that surface. In both cases you would scrub the sail with a soft brush. The sail would have to be thoroughly hosed down with fresh water before being left to dry.

Mildew is difficult to remove. In the first instance scrub the affected area with a stiff brush. If that fails place the affected area in a 1% cold water solution of bleach and allow it to soak for 2 hours. The sail must then be thoroughly washed and rinsed.

Where the stain has been made by oil or grease you need to apply trichloroethylene to it or rub it with Swarfega. If that does not succeed, or if rust is the problem, try a 2% warm water solution of concentrated hydrochloric acid. Where varnish is the problem wipe the stain with trichloroethylene and then a 50% mixture of acetone and amyl acetate. When finished wash and rinse it thoroughly.

Tar or pitch stains should be treated with a solvent such as Polyclens, white spirit or trichloroethylene. Paint can be treated with white spirit or a turpentine substitute, but never use an alkaline based paint remover.

You must carefully read the instructions on any stain remover. Most are either poisonous or inflammable. When using such material do so in fresh air and away from naked heat. Wash yourself thoroughly after using solvents.

When you have laid up the boat at the end of the season wash the sails thoroughly in warm water and a mild liquid detergent. Scrub any marks with a soft brush and treat any stains. Rinse thoroughly and then dry completely. Check the sails panel by panel and seam by seam for any damage. When you are satisfied with the sails' condition stow them carefully in a clean, dry and well ventilated area. The condensation inside a GRP hull during the winter months does not make that a sensible place in which to stow sails.

It would be a good idea to make use of the winter valet service provided by the leading sailmakers. Such service includes cleaning and repairing any damage.

CHAPTER 16

Pollution

Pollution is set to become a major issue for boat owners. The cleanliness of the sea should be of concern to all who use it.

You may have been attracted to sailing by the desire to sail through crystal clear waters and arrive at quiet and unpolluted anchorages, and on passage you and your crew will hope to see a wide variety of marine life. It is a matter of conjecture how much longer we will keep the remaining unspoilt coastal areas. In the UK there is still no clear government policy on the management of the coastline.

There is much the individual boat owner and crew can do to help in the conservation of the coastline. A first step might be to join the local branch of the Marine Conservation Society (MCS) and become actively involved in conservation. Although the next few years will see more regulations come into force to protect the sea we should act as individuals before we are forced by legislation to do that which should long have been common practice.

No other country has the range of marine habitats found along the British coastline. These range from arctic to mediterranean in nature. When deciding upon an anchorage ensure that you are not disturbing the natural habitat. Avoid the nesting grounds of sea birds and the breeding areas of seals at certain times of the year. Make sure that your anchor does not damage rare seabed habitats, and if you go ashore do not pick wild flowers. If you must fish then think of the catch in terms of the rarity of a particular species and the effect on dwindling stocks.

International concern has been expressed since the 1973 International Convention for the Prevention of Pollution from Ships. Annexes III and IV of this convention deal, respectively, with pollution by packaged substances and pollution by sewage. Annex V deals with the dumping of litter and general rubbish. Unfortunately, as with many well-intentioned international agreements, ratification is only voluntary and there is no effective enforcement.

The UK government is currently considering ratification of Annex IV, relating to the disposal of sewage from vessels. If this comes into force boat owners may be forced to fit holding tanks, and marinas and port authorities will have to install tanks to receive raw sewage. This action is vital if inshore waters, especially enclosed bays, are not to become polluted. Apart from being unsightly and foul smelling, water affected by sewage can lead to ear, nose and throat infections as well as stomach disorders. It also leads to the contamination of shellfish and so works its way up the food chain. For these reasons you must not discharge sewage into the water while close inshore. The amount of sewage emanating from private boats may be a small proportion of the total amount affecting coastal waters but it clearly adds to the problem.

Some 300 million gallons of raw sewage are discharged every day from the land into British coastal waters. In certain localities this leads to a hypertrophic environment where the abundance of nutrients produces massive algal blooms. These eventually die and sink to the seabed where their decay leads to the deoxygenation of the lowest layers of the water and the death of bottom-living organisms. The destruction works its way up the food chain and eventually affects mammals and fish. The toxins found in the 'red tides' which affected the coast between the Tyne and Tweed estuaries in 1991 led to severe contamination of certain marine mussels and the official closure of the shell-fisheries along that part of the east coast. To help reduce such problems skippers must insist that only phosphate-free detergents such as Ecover are used (both on land and at sea).

Annex V of the convention makes it illegal to dump most forms of rubbish over the side.

The Merchant Shipping Regulations 1988, No. 2293, oblige marina and harbour operators to provide reception facilities for rubbish. If these are not available you must put pressure on the relevant authorities. The same operators must also provide adequate toilet facilities.

Rubbish dumped at sea is now such a problem that you should report any significant incident. All waste takes a long time to break down in the marine environment. The following rates of material decomposition emphasise the problem:

Paper	2–5 months
Orange peel	6 months
Milk cartons	5 years
Plastic cartons	50–80 years
Plastic foam	never

Plastic is the problem. Some 6.5 million tonnes of plastic are deliberately discharged by big ships each year. Possibly the greatest danger to marine life are the Hi-Cone rings used for multi-packaging tins. These are very attractive to many forms of marine life. Once trapped by putting either their head or a limb through one or more of the rings the animals either drown or are starved to death. You must always cut up plastic rings before putting them in a dustbin and should never take them out to sea.

A photodegradable plastic is now available, but even this takes a minimum of 2 weeks to break down (in ideal conditions). The USA and Sweden have already introduced legislation to force companies to use such material. The UK is still considering the matter.

Smaller fragments of plastic are just as harmful: fish, mammals and birds eat them, thinking they are food. Apart from being toxic they have the effect of filling the stomach so that the animal stops feeding and starves to death. Turtles have died in a similar manner. Do not use plastic at sea.

The alternative to plastic packaging is cardboard. This is more expensive and so reduces profit. However, Coca Cola is to be congratulated because not only has it introduced the litter-free ring pull but it has abandoned Hi-Cone in favour of cardboard packaging.

Oil is an obvious pollutant. More than 60% of birds washed up on the British coast are oiled, and the figure rises to 75% along Channel coasts. When a bird is smothered in oil it attempts to clean itself and so dies from the poison it ingests. Larger animals, such as whales and dolphins, may be able to avoid the obvious danger of a slick but face possible starvation as the food chain is damaged. If you see a slick report it immediately to the coastguard or the Marine Pollution Control Unit of the Department of Transport. Should you find an oiled bird seek advice from the RSPCA or RSPB.

The antifouling paint, Tributyl (TBT), was a problem until its use on vessels of less than 25m (83ft) was made illegal in 1987. TBT had caused deformities in oysters and led to the extinction of entire dogwhelk colonies. The latter, which may become infertile or even die as a result of TBT poisoning, are the subject of an intensive study by the MCS to discover the extent of recovery since 1987. The dogwhelk, a predatory mollusc, is a good indicator of pollution because it is one of the more common intertidal animals. It has no commercial value and lives for about four years in virtually the same location.

The engine of your boat is a pollutant in terms of noise, smell and fumes. Carbon monoxide, which leads to asphyxia, is one of the most poisonous gases emitted by the engine. Nitrous oxides in the exhaust mix with steam to produce nitric acid. This and the various hydrocarbons that are emitted irritate the eyes and affect the respiratory system. Sulphur dioxide is a similar irritant and combines with water to form sulphuric acid. You should think of these things the next time you sit with your engine running in a marina berth.

Answers to Questions

Chapter 4
1. a) Polypropylene.
   b) Prestretched Terylene (Dacron).
   c) Multi-plait nylon.
   d) Three strand nylon.
   e) Sixteen-plait Terylene.
2. Laid up cordage.
3. a) Attaching a rope to a ring.
   b) Temporarily attaching the middle of a rope to a spar or the fenders to the guardrail.
   c) Making a loop in the end of a rope or attaching a sheet to the clew of a sail.
4. a) A reef knot.
   b) A figure-of-eight knot.
   c) Double sheet bend.
   d) A rolling hitch.
5. a) A reef knot.
   b) A figure of eight.
   c) A single sheet bend.
   d) A rolling hitch.

Chapter 5
1. a) Four times the depth of water at high water.
   b) Six times the depth of water at high water.
2. a) Six warps (see p69).
   b) Stern and bow springs (see p69).
3. A – A poor anchorage exposed to the prevailing wind with the seabed covered in boulders. An awkward reverse air current may also be produced by the cliffs on the headland.
   B – Again a poor choice. The water is deep right up to the coastline and although the headland may provide some shelter a strong downdraught is likely from the cliffs.
   C – This is as bad as B but with even less shelter.
   D – This is directly exposed to the wind with the possibility of dragging onto the shallows inshore, or of being blown into the pier. Unless you have a bilge keel you will have a long row at high water and will not be able to get ashore at low water.
   E – A ludicrous position at the entrance to a port.
   F – Prohibited because of a submarine pipeline.
   G – Prohibited because of oyster beds.
   H – An excellent choice with relatively shallow water sheltered by gently rolling hills. The sand and clay bed provides good holding ground while the depth of water would allow easy access to the shore at all states of the tide.
   I – Not a good choice. The low-lying land would tend to funnel the wind through the gap between the higher land to north and south. Mud does not provide such good holding ground.

CONCLUSIONS
   H – By far the best.
   I – A possibility, depending on wind strength.
   D – A poor third, but just viable as long as the wind and swell are not too strong.

   A
   B } These provide little shelter or security.
   C

   E
   F } These are all prohibited.
   G

4. a) i) The anchorage: approach downwind stemming the tide with mainsail lowered. At the anchorage let the headsail fly, or lower it, and release the anchor. The boat will drift back on the tide.
      ii) The mooring buoy: approach from downwind. As you pass the buoy lower the mainsail and make your final approach from upwind under headsail only. Control your speed with the sheets so that you just make way over the tide until you reach the buoy.
      iii) The pontoon berth: sail upwind beyond the berth and drop the mainsail. Run down to the berth under headsail only, again using the sheets to control your speed. When you have sufficient way to make the berth let the sheets go and steer into the berth.
   b) i) The anchorage: hoist the headsail and use that to bring the boat over the anchor. As the anchor breaks free sail downwind slowly until it is secured on deck. Then turn the boat head to wind in order to raise the headsail.
      ii) The mooring buoy: take the buoy to the stern so that the boat will lie stern-to-tide and head-to-wind. Then hoist the sails and cast off in the required direction by backing the headsail.
      iii) The open quay: release all warps except for a spring from bow to stern. Put the rudder hard over to port so that the tide takes the stern out. A backed headsail will assist in this manoeuvre.

Chapter 6
1. a) You should not wear a harness in poor visibility because of the danger of being dragged down by the sinking boat if you are involved in a collision.
   b) Ships converge on headlands, so this is a very dangerous place to be in poor visibility.
2. a) –   · ·
   b) –   · ·
   c) –   · · } At intervals of not
   d) –   · · } more than 2 minutes.
   e) –   · ·
   f) A bell is rung in the bow for 5 seconds followed by a gong for 5 seconds in the stern at 1 minute intervals.
3. a) Close to the galley.
   b) Near to accommodation hatches.
   c) Inside the engine compartment, or at least discharging into it.
4. a) During the day in good visibility and light winds.
   b) When more than 3 miles from land or the nearest boat.
5. – raising and lowering of arms;
   – continuous sounding of a horn;
   – SOS by sound or light;
   – code flags NC;
   – ensign hoisted high in the rigging.
6. Do not touch the line until it has earthed either on the boat or in the water. Take up the slack and haul in the line when directed to do so. The winchman will use the line to guide himself down to the boat. At no stage should you attach the line to the boat.
7. Mayday message must be sent because the casualty is bleeding internally.

Chapter 7
1. Rule 5 states that you must keep a continuous lookout. This is impossible if you are single-handed.

2. a)   b)   c)

3. a) Vessel at anchor.
    b) Vessel restricted in its ability to manoeuvre.
    c) Vessel fishing.
4. a) All round white light.
    b) Either a red, white and green tri-lantern, or red and green side lights with white stern light.
    c) Either red and green side lights, white stern light and white masthead (steaming) light, or an all round white light at the top of the mast and red and green side lights.
    d) The same as c).
5. a) Vessel, motor sailing, underway, starboard side.
    b) Power driven vessel, greater than 50m, underway, port side.
    c) Fishing vessel, other than trawler, underway, starboard side.
    d) Pilot vessel, underway, starboard side.
    e) Vessel between 50 and 100m at anchor.
6. By using a hand compass to take bearings on the target vessel. If the bearing does not alter then a collision is likely.
7. According to Rule 17 the right-of-way vessel must maintain her course and speed. However, if the give-way vessel fails to alter course, or to do so substantially, the right-of-way vessel must take avoiding action.
8. a) I am altering course to port.
    b) I intend overtaking on your starboard side.
    c) Warning signal by vessel approaching bend or obstruction.

Chapter 8
1. a) Lines joining points of equal pressure.
    b) Millibars.
    c) The rotation of the earth causes the air to be deflected to the right of its path in the northern hemisphere.
2. a) A = a trough; B = a ridge; C = a col.
    b) There is a steep pressure gradient so the wind will be strong.
3. a) S = south-south-west; T = north-east; U = north-west; V = east; W = north.
    b) Fog is likely to develop.
4. a) Radio 4, 1515m (198kHz).
    b) 1355.
    c) 0033.
5. Coastguard rescue centres and coast radio stations.
6. a) Pressure has risen or fallen by 0.1–1.5mb over the last 3 hours.
    b) A weather system moving at a speed of 15–25kn.
    c) Predicted change in the weather will take place within the next 6 hours.
    d) Visibility is less than 2 miles.
7. Force 3.
8. Large waves are beginning to form. White foam crests are more extensive with the probability of some spray.
9. a) When the cold front goes through it will bring squally conditions in its wake. Gusts will be unpredictable and may reach gale force. Visibility will be very poor during the showers. These are not ideal conditions for the inexperienced skipper.
    b) Dover is by far the better of the two on this occasion because it will remain in the lee of the land as the wind veers from south-west to north-west with the passage of the cold front. Boulogne will be very exposed as the wind veers to the north-west with a long fetch over the Channel causing a large swell to develop.
    c) A ridge is building from the south in the Atlantic.

This will bring lighter winds after the passage of the cold front. If you are inexperienced you should wait for these lighter winds to develop.
10. If you go direct to Etaples from Newhaven then the cold front will pass over you before you reach the French coast. That will leave you in open water (at night) exposed to the strong and squally north-west wind that follows the cold front. It would be far wiser to go to Folkestone first so that during the night of 21 June you stay in the lee of the English coast. You could then cross the Channel in the lighter winds of the ridge building from the south.

Chapter 9
1. a) The shore station.
    b) The called station.
2. 16.
3. 06.
4. One minute although you should try to be much quicker than that.
5. Using 25W would interfere with other stations.
6. To talk to a marina or yacht club on marina or club business.
7. Yes, but only for matters relating to safety.
8. The nearest coast radio station.
9. This indicates that the channel is engaged. You should try later.
10. This is the end of my working with you; no reply required.
11. The three minutes immediately after each hour and half hour.
12. a) Mayday.
    b) Pan Pan.
    c) Mayday.
    d) Pan Pan Medico.
13. 'Mayday, Mayday, Mayday. This is yacht *Bluebird*, yacht *Bluebird*, yacht *Bluebird*. One four zero from Nab Tower, 1 mile. Hit submerged object and sinking rapidly. Require immediate assistance. Total crew four, taking to liferaft with EPIRB. Over.'

Chapter 10
1. a) 50°34'.60N   01°13'.60E.
    b) 50°57'.40N   01°23'.40E.
    c) 50°54'.00N   00°48'.10E.
    d) 51°02'.20N   01°11'.20E.
    e) 50°59'.40N   01°22'.60E.
2. a) 51°24'.10N   01°20'.50E.
    b) 51°17'.60N   01°30'.05E.
    c) 51°10'.55N   01°32'.35E.
    d) 51°13'.40N   01°24'.65E.
    e) 51°12'.95N   01°34'.55E.
3. a) 4.2 miles.   d) 12.8 miles.
    b) 9.2 miles.   e) 4.1 miles.
    c) 7.8 miles.
4. a) 2.45 miles.   d) 0.5 miles.
    b) 3.0 miles.   e) 1.40 miles.
    c) 1.65 miles.
5. a) 50°24'.50N   00°00'.00.
    b) It is on the Greenwich meridian.
6. 50°52'.00N   01°02'.30E.
7. These are areas that dry when the water is at chart datum.
8. Chart datum.
9. a) Green, white and red.
    b) 2.8m.
10. a) Broken shells with gravel pebbles.
    b) 52m.
    c) 1.9 miles.
11. a) 041°T.
    b) 25.2 miles.
    c) 28 miles.
    d) 50°43'.40N   00°26'.10E.
    e) 7.4 miles.
    f) 275°T.

12. It is a traffic separation zone.

Chapter 11
1. a) 315°.
   b) 225°.
   c) 202.5°.
   d) 067.5°.
2. a) 257°T.
   b) 244°T.
   c) 014°T.
   d) 350°T.
   e) 020°T.
3. a) 013°M.
   b) 169°M.
   c) 325°M.
   d) 139°M.
   e) 086°M.
4. Heading 245°C therefore deviation = 1°E.
   Beacon
     132°C + 1°E = 133°M − 4°W = 129°T.
   Flagstaff
     265°C + 1°E = 266°M − 4°W = 262°T.
   Church tower
     324°C + 1°E = 325°M − 4°W = 321°T.
5.

T	Var	M	Dev	C
046°	1°W	047°	3°E	044°
129°	5°W	134°	3°W	137°
156°	3°E	153°	3°W	156°
152°	5°W	157°	3°W	160°
295°	4°W	299°	3°E	296°
320°	4°E	316°	4°E	312°
045°	3°W	048°	3°E	045°

6. 135°T
   − 3°E variation
   ___
   132°M
   + 3°W deviation
   ___
   135°C
7. 185°C
   − 4°W variation
   ___
   181°M
   − 4°W deviation
   ___
   177°T
8. 04°23′.
9. a) 210°T.
   b) 213°M.
   c) 003°E.
10. a) 338°M.
    b) 298°M.
    c) 183°M.
11. a) 048°C.
    b) 214°C.
    c) 157°C.
    d) 326°C.
    e) 340°C.
12. a) 276°C.
    b) 143°C.
    c) 219°C.
    d) 122°C.
    e) 231°

Chapter 12
1. a) 0746 BST.
   b) 1925 BST.
   c) 3.2m.
2. a) 0.8m.
   b) 4.3m.
3. a) 17.0m.
   b) 20.4m.
   c) No. There will be 1.1m depth.

4. 4.2m.
5. 1.3m.
6. a) 255°T 0.6kn.
   b) 239°T 0.5kn.
   c) 070°T 0.4kn.
7. a) 031°T 1.5kn.
   b) 211°T 0.5kn.
8. a) 2.65m.
   b) 1359 BST.
9. 3.5m.
10. a) 1113 BST.
    b) 0.8kn.

For diagram answers see overleaf

Chapter 13
1. a) 51°15′.80N 01°26′.75E.
   b) 206°T, 4.65 miles, 4.65kn.
2. a) 51°12′.70N 01°37′.10E.
   b) 026°T, 3.0 miles, 3.0kn.
3. 51°17′.45N 01°27′.90E.
4. 51°11′.75N 01°27′.90E.
5. 229°T.
6. a) 51°10′.7N 01°26′.85E.
   b) 028°T, 2.5 miles, 1.25kn.
7. a) 51°21′.55N 01°37′.50E.
   b) 172°T, 2.55 miles, 1.3kn.
8. a) 074°M.
   b) 4.5kn.
   c) 1930 BST.
9. a) 329°M.
   b) 3.2kn.
   c) 0603 BST.
10. a) 155°M.
    b) 6.1kn.
    c) 1957 BST.

For chart answers see pages 227-229

Chapter 14
1. a) A = safe water;
        B = port lateral;
        C = north cardinal;
        D = starboard lateral;
        E = isolated danger;
        F = west cardinal.
   b) A = red ball;
        C = two cones pointing upward;
        E = two black balls.
2. a) Continuous, very quick.
   b) Single flashing.
   c) Group occulting.
3. a) Group flashing (2).
   b) Very quick (9) every 10 seconds, or, quick (9) every 15 seconds.
   c) Any rhythm.
4. a) Very quick (6) plus long flash every 10 seconds, or, quick (6) plus long flash every 15 seconds.
   b) Very quick (3) every 5 seconds, or, quick (3) every 10 seconds.
5. a) Safe water mark – pass safely either side.
   b) Isolated danger mark – give wide berth.
   c) North cardinal – give a wide berth to west or east and do not approach close from the south.
6. Horn sounds once every 30 seconds.
7. West to east.
8. a) You are to port of the leading line.
   b) Alter course to starboard.
9. The depth of water is greater near B1 than B2. Look at the echo sounder and correct the reading for the height of tide to give you the depth of water. It should then become obvious which of the two buoys you are close to.
10. You are close to a very shallow part of the Goodwin Sands. You must immediately head due west.

Chart Answers

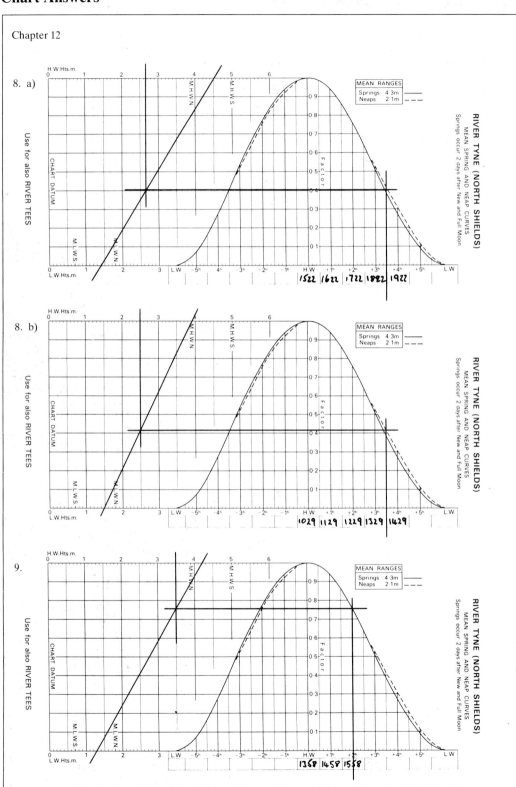

Chapter 12

8. a)

8. b)

9.

Chapter 13

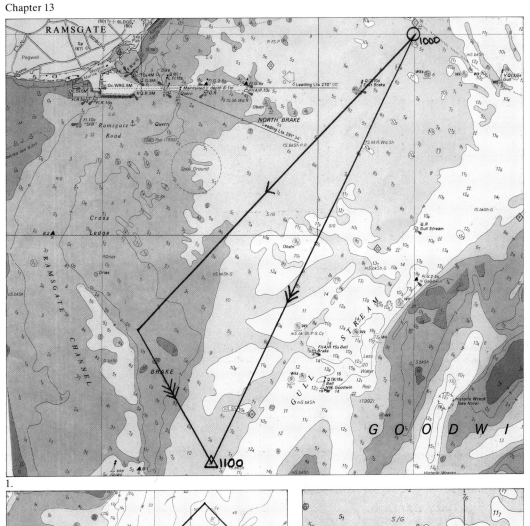

1.

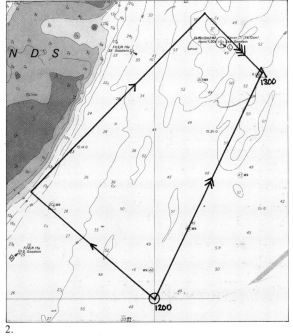

2.

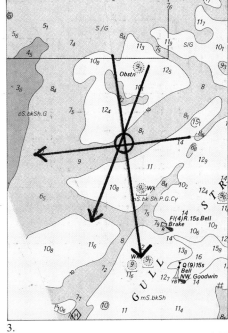

3.

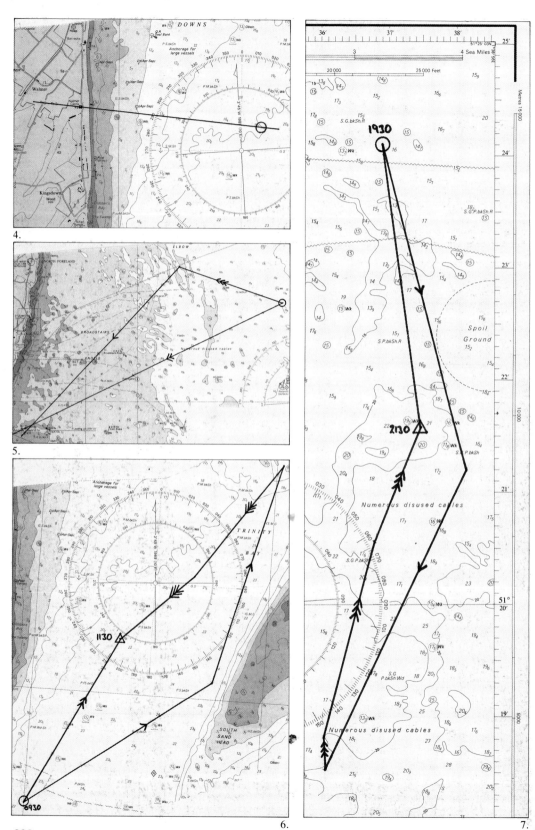

4.

5.

6.

7.

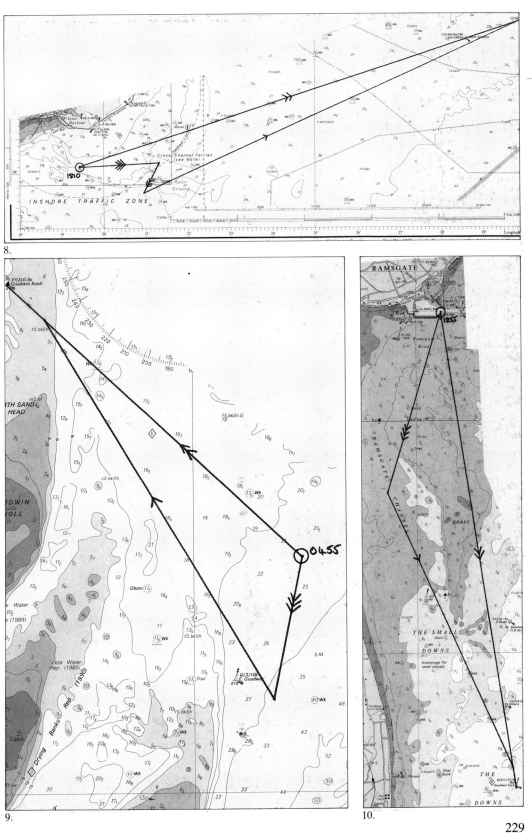

8.

9.

10.

Glossary

Aback This describes a sail which is deliberately set with the wind on the wrong side, as when heaving-to. It is also used if a wind shift or movement of the helm accidentally takes the wind onto the wrong side of the sail.

Abaft A point lying to stern of the named part of the boat.

Abeam A point lying at a right angle to the fore–aft line.

Aft Towards the stern of the boat.

Aloft A position up the mast or in the rigging.

Anchor aweigh This describes that moment when the anchor has just broken free from the seabed when being hauled in.

Anchor buoy A small buoy attached by a light line to the crown of the anchor. It is used for tripping out the anchor or simply marking its position.

Anchor locker Stowage locker on the foredeck for the main anchor.

Anchor roller A roller over which the anchor line passes.

Athwartship A line passing through the centre of the boat from port to starboard at the point of maximum beam. It is at a right angle to the centreline and so separates the fore and aft sections.

Back spring A mooring rope from the aft part of the boat to a point forward of the boat on a pontoon.

Backstay The wire cable supporting the mast, running from the masthead to the centre point of the stern.

Batten This is used to stiffen the leech of sail (usually the mainsail). It is typically made of flexible wood or GRP. It fits into a batten pocket in the leech.

Beam reach Sailing on a heading that is approximately at a right angle to the wind direction.

Beating Sailing towards the wind with the sails hauled in tight.

Bilge The area beneath the cabin floor where water collects, hence bilge pump.

Boom A spar that supports the foot of a sail (usually the mainsail).

Breast line A mooring line led at a right angle from the boat to a pontoon.

Broaching When running before a strong wind and the boat suddenly breaks broadside on to the waves.

Broad reach Sailing on a heading that is halfway between a beam reach and a run. The angle between the heading and wind direction is approximately 135°.

Centreline An imaginary line running down the centre of the boat from bow to stern separating port from starboard.

Cleat A fitting to which a rope or sheet is secured by a series of turns.

Clew The aft end of a sail to which the sheets are attached.

Close-hauled Sailing as close as possible to the wind.

Close reach Sailing on a heading between close-hauled and a beam reach.

Coach roof That part of the cabin roof lying above deck level.

Cockpit That section of the boat, normally in the stern, where the crew are stationed and the boat is steered.

Cutter A sailing vessel with two headsails.

Downhaul A rope or line used for pulling a sail or spar downwards, especially on a spinnaker boom.

Downwind 1) Sailing with the wind astern.
2) Any point or feature that is to leeward of the boat.

Foot The lower part of a sail.

Forehalyard The halyard (line) used for raising and lowering a headsail.

Forehatch The hatch from the bow section of the deck to the forecabin.

Foresail A headsail attached directly to the forestay.

Forestay A wire cable supporting the mast, running from the masthead to the bow.

Forward A point towards the bow of the boat.

Genoa A very large but light headsail used in light to moderate winds. Often the genoa is bigger than the mainsail.

Goose winging Running with the mainsail set on one side and the headsail on the other side.

Guy The line attached to the clew of the spinnaker.

Hand hold A low wooden support close to deck level to give help when moving around the deck.

Hank A catch that attaches the headsail to the forestay.

Head The top part of the sail to which the halyard is attached by a shackle.

Headsail Any sail set forward of the mast.

Heave-to The manoeuvre by which the boat is slowed or stopped by coming head-to-wind with the headsail backed and the tiller lashed to leeward. You would heave-to to ride out rough weather, to wait for the tide or simply to have a rest.

In stays That point during the process of going about when the

bow points directly into the wind with the sails flapping.

Keel That part of the hull projecting beneath the water to give the boat stability and direction.

Ketch A sailing vessel with a small (mizzen) mast set astern of the main mast. The mizzen mast is forward of the steering gear.

Kicking strap A line and block used to tension the boom and mainsail downwards. It is attached from a point near the base of the mast to a point approximately one-third of the way along the boom.

Leech Aft edge of a sail.

Leeward A position downwind.

Luff 1) Leading edge of a sail.
2) To sail so close to the wind that the leading edge of the sail flutters. This may be done to reduce heeling.

Mainsheet The line, usually in a triple loop with a running block, that controls the mainsail once set.

Off the wind A point of sailing downwind or away from the wind.

On the port/starboard bow A position ahead of the boat at an angle to the bow but forward of abeam.

On the port/starboard quarter A position astern of the boat at an angle to the stern but abaft the beam.

On the wind A point of sailing upwind or towards the wind.

Pulpit The stainless steel frame encircling the bow to which the safety lines are attached.

Pushpit As for 'pulpit' but at the stern.

Quarter That section of the hull between amidship and astern.

Reef To reduce sail area, especially the mainsail.

Rudder The control surface for changing the direction of the boat. It is hinged at, or close to, the stern.

Run Sailing on a heading with the wind directly behind the boat, in other words making an angle of 180° between wind direction and boat heading.

Running block A block through which sheets run.

Safety lines Lines, usually of wire, running along both sides of a boat from pulpit to pushpit through the stanchions which support them.

Schooner A sailing vessel with two masts, the smaller of which is forward of the main mast.

Shackle A U shaped metal link closed with a pin and used to connect sheets to sails and chains to anchors.

Sheet A line used to control a sail. It is attached to either the clew or, in the case of the mainsail, the boom.

Shrouds Those parts of the standing rigging that support the mast in a lateral direction.

Skeg Positioned under the hull just forward of the rudder, this acts as a small keel in the sense that it provides directional stability.

Sloop A sailing vessel with one mast, one mainsail and one headsail.

Spinnaker A large bulbous sail set forward of the mast when the boat is sailing downwind.

Spinnaker boom A spar attached from the mast to the spinnaker tack and therefore the spinnaker guy. It helps the spinnaker to keep both its shape and its distance from the boat.

Spreaders Short metal bars fitted either side of the mast at about two-thirds height and at a right angle to the centreline. This allows the shrouds to run taut from the masthead outwards to the side of the boat.

Stem This is the leading edge of the bow.

Tack 1) The lower leading corner of a sail.
2) To change the direction of the boat by turning it through the wind so that the sails fill on the opposite side.

Tacking The process of constantly changing from one tack to the other in order to make progress to windward.

Tiller The short length of wood, GRP, carbon fibre or other material attached to the rudder head in order to control the rudder and therefore the direction of the boat.

Underway Usually used to refer to any vessel moving through the water. Strictly it should refer to a vessel not anchored or tied up.

Uphaul A rope or line used for pulling a sail or spar upwards, especially on the spinnaker boom.

Upwind 1) Sailing towards the wind.
2) Any point or feature that is to windward of the boat.

Winch A rotating circular drum used for hauling in a sheet or rope. A winch handle fitted into the top of the winch turns the drum.

Windward A position upwind, ie the direction from which the wind is coming.

Yawl A sailing vessel with a small (mizzen) mast set astern of the main mast. The mizzen mast is aft of the steering gear.

Index